Every Christian educator can benefit from this book—teachers and administrators alike, whether new to the task or with years of experience. Based on the premise that different persons learn in a variety of ways, all legitimate, the author shows clearly how teachers may recognize students who learn in these different ways, plan and teach lessons that involve all of them through the use of a wide variety of appropriate methods, and at the same time reinforce each student's sense of achievement. The same understandings are applied to leader recruitment and development. The book sparkles with appropriate anecdotes, live cases, and practical suggestions. It will be useful both in workshops and for personal study.

D. Campbell Wyckoff
Thomas W. Synnott Professor of Christian Education, Emeritus
Princeton Theological Seminary

When the stateswoman of Christian Education puts pen to her *magnum opus*, the benefits are all ours: teachers, students, and administrators. What a mother lode of resources this is! Imaginative, thorough, engaging, and accessible—characteristic of Marlene's own teaching style. Lights will come on in your head, and you'll never be the same teacher, or student, again.

Jerry B. Jenkins
Author and Writer-in-Residence
Moody Bible Institute

As Gardner broadened the world of teaching by identifying multiple intelligences which learners utilize in the process of learning, so Marlene LeFever has enhanced Christian education by identifying the presence of four kinds of learners in our classrooms. Good teaching comes from remembering that it's like not to know. Marlene has made us aware of what it is like "not to know" when what is being taught is outside our learning frame. She has given us insight and tools for building learners' esteem and for realizing their learning potential. As anyone who knows Marlene would anticipate she has done such with rousing enthusiasm, captivating flair, and catalytic creativity. This book will enable the exploration of whole new frontiers of learning for those who teach in the church.

Dr. Julie Gorham
Associate Professor
Christian Formation and Discipleship
Fuller Theological Seminary

LEARNING STYLES

Reaching Everyone God Gave You to Teach

Marlene D. LeFever

DAVID C. COOK PUBLISHING CO.
Colorado Springs, Colorado—Paris, Ontario

This book is dedicated to the world's largest volunteer force, Sunday school teachers all 41 million of them!

Published by David C. Cook Church Ministry Resources,
a division of Cook Communications Ministries International
Colorado Springs, Colorado 80918
Cable address: DCCOOK
Cover designer/illustrator: Jeff Sharpton
Edited, designed, and desktop published by Dave and Neta Jackson
Illustrators: Nancy Berg, Kathy Weyna, Dave Jackson
Printed in U.S.A.

ISBN: 0-7814-5117-5
10 9 8 7 6 5 4 3

Foreword

Style is real and it makes a difference. We are each unique and our lives need to reflect that uniqueness if we are to find real meaning in our work and create the best possible communication networks with our families and communities. Our schools need to embrace the need for multiple methods of instruction if we are to reach diverse learners. In diversity, we find not differences that separate but balance and wholeness, the prerequisites of excellence.

The brain is incredibly flexible. Each human being perfects specific cognitive operations and not others as a result of personal adaptations to one's experiences. Additionally, the human brain continues to adapt and expand for the lifetime of the individual. An enriched environment significantly influences brain power and an impoverished environment limits brain power. From this broader perspective, cognitive potential is understood to grow and diversify with use. These findings have understandably prompted a serious challenge to the way we conduct teaching/learning acts. Teaching models that emphasize only knowledge acquisition fail to deal with the developmental reality of learning styles.

Marlene LeFever's work in Christian education and my work with 4MAT are blended here into a powerful and useful tool for the education ministries of Christian churches. Her understanding of learning styles is insightful and her treatment of the topic is delightfully creative. Her lesson unit designs are original and elegantly simple to use. Her insights into learning style implications for teachers and volunteers are right on the mark. The section on worship is worth the price of the book.

For those committed to "reaching everyone God gave you to teach" this book will enhance your ability to both spark the heart and enlighten the mind of the children in your care.

Bernice McCarthy
President of Excel, Inc.

What's in It for You?

During the last decade I have talked about learning styles with many different people. Most of them were church volunteers, serving as Sunday school teachers, vacation Bible school helpers, and youth leaders. Others were paid church staff members: pastors, directors of Christian education, and religious education teachers. Many were parents, frustrated with how their children were doing in school and Sunday school.

Over and over, I heard similar comments from this widely diverse group:

- "Learning styles gives me handles on how to teach Bradford [or Elizabeth or Jeremy]. You don't know how close I've come to giving up."
- "I've got to rethink my teaching. I'm missing kids, even though they're in their seats every Sunday!"
- "If my teachers had only known about learning styles when I was a kid."
- "Learning styles has changed my perspective on who's smart and who's not."
- "What would learning styles look like if I applied the concept to my preaching?"

Volunteer teachers—This book is written first of all to volunteer teachers in the church, those people who Sunday after Sunday share God's love with others. Chapters 1—12 will be especially helpful to those people who got their assignment to teach from God, but who may not have had a lot of formal teacher training.

Professionals in the church—Professional educators in the church and Christian school teachers will want to go a little deeper into learning styles. Chapters 17 and 18 will help them do that. Chapter 14 applies learning styles to teacher recruitment.

Worship leaders and pastors—Pay special attention to Chapter 15.

Spouses and parents—Anyone who is married or raising children may want to memorize Chapter 16!

Acknowledgements

Dr. Bernice McCarthy, designer of the 4MAT System and president of Excel, Inc., turned me on to individual learning styles and the complete learning cycle. Thank you, Bernice, for your research, your determination to share what you have learned in the secular arena, and your willingness to allow me to piggyback on what I learned from you and present it to Sunday school teachers.

To Dr. Rita Dunn and Dr. Kenneth Dunn I owe special thanks for their research into the twenty-one elements of learning.

Five people have helped edit this book, forcing me to rethink concepts and get rid of as much "educationalese" as possible. The Apostle Paul didn't add "editing" to his list of spiritual gifts, but in my opinion God certainly does *gift* good editors. Thank you, Carrie Salstrom, for your first reading and your sensitive way of asking, "Does this sentence really make sense to you?" Ardith Bradford and Terri Hibbard, thanks to you for looking at the broad picture, shifting chapters, and demanding rewriting. You were right! Finally, thank you, Dave and Neta Jackson. You are both gifted editors and writers, and I'm glad we got to work together again.

Contents

Introduction to Learning Styles

Just as each of us has one body with many members, and these members do not all have the same function, so in Christ we who are many form one body, and each member belongs to all the others. We have different gifts, according to the grace given us.
—Romans 12:4-6a

The elderly, sun-weathered man didn't look like the typical attendee at a Sunday school seminar. Throughout the whole day, as I interacted with the rest of the group on learning styles, he sat. I never saw him make one note or join in any of the group discussions. He just sat. Even after the meeting ended, he remained seated until everyone else was finished talking with me. He stood up, and as he walked up to me, he pointed his finger directly in my face. His voice was angry, and he had tears in his eyes.

"Teacher!" he said. "Iffen somebody'd a tol' me when I was a kid that God made my mind right, I 'da' done something for my Jesus."

He turned and walked out, leaving me with tears in my eyes.

Somewhere, years before, perhaps based on what a teacher had said about him or the grades he had received, that man had concluded that he had limited potential. Those limits became self-fulfilling. Now, too late, he suspected he was incorrect about those limits. What a waste of a lifetime!

Individualized Teaching

When teachers understand students' learning styles and adjust their teaching to those styles, students will learn. Teaching to style enables teachers to begin reaching *everyone* God gave them to teach.

In a secular sense, students will find that subjects which were closed to them in the past open up. They may not suddenly become star students, but their performance will improve. Scholastic success becomes possible.

From a Christian perspective, people who thought they had nothing to offer will be more open to expanding their talents and developing their gifts.

I was in a university town, leading a teacher training session that included information on learning styles. After the session a woman shared her reaction to what I had taught. "I know you are here to make us better teachers, but I think God may have sent you to save my self-image. I'm not school smart, but I am a friendly person and people seem to like me. I can make these university types feel comfortable enough to talk to one another—to create an atmosphere in which they can learn from one another. But everyone in our circle has an earned doctorate, some even two. I've always felt inferior to them. Until today, I never realized that my ability with people—my friendship skills—are a type of intelligence. Now I'm walking taller."

When teachers adjust their teaching styles, students learn.

I've been following the research about learning styles for over a decade. My first exposure came though the Association of Curriculum and Supervision Development (ACSD), and as I listened to educators Bernice McCarthy, Rita Dunn, Kenneth Dunn, and Anthony Gregorc, I found myself saying, "Makes sense. Yes, I can see the value of what they are preaching." And preach they did! These secular educators saw the difference that teaching based on learning styles made in their students' grades and attitudes. They wanted every classroom teacher to benefit from what they were learning. "When you find something that works," Rita Dunn of St. Johns University, Jamaica, New York, said, "you have a responsibility to tell others about it. I'm very missionaryish about this!"

Me, too! My passion for educating teachers includes the world's single largest volunteer group—Sunday school teachers and those who volunteer in all Christian education ministries.

Learning Style Action

This book shares some basic information about learning styles in terms of action. It is not enough to know that each of us has a specific style and that when we are taught in that style, we are more likely to succeed. Knowledge is not my primary goal. Action is. I want Sunday school teachers and club leaders and vacation Bible school volunteers—anyone who teaches for Jesus' sake—to identify his or her own preferred style and then take steps to teach not only to those students who have similar strengths, but to *all* students.

To facilitate learning style action, I encourage you to study the sample lessons in Part III. See how learning styles look in a teaching setting. Then, in Part IV, experiment with the methods suggested (Chapters 9—12) in designing your own "Do-It-Yourself Lesson Plan" (Chapter 14). See if teaching to students' styles revolutionizes the way you present your message. We Christians have a life-saving truth. We dare not allow an ineffective presentation of that truth to hide what we have to say.

When we don't pay attention to how God made students' minds, we are in effect saying, "I don't care about this child. I am content not to teach him." The United Negro College Fund has a motto that all teachers should place where they see it frequently: *"A mind is a terrible thing to waste."* That motto is true both educationally and spiritually.

My brother Jim hated school. He graduated over thirty years ago, and he still shudders when he sees a school bus. When he was in tenth grade the guidance counselor suggested to Mother that he be allowed to quit. She knew her boy was smarter than his report card or his enthusiasm for school indicated. She crossed her arms and said, "My boy will stay in school until he graduates, even if it takes until he is fifty-seven." The counselor believed her and Jim was moved along, even though his grades did not improve.

Let me tell you about my "dumb" brother. He hated the senior history class, Problems of Democracy. He was an action sort of fellow, and history bored him. He certainly couldn't care less that the roots of the present were deep in the past. What happened today was important. He didn't study for tests. He failed, while helping to start a Boy Scout troop to train kids in sportsmanship and values.

English was another useless subject, in his opinion. He never did meet an adverb or pronoun he could relate to, so he flunked. At the same time he was writing to mechanics magazines on how to convert a Volkswagen into a dune buggy. The letters, word perfect, were being published and the editors didn't know he was just a kid.

Chemistry seemed silly to him, all that stuff to memorize. Why didn't the class get busy and do something worthwhile? So his mind wandered and his grades plummeted. In his off time, he rewired a lady's house for electricity, because she couldn't afford a "real" electrician. Her home is still lit!

The high grade on his report card was shop, a D–. He did a sloppy job on his wooden book rack because he hated books, and he certainly didn't want some place to keep more of them. In metal shop, in the late 1950s, the class was making ash trays. We were a nonsmoking family, so the project seemed dumb to him. But helping his buddy who drove a large truck made sense. To make the cab more comfortable because the truck didn't have air conditioning or adequate heating, he developed a grill that would allow the engine to heat more quickly in the winter and remain cooler in the summer.

I tell Jim's story to a lot of Christian educators, and I often find them nodding assent as if to say, "The school system blew it. Isn't that just like professional educators—missing a kid who wasn't dumb, just different?"

But the story isn't just about what happened in school Monday to Friday. It's also about Sunday. My parents forced Jim to go to Sunday school. There the teacher talked at the class and later had students write in their workbooks. The hour stretched interminably. Jim always sat quietly as near to the door as possible. Then when the bell rang, he was able to dash out of the door two seconds earlier than anyone else and the ordeal was over for another week. When he was old enough to quit going, he did.

He and his wife are now actively involved in their church—not only in the worship, but also in Sunday school. What happened? A pastor inadvertently captured Jim's interest by appealing to his learning style. "I'm going to build a church in the meadow across the way," he said to Jim. "Would you like to contribute and attend when it's built?"

Jim heard the word *build*, and it was as if God and he smiled at each other for the first time in a long time. Building he understood. Building made sense. He learned by using his hands along with his head. Sure, he would give money, but he could also help put up the building.

Every night after work and on weekends, Jim helped build his church.

I got a long tour through it when it was finally finished—a very long tour, even though the church could be a model for the little church in the dell. I saw the type of insulation, the electric wires, the Sunday school classrooms. I wondered about my brother's continued enthusiasm in things of God now that the church was built. Would he be willing to sit when the "hands-on" part was finished. "Finished?" Jim said, when I asked him. "It's not finished. We've got a sister church in Hershey that's adding a nursery, and I've got to get up there by 6 A.M. next Saturday to make sure they put in the right amount of insulation. Wouldn't want the kids catching cold."

At this rate my brother and God will keep smiling at each other.

Finding a place where his unique learning—hands and head together—is appreciated has made all the difference. Jim knows he's respected in his church for what he can do, and that knowledge frees him to participate in areas where he may not be as gifted. He's willing to sit through sermons and adult Bible studies, even though sitting is not involved in his preferred style of learning.

"A mind is a terrible thing to waste." —United Negro College Fund.

As a kid, Jim could have been lost educationally if a parent had not stood up against the system. As an adult, he could have been lost to the church if God had not provided a way for him to share the gifts of his mind and hands.

How we learn affects everything else in our lives, our feelings about ourselves, our willingness to try new things, and our contributions to society and to our Savior.

Learning styles will make our assignments as Christian educators more difficult. No longer can we teach the way we like to learn and assume everyone will learn. No longer can we make an easy judgment about who's smart and who's not. Learning styles force us to rethink how we teach and adjust to the way God made people—not the way we used to think He made them or even the way we wish He had made them.

Part I

UNDERSTANDING LEARNING STYLES

Some people learn by listening and sharing ideas,
Some learn by thinking through ideas,
Some learn by testing theories,
And some learn by synthesizing content and context.
—Susan Morris, Excel, Inc.

Effective learning follows a natural process: (1) Learners begin with what they already know or feel or need. What happened before must provide the groundwork for what will happen now. Real learning cannot take place in a vacuum. (2) This real-life connection prepares them for the next step—learning something new. (3) In the third step, learners use the new content, practicing how it might work in real life. (4) The final step demands that learners creatively take what they have learned beyond the classroom. This final step moves students out of the church into their Monday-through-Friday lives.

Learning Styles in the Cycle

Each student will have a place in the cycle where he or she is most comfortable and can contribute the most excellent work. But even though different students prefer different places in the cycle, it's important for all students to go through each of the four steps in the cycle.

To help explain the characteristics of people who prefer different places on the cycle, educator Bernice McCarthy has given them names. We will use these names throughout the book.

1. *Imaginative Learners* easily share from their past experience, providing a context for learning.

2. *Analytic Learners* need to learn something new in the lesson.

3. *Common Sense Learners* need to see if what they learned makes sense now.

4. *Dynamic Learners* find creative ways to use what they've learned.

Each Style Contributes

Not only is each person most comfortable in a particular style, but each style benefits the whole learning process.

Imaginative learners help answer the question, "Why do I need this?" They enjoy talking and sharing their life experiences. Without them, other students may not grasp the personal value of what will be taught.

Analytic learners help answer the question, "What does the Bible say about my need?" They enjoy learning new facts and concepts. Without them, other students may not build an intellectual understanding of the Bible.

Common sense learners help answer the question, "How does what the Bible teaches actually work?" They enjoy experimenting. Without them, other students may not practice how biblical values work today.

Dynamic learners help answer the question, "Now, how will I use what I have learned?" They enjoy finding creative ways to put faith into action. Without them, other students may not discover a "practical" faith.

Problem—Missed Steps

When any step is missed, the children, teens, and adults who prefer that step are also missed. There is no opportunity for them to show their natural abilities or to develop those abilities.

Is it any wonder they drop out of our church programs, and in many different ways, announce, "God didn't make my mind right"?

These first two chapters provide an introduction to learning styles—your own and the styles of those you teach.

1

What Are Learning Styles?

Each person is given something to do that shows who God is:
Everyone gets in on it, everyone benefits.
All kinds of things are handed out by the Spirit, and to all kinds of people!
The variety is wonderful (I Corinthians 12:6).
—Eugene Peterson in The Message

"God made my mind right!" I end many of my learning style training sessions by asking participants to say this sentence aloud three times, "God made my mind right!" The first time they say it to themselves as an affirmation of their own special style of learning. The second time, they turn to their neighbor and tell him or her in no uncertain terms, "God made my mind right!" Finally they say it as a prayer of thanks to their minds' Maker.

Sometimes people break into spontaneous clapping after the three sentences. "I've never thanked God for my mind before," a Sunday school teacher said. "I've really got a pretty special one, you know!" Sometimes people will cry. "I thought there was something wrong with me. Now I know God can use my unique 'smarts'!"

Knowing about your learning style can change your opinion of yourself and what you are willing to attempt for Jesus. Knowing about learning styles helps you teach all the children, teens, and adults God put in your classroom.

A learning style is the way in which a person sees or perceives things best and then processes or uses what has been seen. Each person's individual learning style is as unique as a signature. When a person has something

Students learn faster and enjoy learning more if their unique learning styles are affirmed.

difficult to learn, that student learns faster and enjoys learning more if his or her unique learning style is affirmed by the way the teacher teaches.

As Christian educators, teaching to our students' learning styles can help all students get more excited about the subject, explore and understand the facts, enjoy grappling with the implications and, most importantly, be more willing to put what they have learned into practice.

The heart of our curriculum, what we want to teach, is the message of Christ—His love for us, His willingness to accept us into His family, and how we live out our responsibilities as His family members. What a challenge! Christ gives us what we are to teach—the content—but the "how" of teaching He leaves up to us. We must make the most of what we know about learning and the methods that communicate effectively with students. Often the wrong "how" can keep our students from hearing the "what."

I was helping to serve a Thanksgiving dinner to a group of street people at a mission in Chicago. Throughout the meal a man wandered around the room muttering to himself. Much of what he said was gibberish. Then his eyes focused on me. He came charging at me, his voice loud and his English clear. "Who do you think I am?" he bellowed at me. "Somebody?"

I was too surprised and frightened to make any response, and almost immediately he went back to muttering words only he could understand. Later that day, I was rethinking what happened and wishing I had had the presence of mind to answer his question. "Yes, that's exactly what I think," I wish I had said. "I think you are somebody—somebody Christ loves. That's why I'm here."

His question is asked in many different ways by our students, and often by members of our own families—"Who do you think I am?" their participation, attitudes, and body language ask. "Somebody?"

We answer each one, in part, by the way we respond. When we teach in ways that capture a student's strengths, we are indeed saying, "Yes, that's why I'm here. For Jesus' sake, I believe you are somebody. I will teach you in a way that affirms your strengths and helps you believe, as I do, that you are someone special."

"When we decide we want to value differences," writes educator Pat Burke Guild, "we will make decisions that expand diversity rather than seek uniformity and inappropriate conformity."[1] Successful teachers no longer believe that what's good for one is good for all. Likewise, we must stop looking for the one best way to do Christian education.

Enlarging Our View of Learning

Everyone has a learning style.

A person's preferred style has nothing to do with IQ, socioeconomic background, or achievement level. It doesn't matter if Janet, for example, has the potential to make A's or C's in school. If she has opportunities to show what she can contribute within her preferred style she is more likely to succeed to her full potential. Each person's style contains clues for developing natural abilities to the highest level. When Janet is successful in her preferred style, she will be willing to dare things that fall outside her strength area. On the other hand, if Janet is never taught within her preferred style, she may assume she's dumb or that her contributions have no value. She may give up, or even drop out.

Until recently, many Christian communicators assumed that the most effective ways to teach were teacher-centered—through lecture, story-telling, or sermon. *If the teacher is talking,* teachers thought, *the students must be learning.* We taught as if we could just slice off the students' heads and pour in everything they needed to know. That assumption contains some truth for some students, but is absolutely false for others. For most students, as we poured in the need-to-know stuff, it dribbled right out of a hole in their big toes! Learning styles is a new tool that Sunday school teachers, youth leaders, pastors—all of us involved in Christian education—can use to better teach all the people we serve.

Along with enlarging our view of learning, learning styles has also enlarged our view of our Creator. We've affirmed God's creativity and diversity in many aspects of life, but assumed for too long that all great minds worked pretty much alike. We were wrong; minds are uniquely individualized. What we now know about learning is just the beginning of what we may someday know.

Exchanging Noses?

Consider noses! Take a look at your best friend's nose and imagine what your face would look like if it had your friend's nose on it. The results are ludicrous. Minds are like noses—very, very different. It is just as silly to look at a group of students and assume that all of them are going to learn in exactly the same way. In actuality, what works for one may be incomprehensible to another.

God's creation is much more creative than we realized even just fifteen years ago. Now we need to expand our elite measure of who is smart and who is not. Janet's teacher was wise to learning styles. She said, "I didn't want to know how 'smart' Janet was according to some predetermined standard; I wanted to know *how Janet was smart.*"[2]

Previewing the Four Learning Styles

Educator Bernice McCarthy identifies four primary learning styles: Imaginative, Analytic, Common Sense, and Dynamic. None of these four styles will fit a student perfectly. (Just as God did not use just four types of noses on our faces, He didn't create just four mind patterns.) We are all mixes of the four styles, but most of us will have one that feels like our best fit. For some of the students we teach, one style will be so predominant that they will not learn if that style is left out of our teaching plans.

Imaginative Learner

Imaginative Learners are feeling people who get involved with others and learn best in settings that allow interpersonal relationships to develop. These curious, questioning learners learn by listening and sharing ideas. They see the broad overview or big picture much more easily than the small details. They learn by sensing, feeling, watching. They can see all sides of the issues presented.

Analytic Learner

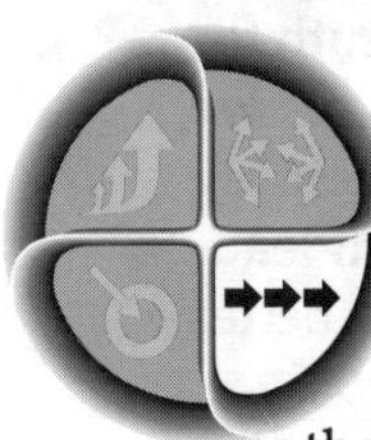

Analytic Learners learn by watching and listening. They expect a teacher to be the primary information giver, while they sit and carefully assess the value of the information presented. These are the students who learn in the way most teachers have traditionally taught, and so they are often considered the best learners. They are strategic planners, and they aim for perfection—the right answers, the A's in school and in life. These learners want all the data before they make a decision.

Analytic Learners are often defined as the best students since they fit the teaching/learning methods traditionally used in Western education. They grow uncomfortable when a teacher veers from these methods. Exact and accurate in their thinking, they are mainly interested in "just the facts, nothing but the facts."

Teacher William Davies told of a classroom encounter with a girl who may have been an Analytic Learner. "As I began to say, 'I'm going to divide the class up into . . . ,' the plaintive voice of a girl in the middle of the room called out, '*Please* don't do that. Everyone's doing that. Couldn't you just teach us—like a *real* class?'"[3]

Common Sense Learner

Common Sense Learners like to play with ideas to see if they are rational and workable. These students want to test theory in the real world, to apply what has been learned. They love to get the job done. They are hands-on people who, using their own ideas, can analyze problems and solve or fix them. Common Sense Learners, as the name suggests, excel when dealing with what is practical and of immediate importance to them. They learn best when learning is combined with doing. They would agree that Jesus "was not a sweatless wonder, but a hard-working savior."[4] Until the late sixteenth century, "faith" was a verb in the English language; to the Common Sense Learner it still is.[5]

Dynamic Learner

Dynamic Learners also enjoy action as part of the learning process, but rather than thinking projects through to their rational conclusion, Dynamic Learners excel in following hunches and sensing new directions and possibilities. These risk takers thrive on situations that call for flexibility and change and find real joy in starting something new, or putting their personal stamp of originality on an idea. Dynamic Learners might agree with Frederick Buechner's character Laughter who affirms that God has a "fire He is trying to start with us [that] is a fire that the whole world will live to warm its hands at. It is a fire in the dark that will light the whole world home."[6] Dynamic Learners feel that fire and come up with an amazing array of ideas for fanning the flame.

Teaching to Styles Helps Students Succeed

As teachers of God's Word, we must give each student an opportunity to demonstrate his or her preferred way of learning at some point in every lesson. Such affirmation helps each student:

- believe that God made his or her mind right.
- be motivated to learn.
- actively participate in the class.
- learn faster.
- understand others better and find ways to communicate effectively with them.
- affirm personal gifts and talents that he or she can use for God's service.
- relate better in group situations.
- make career choices in which he or she has the best chance to be successful.
- build tolerance and empathy for those who are least like him or her.

Four primary learning styles! How does a Sunday school teacher, for example, teach all four every Sunday? "I've got just forty-five minutes every class period to raise the dead," a teacher quipped. "Help! I don't want to miss anyone."

The four different learning styles actually fit together into a learning cycle. If this teacher follows the four steps in the cycle, every student will have an opportunity to learn and share his or her contributions with the whole class. Chapter 2 will take us around that cycle.

NOTES

1. Pat Burke Guild and Stephen Garger, *Marching to Different Drummers* (Alexandria, Vir.: ASCD, 1985), introduction, p. 10.

2. Patricia Lee, "To Dance One's Understanding," *Educational Leadership*, February 1994, p.83.

3. William G. Davies, "Worship and Learning: A Case for the Liturgical Classroom," *Religious Education*, Vol. 88, No. 4, Fall 1993, p. 577.

4. William Griffin, "Morning Prayer," *Image: A Journal of the Arts*, No. 4, Fall 1993, p. 87.

5. Eric Thurman, "Releasing Faith," sermon, Church of the Resurrection, Glen Ellyn, Illinois, April 2, 1995.

6. Frederick Buechner, *The Son of Laughter* (San Francisco: Harper, 1993) from James I. Cook, "A Touch to Light the Way," *Perspectives*, January 1994, p. 21.

2

Teaching to All Four Learning Styles

Don't be afraid to take a big step if one is indicated.
You can't cross a chasm in two small steps.
—David Lloyd George

Did you see the cartoon of a Sunday school teacher with her class of very young children? The teacher is announcing, "Okay, kids, have these verses memorized by next Sunday or you can kiss your snack time good-bye!" We all laugh, but many teachers have the same mindset. They think, *If I just teach the content of the Bible, its facts, stories, and principles, my students will have learned.*

Wrong! Students may be able to repeat the facts, stories, and principles—although even that is doubtful—but they won't have learned how they might use those facts today. At best, teachers will have reached some Analytic Learners, but what about students in the other three styles? Real learning requires teaching around the Learning Style Cycle. Real learning requires each student to succeed in his or her preferred style and to participate in the other three styles as well.

A Curriculum Pattern

David Kolb[1] and Bernice McCarthy[2] have provided educators with a basic learning style model. Their research provides a structure or pattern that can help us be more effective.

This pattern does not tell us anything about the content we want to teach. Instead, it helps us better communicate any subject matter. When we place Christ's message at the core of our teaching, the Learning Style Cycle becomes a structural, methodological tool that can help us teach every child, teen, and adult, each made in the image of God and each made uniquely.

Each teacher is responsible for doing the best job possible. We use all the research and tools at our command. These don't diminish our affirmation of the power of the Holy Spirit in our classrooms. He can use everything, including learning style research, to make us more fit to teach. Through learning styles, He may help us reach students that no one has reached before. Just as surely, He can choose to work in students' lives in spite of what teachers have not known or have done wrong.

The Learning Style Quadrants[3]

Bernice McCarthy's system,[4] called the 4MAT System, divides learners into the following four quadrants. Her process is a tool that helps us better teach the Christian message.

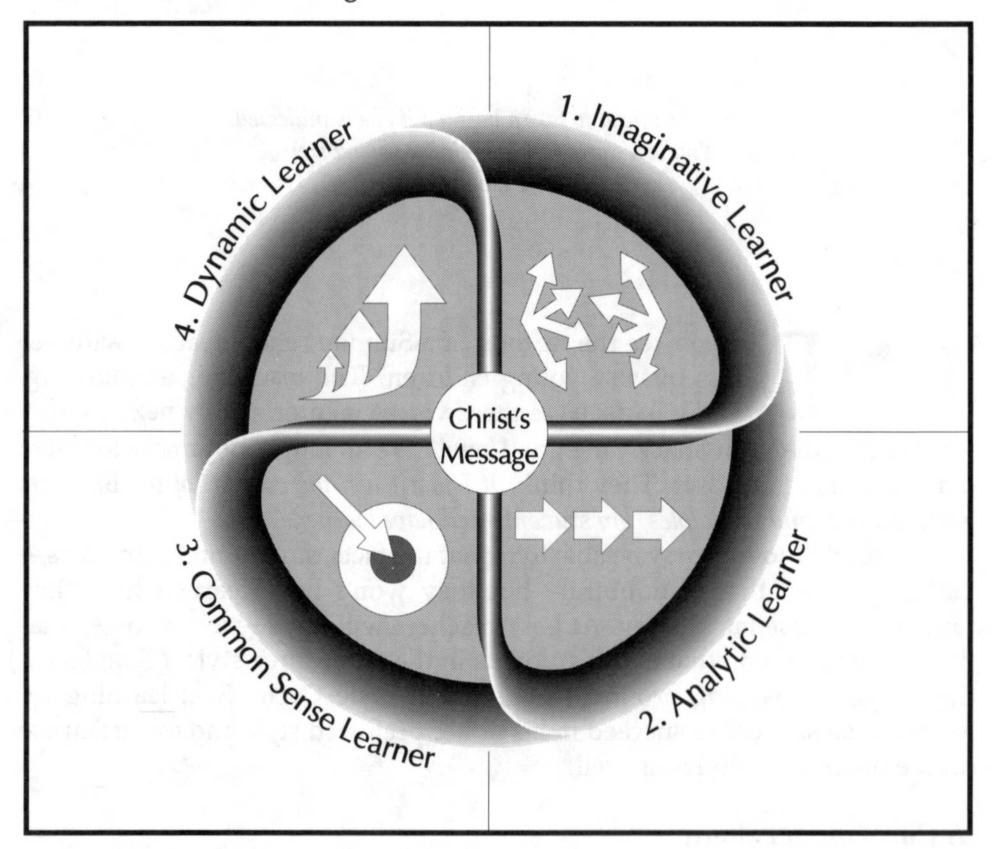

The Learning Style Questions

"How can I possibly teach a lesson that meets the needs of Imaginative, Analytic, Common Sense, and Dynamic Learners?" a teacher asks.

The answer is, "Knowing there are learners in each of the four learning style quadrants can actually give you a teaching structure that helps you succeed class after class." The four styles provide a skeleton on which learning can be hung.

An individual lesson or an entire curriculum can be built around the four types of learners. The lesson starts with Imaginative and moves to Analytic, then on to Common Sense, finally finishing with Dynamic. You can see how this logical progression works by looking at the questions each learning style group is best at answering.

Learning Style		Key Questions
1. Imaginative	→	1. Why do I need to know this? (meaning)
2. Analytic	→	2. What do I need to know? (content)
3. Common Sense	→	3. How does this work? (experiment)
4. Dynamic	→	4. What can this become? (creative application)

The strengths of all students come to the fore when the teacher follows this four-step pattern in each lesson. Every student participates in the whole lesson. Every student is affirmed because there will be one part of that lesson that spotlights his or her strengths. A Dynamic Learner will enjoy the fourth section of the lesson most. However, he or she will be willing to first participate in the other three sections of the lesson to get the information needed to do his or her part. Throughout the lesson, the student knows that the chance to show his or her unique intelligence is coming.

Note that in a natural sequence of teaching, you develop a lesson by starting with 1 and progressing to 4.

> By examining the primary characteristics in each quadrant of the cycle, the role shifts of teachers and learners become apparent. Each quadrant has a different emphasis. Quadrant One's emphasis is on meaning, or how the material to be learned is connected to the learners' immediate lives. Quadrant Two's emphasis is on content and curriculum and the importance of delivering instruction through an integrated approach. Quadrant Three addresses the usefulness of learning in the lives of the learners both in and out of school—it emphasizes the transferability of learning. Quadrant Four encompasses creativity, how the learner adds to the original learning in new and unique ways.[5]

1. Imaginative Learning: Part 1 of the Lesson

Question: Why study this lesson? Why do I need to know this?

In the first quadrant, you, the teacher, will begin by using what students already know. Students approach a subject with a wealth of knowledge. Starting with students' prior understanding gets their attention immediately. It focuses them on the direction you wish to take them.

The Imaginative Learners can help the whole class establish the "why" of the lesson. Why study this subject? Why is it important? They can draw on

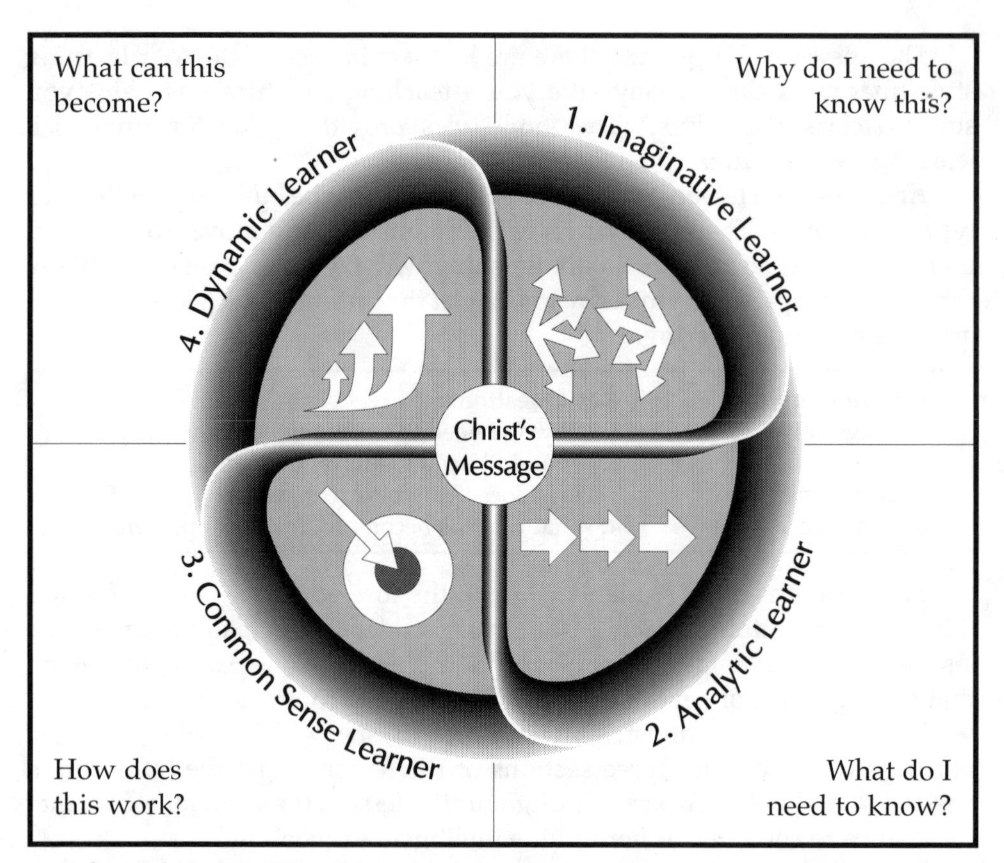

past knowledge and experiences and share with their peers why everyone should pay attention to this subject, because it's really important.

For example, let's consider how a teacher might structure a lesson on a Christian's responsibility to grapple with the problem of world hunger. The teacher asks the students not to eat supper on Saturday night or breakfast on Sunday. When they come to class, the obvious topic is hunger. What does it feel like? What were some of their thoughts about going hungry? Everyone in the class participates in this discussion, but the teacher usually finds that Imaginative students take the lead. The learners find it easy to discuss feelings and give the context into which the rest of the lesson will fit.

2. Analytic Learning: Part 2 of the Lesson
Question: What do I need to know?

In this second quadrant, the teacher needs to add new facts and concepts to what is already known. Analytic Learners will excel in learning information in Scripture that brings content to feelings. Now the students have seen that not only is the subject relevant to them, but they also have new information to help them deal more effectively with the subject.

In our classtime on world hunger, Analytics would be interested in studying what the Bible has to say about hunger. How involved are Christians supposed to be in helping the poor, powerless, and oppressed? What did Micah say? Are there specific principles that Christians need to know before they can make moral choices? The teacher guides students in finding what they need to know or, depending on the age level, provides direction to students to study God's Word for themselves.

3. Common Sense Learning: Part 3 of the Lesson

Question: How do I use what I know? How does what I've studied actually work today?

The third quadrant students would pick up on the practical side of the problem. The Common Sense Learners do not feel that it is enough to know the content about the subject. They must find how to put what they know into practice, to make it usable. "Okay," the Common Sense Learner may say about this study on hunger, "we've been through a mini-simulation on hunger and we now know what God has said about the subject. So what is this class going to do about it? Let's see more action around here." Common Sense Learners might get excited about marking the hunger spots on the world map and using biblical passages to suggest some possible solutions in which this class might get involved. The teacher could help students check if the direction in which they are going is valid.

4. Dynamic Learning: Step 4 of the Lesson

Question: What can this become? What if I added this—or that—to what I know?

The fourth quadrant question asks students to add a part of themselves to what they have learned, to find creative ways for the whole class to take the lesson home with them. Dynamic Learners want to enlarge what they have learned, adding creative ideas and perhaps teaching what they have learned to others. They are great at suggesting lots of ideas for expanding what they know, and they often hit on something that excites the whole class to action. The teacher partners in helping students explore the possibilities of what they know.

Because they are so creative, it is hard to predict what response the Dynamic Learners would make in expanding what they know about world hunger. Perhaps they would lead the whole church in fasting two days a month and contributing the money from those uneaten meals to a world relief organization. They might get the class involved in writing and putting on a church-parking-lot drama about the ongoing problems of hunger.

In an effective learning environment, all students participate in all four parts of the lesson, not just the part for which they are best suited. They know that their learning style will be affirmed at some point in the lesson. That knowledge frees them to participate in activities that will not be in their strength areas.

"These four quadrants represent the natural cycle of learning. Learning has a 'from here to here' flow," says researcher McCarthy. "We start with the broad picture, what we know ourselves, and we move to newness."[6]

The four-stage cycle "begins with (1) here and now experiences followed by (2) collection of data and observations about that experience. The data are then (3) analyzed, and the conclusions of this analysis are fed back to the learners in the learning experience for their use in the (4) modification of their behavior and choice of new learning experiences."[7]

When a teacher teaches in all four learning styles, the teacher knows that all students' strengths will be affirmed, even if the teacher is new or has first-time visitors in the class. Of course, the better we know those we teach, the more likely it is that we will be able to identify their strengths, especially when students have strong learning style preferences.

Effective Teachers

The most effective teachers are those who are able to teach within all four quadrants. They can use methods and processes that are appropriate to each. While they may personally prefer one learning style over another, they know the importance of teaching to every style, perhaps especially those outside their preference.

Effective teachers teach within all four quadrants.

Excellent teachers resist the tendency to teach to only one type of learner, using the same methods week after week.

Phrases that limit teacher effectiveness:

1. "I teach the way I was taught." This usually means the teacher is lecturing or using teacher-centered storytelling as the primary teaching tool. Many teachers believe that teaching is only really taking place when they are talking. The content may have been presented *at* students, but it makes little internal difference to them.
2. "I teach the way I like to learn." If teachers teach according to their own preference, students who learn in the same way the teacher does will love class, and those who don't may quit coming. This explains why one year Joshua loves going to Sunday school and the next year he is turned off by it and tells his parents, "Sunday school is boring." What Joshua may be saying is that this teacher is presenting information in a way that never affirms his preferred way of learning.

A teacher's personal learning style preference dare not dictate how a lesson is taught. The class is successful only when the teacher teaches to all four learning styles. Until each teacher is convinced of the importance of teaching in ways that reach all students, some will be missed. Some will vegetate until the class is over. Others will leave the church completely, assuming that whatever others find there is certainly not available to them.

Predicting Your Learning Style

Use the following tool to predict which learning style is most and which is least like your own. Knowing this will make you a better teacher if you pay extra attention to those styles which are least like your preference. Students who have your least preferred styles are the ones you are most likely to miss.[8] They may be at risk, not because of how intelligent they are, but at risk because of the way you are teaching. Conversely, in a class where the teacher is teaching to style, the teacher's preferred learning style will make no difference to any of the students. They may not even be aware of the teacher's preference.[9]

What's My Learning Style?

Directions: After reading each sentence, indicate if that statement is:

VM Very Much like me.
MM Moderately like me.
SM Somewhat like me.
NM Not at all, or very little like me.

After completing the statements, decide what predicts most closely the way you learn. For example, if you have three VMs in Imaginative and none in any of the other categories, you may be an Imaginative Learner. This prediction may confirm what you already know about how you learn best. For more valid testing, order the instruments suggested in footnote 8 on page 35.

Imaginative

_____I do my best work when I'm with other people.
_____I like a colorful working environment.
_____I like to give essay-type answers to questions, rather than specific fill-in-the-blank answers.
_____I see myself as a friend to my students.
_____The worst thing that could happen in my class is that students wouldn't get along well together.
_____People describe me as a really nice person.
_____Part of my self identity is wrapped up in the number of friends I have and the strength of those friendships.
_____Three words that describe me are *friendly, sharer, hugger*.

Analytic

_____I do my best work alone, after gathering information I need from books or other teachers.
_____I like to work at a desk or table.
_____I like to solve problems by finding the right answer.
_____I see myself as an information giver to my students.
_____The worst thing that could happen in my class is that students won't learn the basics of their faith.
_____People describe me as a really smart person.

_____Part of my self identity is wrapped up in how smart others think I am.
_____Three words that describe me are *rational, analytic, smart*.

Common Sense
_____I do my best work alone, putting together information so it will work.
_____I like to work with my hands, as well as my mind.
_____I like to solve problems by checking out my own ideas.
_____I see myself as a trainer, helping my students do what needs to be done.
_____The worst thing that could happen in my class is that students wouldn't learn to live their faith in practical ways.
_____People describe me as a hard worker, a results-oriented person.
_____Part of my self identity is wrapped up in how well my creations work.
_____Three words that describe me are *active, realistic, practical*.

Dynamic
_____I do my best work brainstorming new ideas and trying things not many people would dare to try.
_____I like playing with new ideas, making intuitive guesses on what works.
_____I like to solve problems by making guesses or following hunches.
_____I see myself as a facilitator or idea-stimulator for my students.
_____The worst thing that could happen in my class is that students wouldn't take what they have learned and make this world a better place.
_____People describe me as a highly creative person.
_____Part of my self identity is wrapped up in how many new ideas I have.
_____Three words that describe me are *curious, leader, imaginative*.

Based on these predictive lists, I suspect:

- My strongest learning style is:____________________.
- This quadrant may be your "home base," the place where you are most comfortable teaching and learning.
- The students I am most likely to miss are those who are strongest in these two learning style quadrants:

  ________________________ ________________________

As you continue to work your way through this book and learn more about learning styles, you may want to change your prediction.

Study the learning style diagram on the following page. Usually the students that we most often miss are in the quadrant opposite our strength. An Imaginative Learner teacher, for example, might find it difficult to teach Common Sense Learners. The teacher might lean toward group activities that encourage free-wheeling discussion and personal anecdotes. The Common Sense student might enjoy working alone to develop a computer game that demonstrates what she has learned. If the teacher continues to teach to his or her own strength (Imaginative) only, the Common Sense student may appear to be quiet, uncooperative, and not very smart.

The Analytic Learner teacher might have difficulty teaching the Dynamic student. The Analytic wants to have Bible drills and memory verse quizzing, but the Dynamic wants to develop and perform dramas that share the truth of those Bible verses. In protest to never having his or her abilities affirmed, the Dynamic Learner may become a discipline problem.

Many children and teens would prefer to be labeled "bad" than "dumb."

The importance of identifying your learning style as a teacher is not so much to know what your style is. Rather, it is to use that knowledge as a caution: Don't allow your teaching to ignore those students whose learning styles are different from your own.

As you go around the four-quadrant cycle week after week, students in all four groups develop a greater ability to think and reason both inside and outside their own quadrant.

Assignment

Place your students' names in the quadrant where you think they have the most strengths. Does this placement give you any clues about which students you are most likely to lose? What are you willing to do about it?

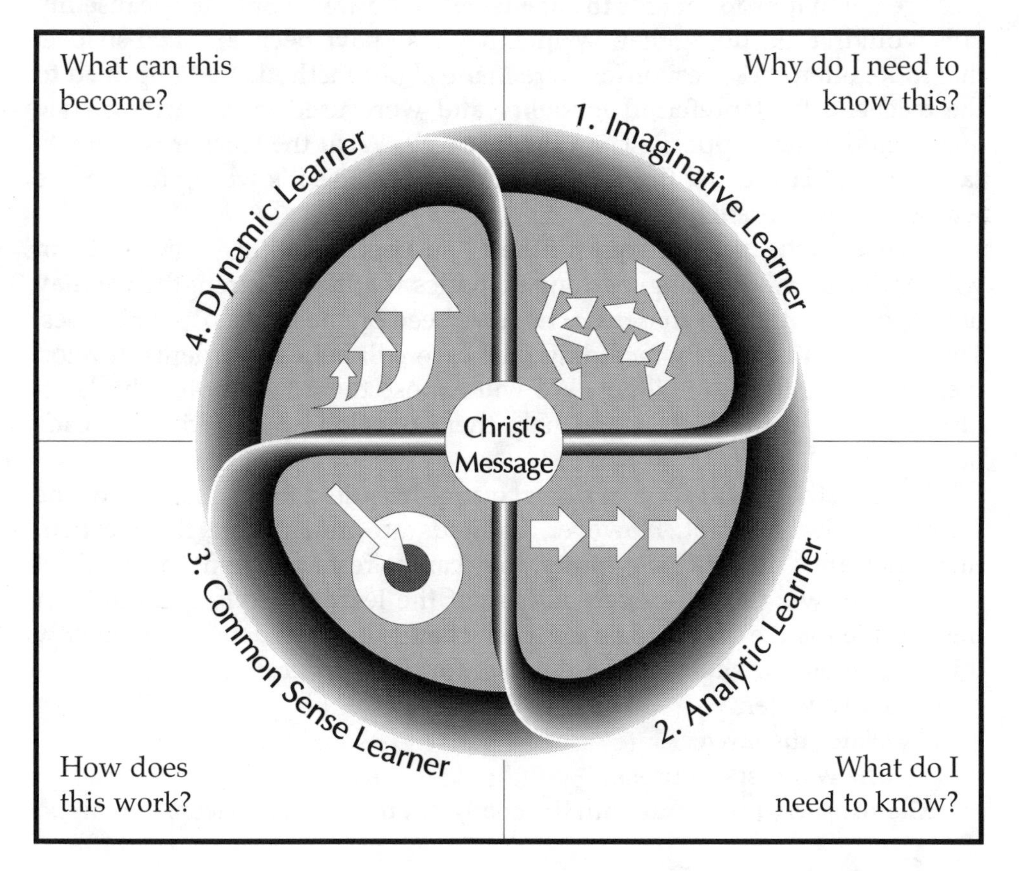

Auditory, Visual, and T/K Preferences

Within each quadrant, students also have auditory, visual, and tactile/kinesthetic (T/K) preferences. (See Chapter 9.) These preferences, called modalities, are sensory channels through which we receive information.

Some students in all learning style quadrants are auditory learners. They like listening, singing, clapping, dramatic reading, hearing music.

Others in all learning style quadrants are visual learners. When they see what they are learning, through words or pictures, they learn better. They love drawing, coloring, photographing, patterns, and forms.

Still others, tactile/kinesthetic students, need to move as part of the learning process. Many Common Sense Learners will have this preference, but students in other quadrants will also have T/K preferences. They will enjoy methods that involve physical action as part of the learning process.[10]

Methods

Knowing your learning style and your preferred modalities will help you understand why you like some methods and dislike others. (Refer to Chapters 9 and 10.) Perhaps you dislike some so much that when they are suggested in a teacher's guide you reject them immediately.

I've had Sunday school teachers complain that such-and-such a method was "really inappropriate for the age level" or "a waste of time because my kids wouldn't like doing that." While they may have been correct, I suspect that more often these responses were made about methods that appealed to the teacher's least preferred modality and were used in a learning style quadrant that was opposite from the teacher's. What the teacher was really saying was, "This is not the way I learn, and because it's wrong for me, it's wrong for my students, too."

A wise teacher will try some of these "suspect" activities—and try them with enthusiasm. By using learning activities that fit the strengths we may not have, we will reach students who have been on the fringes of our classes. They just didn't fit in. By including them, we will help all students develop their natural gifts and abilities. We will expose them to people who learn differently from themselves and help them develop appreciation for each other.

Some methods will seem at first glance to be suited for use with only one learning style quadrant. However, methods are much more flexible than that. They are a little like silly putty; they can be reshaped to fit the needs of students in two, three, or even all four of the learning style quadrants. A method is a lot like the word *water*. It can change its form depending on how it is used. Note the slightly different uses for the word *water*.

I love water.
Water the lawn.
The water spout broke.

All are *water* words, but with the change in the part of speech, we can do different things with the meaning of *water*. The same is true of methods. When we change the method slightly, we can do different things with it, and it just might be perfect for an altogether different learning style group.

Picture Watching—An Example

Picture watching is a method that students with a visual modality preference will enjoy. This one method can be tweaked so that visual people in all four learning styles can enjoy it.

The following lesson ideas are all aimed at youth and adults.

IMAGINATIVE LEARNERS

Focus: Our need to feel Christ's presence.

Students will sit in groups of three or four and study a picture of Jesus surrounded by children. Students think back through their week and consider which child in the picture is most like they were—the child on Jesus' lap, the one hanging back a little, or the child reaching out to Jesus. Students explain their choices.

This activity brings to the lesson the past experiences of the students. It prepares them for the topic of the morning. It answers the question, "Why study this lesson?"

ANALYTIC LEARNERS

Focus: The servanthood of believers.

Students will do a biblical study of the post-resurrection story of Jesus making breakfast for His disciples. They will then look at several pictures of the event and determine which is the most true to the Bible's content and what can be learned from the pictures.

Visual students will enjoy this inductive study that combines the study of pictures with the study of Scripture. They are good at analyzing pictures and words. This picture watching activity helps answer the question, "What do we need to know? What forms the foundation of our faith?"

COMMON SENSE LEARNERS

Focus: Christians are called to be the salt in today's society.

Students will review the lesson from Scripture and construct collages from magazine pictures that help to illustrate where "salt" might be poured. These posters will be placed in the foyer of the church to encourage the whole church to consider the place of the Christian in social action.

DYNAMIC LEARNERS

Focus: Salvation, emphasizing that God has no grandchildren. Christianity is a personal choice.

Students develop a slide show from famous paintings and use it to teach twelve- and thirteen-year-old children what it meant for Jesus to be crucified for us.

Each of these methods involves visual learning through pictures. But note how the use of the method changed to fit the different learning style quadrants.[11]

Methods support the curriculum structure, not the other way around. The right methods used effectively within the four-quadrant learning style pattern will help us discover that God gave us students who are a lot smarter than we thought they were.

When we add the three modalities of learning to the curriculum pattern, the pattern looks like this.

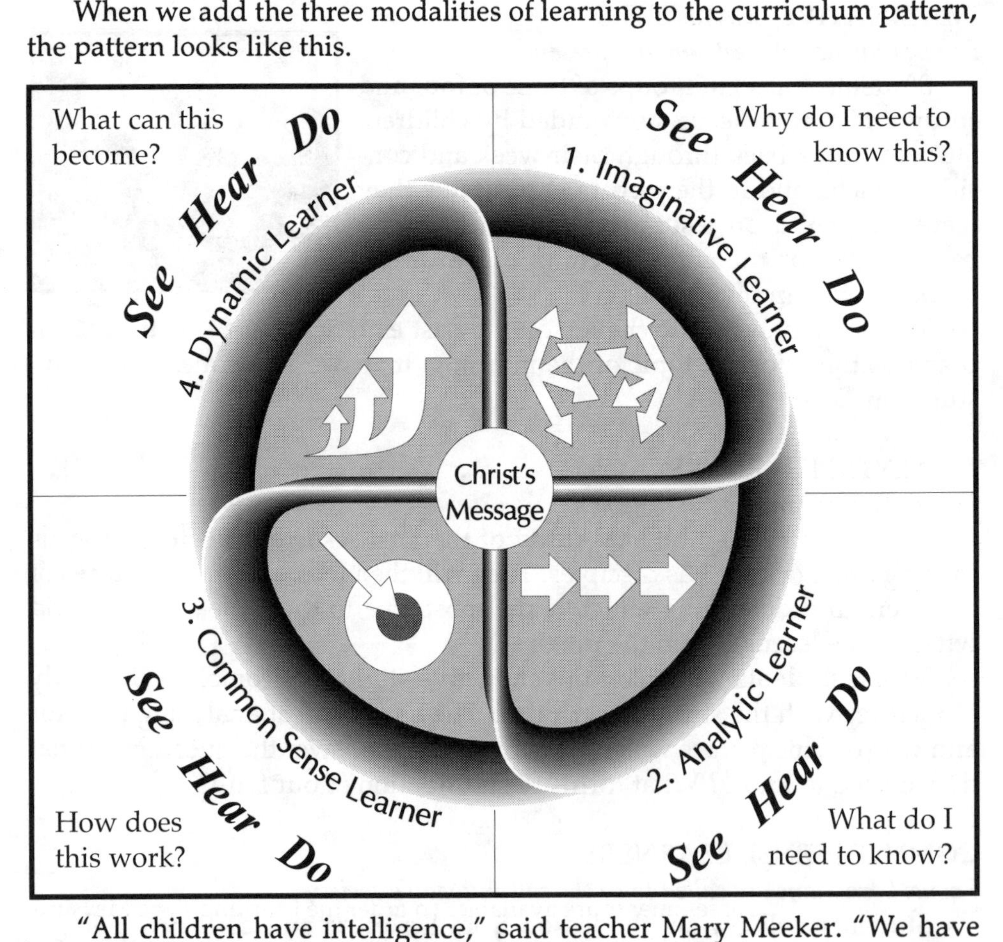

"All children have intelligence," said teacher Mary Meeker. "We have asked the wrong question. We have asked, 'How much?' and we need to ask, 'What kind?'"[12]

Assignment

Apple Learning Solutions printed an ad showing two identical twins. The caption read, "To us, they look very different." Within the ad for Apple Macintosh personal computers, the copy asserted, "No matter how similar they may appear, every child is unique. Each has different interests, different abilities, and a different way of learning."[13]

Develop an ad to educate a volunteer who has never taught a Sunday school class on what he or she needs to know about learning styles before starting his or her exciting assignment.

NOTES

1. For further information, see David Kolb's book, *Experiential Learning: Experience as the Source of Learning and Development* (Englewood Cliffs, N.J.: Prentice-Hall, 1984).

2. McCarthy's model expands the Kolb model into eight steps. Her unique approach involving hemisphericity will be expanded in Chapter 18, "Bernice McCarthy and the 4MAT System."

3. The characteristics of people who fall into these four quadrants will be expanded in Chapters 10 through 13.

4. I have used Bernice McCarthy's terms, as they are explained in her 4MAT® System (Excel, Inc., 23385 Old Barrington Road, Barrington, IL 60010. Phone: 708-382-7272, FAX: 708-382-4510) because they tell us something about the learner. Her terms require less explanation than Kolb's. Kolb's terms for the same quadrants are Diverger (Imaginative); Assimilator (Analytic); Converger (Common Sense); Accommodator (Dynamic).

5. Bernice McCarthy, "Using the 4MAT System to Bring Learning Styles to Schools," *Educational Leadership*, Vol. 48, No. 2, October 1990, p. 33.

6. Bernice McCarthy at ASCD Action Laboratory, "Using 4MAT as a Framework for Connecting Content and Learners: Meeting the Instructional Challenge of Cultural Diversity," ASCD Action Lab, March 19, 1994.

7. C. Ted Taylor, "Experimental Learning: The Learning Style Inventory Experiential Learning Model," *Adult Leadership*, April 1989, p. 6. Based on the work of David Kolb and Ronald Fry, "Toward an Applied Theory of Experiential Learning," *Theories of Group Processes*, Cary L. Cooper, ed. (New York: John Wiley and Sons, 1975), pp. 33, 34.

8. Learning style assessments are available. To order the Learning Type Measure (LTM) or Teaching Style Inventory (TSI) by Excel, Inc. (both sold in packets of 25), contact Excel, Inc., 23385 Old Barrington Road, Barrington, IL 60010. Phone: 708-382-7272. The LTM not only helps identify an individual's learning preferences, but also provides a method for applying this knowledge to develop strategies for improved teaching, communication, or management. Educators can order the Learning-Style Inventory (LSI) by David A. Kolb ©1981. Write McBer & Company, Training Resources Group, 137 Newbury Street, Boston, MA 02116. This excellent predictive inventory will help you identify your primary style and the strength of that style.

More importantly, it shows the cycle of learning that indicates the strength of your style in each of the four quadrants. The weaker your strength in a quadrant the more important it will be for you to make the extra effort to teach in ways that students who learn in that quadrant prefer.

9. "Teaching style should never be treated as a mere corollary to learning style. Teaching/learning styles are distinct, though complementary, and should be studied separately. They bear completely different objectives, goals and criteria. The nature of learning style describes the learner's learning: the nature of teaching style is not to describe the teacher's learning or even primarily the teacher's facilitation of the student's learning; rather, it is to describe the teacher and his or her behavior as a vehicle for teaching." Grace M. H. Gayle, "A New Paradigm for Heuristic Research in Teaching Styles," *Religious Education*, Vol. 89, No. 1, Winter 1994, p. 9.

10. Learning style experts give different percentages of students who have strong modality preferences. Recent information suggests that 70 percent of our students have a strong preference. This 70 percent learn best when methods that are used within their learning style quadrant match their auditory, visual, or tactile/kinesthetic preference. They learn even better when their primary preference is backed up by their secondary preferences. For the other 30 percent who do not have strong modality preferences, how well they do with methods involving sight, hearing, and movement will depend on how interested they are in the subject. See Rita Dunn, Jeffrey S. Beaudry, and Angela Klavas, "Survey of Research on Learning Styles," *Educational Leadership*, March 1989.

11. For a listing of methods and the modalities for which they are appropriate see Chapters 9, 10, 11, 12, and 13.

12. Quoted by Mary Meeker at ASCD Action Lab, "Using 4MAT as a Framework for Connecting Content and Learners: Meeting the Instructional Challenge of Cultural Diversity," March 19, 1994.

13. *Teacher Magazine*, September 1993, pp. 4, 5.

Part II

Stories of the Four Styles

THOU alone, O Lord, art able to move a man; from the moment that I think of Thee, my life is at Thy service; my weak talents are perhaps great in the eyes of men, but for Thee they are nothing and in every case they are the gifts Thou hast given me. When I think of Thy sufferings, Thou, my Lord and Saviour, I do not want to spend my days whimpering in a pulpit, but I want to be surrounded by insults, losing everything which is of earthly order—if it is Thy will.
—Reprinted from The Prayers of Kierkegaard *by Perry D. LeFevre*

The next four chapters include stories of four students and four teachers (their stories representing compilations from a number of people). Each person represents a very different view about faith and teaching and learning. These views reflect a strong learning style preference. Note the experiences they considered pivotal in their learning/teaching experience. What gave them joy? What hurt them? What helped them learn and what turned them off to learning? Spend more time with those people who do not learn like you do. These are the people you most need to understand.

The students' stories may allow us to say, "Oh, that's why she acts the way she does." Or, "Now I understand that student."

What is true in these stories will not duplicate exactly what you see in your students. But look for similarities. Each learner can say, "My learning style is like my fingerprint—similar, perhaps, to many others—but unique."

Pay particular attention to the four teachers' experiences. Each is an excellent teacher—to the students who learn like he or she does in the same learning style—but each needs to be more aware that there are students in the class who are getting very little out of their Christian education.

Success

To demonstrate how differently people from various learning styles approach teaching, four youth leaders defined success. Their definitions determine the goals and design of their youth programs.

Success to an Imaginative youth leader: "I succeed when my kids learn to know themselves and their God. I want them to care for each other, to be honest and fully open. I want them to see me as a caring person. I judge success in terms of what happens in the lives of those young people."

Success to an Analytic youth leader: "My teens want highly ordered, disciplined structures. They love Bible quizzing. They enjoy studying solid content and participating in in-depth discussions. They will see me as the master scholar. I will know my class has succeeded when the students are prepared to wisely give an answer to anyone who asks what they believe and why."

Success to a Common Sense youth leader: "My kids enjoy working on projects that show faith in action. I want them to test if what I say is really true, and when they do, I'm successful. Perhaps you could call me a provider. I give them what they need to do an important job, then I step back and allow them to do it."

Success to a Dynamic youth leader: "My kids need to be involved in their faith. They need to respond to the pain they see in our world. A growing Christian is an active Christian looking for new ways to live his or her Christianity. I'm a success when I am a catalyst for their action."

Unfortunately, teachers who are unaware of learning styles or ignore their implications ignore the just-as-excellent concepts that are part of their peers' definitions. When they do this, they are in danger of missing people.

It is not the learner's responsibility to adjust to the teacher's preferred style, although—in order to survive—some do.[1] Most, however, especially in the Christian education setting, will simply stop participating.

Why not write your own, better definition of success?

Assignment

Before you work your way through the next four chapters, fix in your mind a picture of a student you've missed. Somehow this boy or girl, man or woman, just never heard what you were trying to communicate. Perhaps you felt there was a wall fixed between you. Take a paper plate and draw that person's picture on the plate. Keep the plate in front of you as you continue to read.

Susan Morris suggested this activity during a workshop on the 4MAT System (ASCD, 1994). As a roomful of educators, we drew on our plates, and—since we were seated by our preferred style—the reactions to this activity were easy to see. The Analytics and Common Sense Learners thought it was a waste of time, but many of the Imaginatives and Dynamics loved it. But the exercise stimulated our learning, even for those of us who didn't enjoy drawing faces on plates! Every time I looked at my plate, I determined anew to do everything possible to reach all my students.

Questions for the Next Four Chapters

As you read the stories of learners and teachers in Chapters 3—6, consider these questions:

Student Stories

- What are this student's strengths in a Christian education setting? In the home setting?
- How would these strengths be captured in a Christian education setting? In a home setting?
- How might a parent who wants to help this child do better in school structure homework situations?
- Describe a teacher who would help this student develop his or her strengths, as well as skills in the other three quadrants.

Teacher Stories

- What are this teacher's strengths in the classroom?
- What students would this teacher be most likely to miss in the teaching process?
- If you were the Christian education director working with this teacher, how would you guide him or her toward greater excellence?
- If this teacher were a parent, what dangers do you see in his or her relationship with the family's children, especially if the children had strengths in other quadrants?

Note

1. Most children are not willing or able to adjust to a teacher's learning style. Susan Harter, a psychology professor at the University of Denver who studies social development in children said, "By the second or third grade children know precisely where they stand on the 'smart or dumb' continuum, and since most children at this age want to succeed in school, this knowledge profoundly affects their self-esteem." From "Tracked to Fail" by Sheila Tobias, *Psychology Today*, September 1989, p. 57. "Education in this country," writes the author, "is becoming a process of separating the 'gifted' from the 'average,' the 'intelligent' from the 'slow'—one is tempted to say, the wheat from the chaff" (p. 55). Learning styles is one way to remove negative labels and restructure education to fit the way God made children.

3

THE IMAGINATIVE LEARNER

To banish the imaginative side of life to the illogical, insignificant, or meaningless is to accept a crippling restriction on what counts as meaning.
—Harvey Cox

"Big contest!" the teacher announces. "All of you who memorize fifty Bible verses this quarter will win points toward a free trip to camp."

Imaginative Learners can assume that they will be staying home this summer—no free trip for them. Reciting something they have memorized is not the way they show they have learned. Memorizing is extremely difficult for them. They could tell teachers what those verses mean and how Christians could put them into practice, but most Christian educators don't give free camp experiences for *living* God's Word!

All too often, the Imaginative Learner's brain power goes under-utilized and under-appreciated. But Imaginative Learners are able to make use of their life experience as a foundation for gaining new knowledge. They tend to paint life and learning with broad strokes, placing more worth in the whole picture than in its individual parts. They think in paragraphs rather than short answers. As they talk, their base of knowledge grows.

I had a boss some years ago who was an Imaginative Learner. A brilliant man, he would often call meetings that would go on and on and on as he talked through a problem. If a meeting was called after 2 P.M. I would let my husband know that dinner that evening would probably be late. This man had to have the give and take of conversation in order to effectively lead. The longer he talked, the smarter he got. He was a lot like the elderly lady who asked the novelist E. M. Forster, "How do I know what I mean until I see what I say?" The answer for this type of learner is, "You don't. It is in the act of verbalizing that you discover what you think."[1]

In a school or Christian education setting, the student rarely has the advantage of being the "boss." So the Imaginative Learner is encouraged to not bother his neighbors or to sit quietly for a change so he or she can learn something. But this student's mind works most effectively when his or her mouth is also working. The student functions through social interaction.

A logical spin-off of this need to see and generalize is a sensitivity to and interest in others. Imaginative Learners are people people. They focus on facts primarily in terms of people. Imaginative Learners are keen observers of human behavior and are able to show real interest and empathy for others.

"If my house were on fire," an Imaginative Learner quipped, "I would save my telephone directory first. It's my link with my friends, and my friends help me define who I am."

Imaginative Learners would relate to Marchiene Vroon Rienstra's poem on the spirit of friendship.

The Spirit Blows Where She Wills[2]

I had lunch with a friend today.
What really happened
was that she got down on hands and knees
and crawled through the narrow doorway
of my heart
to the hearth, where, she knew
(though I did not)
a divine spark
still glowed within
under a mound of sad, gray ash.

She wasn't afraid to get herself sooty.
She gently separated the ashes,
uncovered the glowing spark,
and softly blew her love
into its orange heart
until it burned bright as the sun
and burst into dancing flames.

Every church committee needs an Imaginative Learner. When people-trouble erupts, the imaginative person acts like oil on troubled water. This person can hold the group—or church—together and bring people into harmony.

The Imaginative Learner closes the back doors to our churches where visitors escape because they feel that "This church is so unfriendly. We're going to try that brick church down the street." Many Imaginative Learners make others feel hugged and appreciated just by talking with them.

These students prefer to make decisions based on feelings and hunches, and they may ignore the cold, hard facts if they feel strongly about an issue. They want to know how much you care before they care how much you know.

Tony Campolo tells the story of a little boy who just might have been an Imaginative Learner.[3] He got a part in the Christmas play and was thrilled about it. All week he practiced and he had his lines down pat. "No room!" "No room!" The night of the pageant, the lights in the church were dimmed. Down the aisle came Joseph looking so tired in his daddy's old bathrobe. Beside him was pregnant Mary with a huge pillow stuffed under her robe. The little boy stared, not saying a word.

His mother knew he knew his lines and from her front row seat, she mouthed them, but he paid no attention to her. His heart went out to the couple. The teacher was worried that the pageant would come to a total stop if she didn't get the innkeeper off the stage. "The words are 'No room,'" she whispered. And still he stared. "No room!" the teacher prompted again. Finally the boy turned toward the teacher and with complete conviction cried, "I know what the words are, but she can have my room!"

Along with their people skills, Imaginative Learners show great innovation and imagination, especially in areas that involve people contact.

The Flip Side

The flip side of our strengths is often our weaknesses. This is true for learning styles, especially among children and teens who are immature in their Christian faith.

In class, these learners can monopolize conversation or disrupt the class with their constant talking.

Imaginative youngsters also depend on others for part of their identity. Often this can lead them to be awkward in social situations because they are too dependent on what others think of them. They want so much to be loved that, when this love is denied, they doubt their self worth.

They can be overly pliable. As young teens they can be talked into conforming to group values rather than standing up for their own convictions.

Meet Two Imaginative Learners

Gift of Gab: A Student's Story

When I was in elementary school, my mom used to call me her Chatty Cathy doll—pretty embarrassing for a boy. She was right. All my life I've liked to talk—about anything. I get my best grades in classes where I can talk. Of course, not all my teachers are thrilled with my mouth. In fifth grade, my teacher moved me right up to the desk under her nose because I wouldn't shut up. That was embarrassing, but I still found ways to talk.

Whenever I get an idea I want to hear how it sounds. I just want to bounce it off someone.

I like people. It's fun to talk with different ones and find out what they like to do and why they do it. I don't understand people who sit quietly by themselves and work on stuff. For me, that's no fun. I do better with people.

I have a group of other kids I hang out with. We do things together, and I like everyone in the group. They like me too. Whenever we have fights and some kids want to go off on their own, I try to talk them out of it. I'm a pretty good talker, so usually they'll stop being mad and come back.

That works in sports, too. Even if I'm on a team where no one likes each other, I can pull us together and make us score. My father says I have a gift in this area and will probably end up in the diplomatic corps. Maybe.

Whenever I get an idea I want to hear how it sounds.

I may not have the brain for that. I'd have to learn another language, and I'm not good at stuff like that. At school I get low grades when I have to give exact answers to questions. I do just fine on essay questions—lots of room to tell stories and share ideas about what I've learned. We don't get essay tests often because it takes the teachers so long to grade them. But when we do, I've had teachers read my answers to the rest of the class because they were so good.

My favorite class in school is history because the teacher breaks us into groups to do projects. I don't always get the best grades, but I have fun. Once we made a Mexican meal. I worked with three other people on the hot sauce. It was my first time for Mexican food. I'm a picky eater and I probably wouldn't have tried it on my own. But all my friends were there, so I ate up.

Another time that teacher had our teams do relief maps. My team picked Rhode Island, because it's little and we figured it would be easy. We got a good grade and the teacher put it on display. It helped dress up the classroom. I like classes where teachers make the room interesting.

My church—now talk about an ugly building. The people are nice, but I would like to have banners or even one stained glass window. I told my father that once, and he said I was shallow, that we could worship God in our church and save money to send to missionaries. Maybe, but I think God would like a little color, too.

I complained to our youth leader about the four blank walls in our church basement. She said, "Challenge! Do something about it." So I did. I got the carpet store to donate some large samples, and my friends and I put the samples on the floor and up one wall. Talk about color, and everything was almost free. I got some plexiglass frames and put posters in them. We change the posters whenever someone finds new pictures.

I like to talk with adults. Some try to pretend they're perfect, but I can see through them.

This year my math teacher is going to have a baby. She doesn't feel good some days. It's funny, but I can tell. Sometimes I try to get the other kids not to act up on her down days.

Last year I had a teacher who didn't know how to teach. He had just gotten out of college, and I don't see why they let him out. When I was in his class I would try to answer questions and stretch them out. I'd gab on and on because I knew he didn't know how to fill up the time. At the end of the year, he told me he was grateful for my participation. He didn't come back this year. I didn't learn anything in his class, but I helped him out.

I was definitively not one of my art teacher's favorites. One day she took our class to a contemporary art museum and told us we could go anywhere we wanted. So my friends and I looked at the pictures for two minutes and then decided we'd walk downtown. "After all," one of my friends pointed out, "she said we could go anywhere we wanted." When she found us, she yelled and screamed about what awful, sneaky kids we were, and she flunked us all. My dad was furious, and kept asking, "Why did you go along? Why did you do such a stupid thing?" I went because everyone I knew went. I'm sorry about the grade, but my friends still like me, and that's more important.

I concentrate better when I'm sitting in a circle.

I've got a lot of friends in my church youth group, too. We do things after church and on weekends and that's fun.

Class time at church is looking up, too. We got rid of those long tables and sit in circles now. Some of the kids don't like it, but I concentrate better when I'm sitting in a circle. It's easier to share my ideas and hear my friends' ideas. The Sunday school teacher I had last year was about the death of me. He would get these workbooks, and we would sit in class, after his little presentation, and fill in the books. Then he'd go over the answers and tell us what was right or wrong. He did everything except run around and put letter grades on all the books. I hated Sunday school and I hated that teacher. I'd ask, "Why can't we talk about something important?" He'd respond, "What's more important than knowing what the Bible says?" Now I'm old enough to have an answer for him, but at the time I just looked for ways to be sick on Sunday morning. My father understood and would let me skip, but not my mother. She'd say, "I loved those workbooks when I was a kid. They're a great way to learn. You're just in a trouble-causing mood."

At the same time, I was in a kids' club program that I never wanted to miss. We'd play games, and even those kids who weren't very athletic had a good time. There weren't winners and losers. Some of the less athletic guys and girls wouldn't have come if everything was competitive.

A lot of the kids I know have bad self-images. That's too bad. I wish our youth leader would do more to help kids feel better about themselves.

One of my friends tried to commit suicide. He said he didn't, but he took a lot of pills, and his folks had to take him to the hospital. I talk to him every chance I get. I don't think he has anyone else to talk to. He goes over and over the same stuff all the time, but I listen, even though it gets boring.

I'm not all that serious about my Christianity, but this is something I can do—listen. When he first started talking, I wouldn't say much. Then, little by little, I would think of things to say and he would answer. At first, what I said sounded dumb, but the more I talked the smarter I became. I'm good at pulling ideas from here and there.

He's a valuable person. All my friends are. I believe that if people don't see people as important, they shouldn't call themselves Christians.

Noise and Learning: A Teacher's Story

My wife and I are team teachers. She does most of the work getting ready for our Sunday school class. She's good at it. She loves books and facts and putting everything in order so the kids learn effectively. I'm more the Mr. Nice Guy. I know that bothers my wife. She's the one who works hardest on the lesson, and I'm the one the kids come to when they have problems. It's not that the kids don't like her. It's just that I'm more approachable. My wife and I both believe that Christian education is a people business, but I'm better at showing that belief to the kids. I think the kids suspect that she's the answer person and I'm the listener, so they come to us for different things.

A couple of Sundays ago, we were taking one of the kids out after class for Sunday dinner. Each week we take a different student. It's a great way to get to know each person as an individual.

My wife had to run into the drug store, and I stayed in the car with Gary. She was no sooner out the door than he started telling me about his date the night before. He had been out with one of the girls in the Sunday school class. Gary said, "I didn't get in until 3:30." I just smiled and shook my head. He continued, "We had a good time." I made a sort-of noise. Finally he got to the point of the conversation. "But nothing happened." He wanted to talk about sex, but didn't know how to get started. This was the perfect opportunity. He didn't have to tell me about his date or the time they got home or that they hadn't had sex. But he wanted to. We got started talking and kept going even after my wife got back. She was smart enough not to interrupt.

I was hesitant about this team-teaching experience going in, but I'm pleased now. You see, I'm artistic. One of the guys in our class told me, "Hey, you're the first artistic man I've ever met in this church." He's exaggerating, but I do know that the church can find artistic and creative people suspect. We do things that seem a little weird, like wanting to spend money on beanbag chairs for the classroom.

One month my wife and I planned to take the Sunday school class to the art museum. We live near Chicago, and yet none of those kids had ever been there before. Very sad. A couple of the kids tried to talk me into switching the museum for a ball park, but I wouldn't give in. At the museum, one of the exhibits was a screen-topped card table. One chair was placed at each side of the table. Kids would sit there and watch a movie of a meal being eaten. A hand holding a fork would appear and spear a piece of meat. Next some peas would disappear. It was great fun for them, and some of those food-crazy boys sat through three meals. Three of the boys went back to their high school after that visit and signed up for a movie-making course. A class several months later included their first movie—a genuinely awful production filled with knights and blood and screams. They were practicing with art forms. Perhaps one of those young men will go on to make excellent movies that God will use to point kids in their generation to Him.

We need to "unlimit" our Sunday school class. Our kids aren't dumb. They've lived a lot of life already. They need to know we value what they already know and we want to help them add more knowledge to that base. Sunday school is not a little classroom. It's preparation for living for Christ in a difficult world.

I enjoy using roleplay in our class. My wife will present some information and I'll break the kids into little groups to practice using what, until then, was only a theory. Roleplay is a great way to make sure the kids listen. They know that Bible study is not just words. It's usable stuff. I've noticed, however, that this is not the universal opinion of roleplay. One girl said, "Why are we just sitting around here talking to ourselves? Why don't you really teach us something?" But I think we need to talk to ourselves in preparation for talking to others who need to see Christianity in action.

Another thing my wife and I do is send kids out into the community and into their schools to gather information for class. I'll do just about anything to get them interacting with faith principles. Once we had them interview several people in the community. They talked to unchurched kids at school about their views of God. They taped the answers. We started class by listening to those tapes. My wife led them in a study of the biblical view of God. We spend a lot more time talking in our class than some of the other classes do. Talking is important. My wife doesn't feel that strongly about it, but she goes along with me. She does make sure they get their facts right before they get too far off the track.

I have some problem with noise in my class. Well, I don't have the problem; the other teachers have it. The kids make more noise than my wife or I do. I've had adults poke their heads into our room and ask us to keep it down so other groups can study. That's embarrassing. But I don't want to tame things down too much. That noise is a sign that some real learning is going on. How's a kid supposed to learn without talking?

The second part of my ministry is to the kids' parents. We let the teens know that it is not us against their parents. I encourage them to talk to me, and I promise that I will keep their confidences unless there are things that would be harmful to them or harmful for their parents not to know. I promise I will tell them before I share anything with their parents. This gives them a chance to go with me or prepare the way for what I'll say. It's amazing how often our kids from Christian families share potentially devastating things with us. If I didn't allow time for these conversations, Christian adults would never be able to help.

My wife was leading a study on crisis, all the big and little crises that enter the lives of teenagers. (The little ones aren't all that little in kids' eyes.) Even we were unprepared for some of the big ones the kids shared. One girl told us that she had cancer and would have to take treatments. She would miss class every other Sunday. The class promised to support her in prayer and with cards. Even though she was relatively new to the class and few of the kids really knew her, they responded in love.

Another girl shared in class, "My girlfriend's father is trying to rape her." There was dead silence. Since she brought up the situation, I couldn't say, "Sorry, but we don't talk about rape in class. I'll talk with you about this later." That was my panicked inclination, but again, I've told the kids that they're free to share whatever they want, and I couldn't back down because I was nervous or unprepared to deal with the subject. So I said to the whole class, "What do you think she should do?" The response was mixed. Teenage boys shared some excellent ideas, and they also tossed in an equal number of really crude ones and a few sick jokes. I suspect this was the adolescent male's way of handling a loaded issue. After class, I asked the girl to stay, and my wife and I talked with her further. Eventually, through this discussion, her friend's father was removed from the home. Without talking, none of this would have happened. I honestly can't understand how people can think teaching is just standing up in front of a class and providing information. Teaching is opening the class to talking about their own experiences and their own needs.

If I were to answer the question, "What do you want your kids to get from your class?" I think I could answer in one word—love. I want my kids to become Christian lovers—to be able to show through their actions just how much love Jesus has to offer.[4] I've seen Christian love grow in the lives of some of the kids, not by leaps and bounds, but by the little things the kids do. For example, they write little encouraging notes to people who need them. I started to do that for them, and they copied my idea. I make free stamps available.

Sunday school is preparation for living in a difficult world.

Sometimes their love acts are secret, and those are the best. For example, Jananne told my wife that she had helped Alice with her hemlines and accessories. Alice had never cared much about clothes and Jananne comes close to being a fashion plate. After my wife told me about this secret act of love, I watched Jananne for several weeks. She tended to ignore the unpopular Alice in class. I guess it's unfair of me to expect her to be totally mature. She's in the process of learning what it means to be a lover.

Christian love is a funny thing. It's got to be natural or the kids will pick up on it. I remember a preacher I admired when I was in college. He seemed to be warm and loving from the pulpit. Then, unfortunately, I got to know him and in person he was cold and unfeeling.

I don't want to ever be two-faced with my kids. What they see is what they get. I love each and every one of them, and I tell them so every week.

Learning Style Worksheet

- What are the characteristics of the Imaginative Learner?

- Of the above characteristics, which are:

  Most like me

  Least like me

- In my teaching (or parenting) which students (children) may be strongly Imaginative Learners?

• Based on how I teach, which one of the following applies to me?

_____I capture these students' strengths weekly.

_____I capture these students' strengths occasionally.

_____I hardly ever capture these students' strengths.

Imaginative Learners

Following is an incomplete list of characteristics that helps define people who have a strongly imaginative learning style.

Imaginative Learners often . . .

- Talk in broad overviews
- Learn by listening and sharing ideas
- Answer the questions "Why?" "Why not?"
- Are sociable, friendly, sensitive
- Are emphathetic
- Keenly observe human nature
- Enjoy listening and talking
- Work best in a noisy setting
- Dislike long lectures, memorizing, working alone
- Are idea people
- Are in tune with their feelings
- See facts in relationship to people
- Learn by talking
- Like the feeling of "my gang"
- Get smarter the longer they talk
- Enjoy roleplay, simulation, mime
- Dislike win/lose situations
- Value people above product, friendship above grades
- Love a colorful working situation
- Define themselves in terms of friendship

Notes

1. Alan Jacobs, "Preferring the Fog," *Perspectives*, February 1994, p. 6.

2. Marchiene Vroon Rienstra, "The Spirit Blows Where She Wills," ©*Perspectives*, January 1994, p. 18. Used with permission.

3. From a plenary session by Tony Campolo, National Youthworkers Convention, October 1990.

4. Father Peter G. van Breemen, Dutch Jesuit theologian, wrote about love in a way that this Imaginative teacher would understand. "The love, the acceptance of other persons makes me into the unique person I am meant to be . . . When I am not accepted, I cannot come to fulfillment" (*As Bread That Is Broken* [Denville, N.J.: Dimension Books, 1974]).

4

THE ANALYTIC LEARNER

If I had only three years to serve the Lord, I'd spend the first two studying.
—Dr. Charles Barnhouse

The Analytic Learner is the type of learner every mother prays her baby will be. The child begins to drool over books at a very young age and continues to devour them for the rest of his or her life. These diligent students are the thinkers and watchers of our society and, in the process, they collect more than their rightful share of the A's that life distributes. For this reason, we often assume that these are the smartest people. This is not necessarily true. There are geniuses in each learning quadrant, but the Analytics are easiest to spot. School, and often the teaching aspects of our Christian education programs, were made for them. They learn best when seated at chairs and desks in straight rows listening to a teacher share from his or her vast amount of information.

They are very rational and sequential in their thinking. They like to sit back, listen, watch, and examine all sides of an issue before they venture an answer or conclusion. They start with an idea or an abstraction and allow their minds to play with it in order to make a personal, "right" observation.

In western culture, approximately 30 percent of our students will be analytic. The other 70 percent of the students fall in fairly equal numbers throughout the other three quadrants. Teacher-centered presentations will reach 30 percent of our students, and that's great for that 30 percent. But we teachers need to remind ourselves that 30 percent isn't passing!

When it comes to making a decision for Christ, Imaginative Learners are often very quickly attracted to the love they feel is available through Christ. Analytic Learners, however, will weigh all sides of the Christianity issue, often for a very long time.[1] They will read Scripture, study respected theologians, and make certain that Christ's offer makes sense. They are unlikely to be convinced by anything but reason. They seek all the facts before they are comfortable. Only then, after long and rational thought, will they be willing to consider a leap of faith.

Teachers love Analytic Learners, primarily because Analytic Learners love teachers. They are quiet in class. They are listeners. They follow directions. Unlike Imaginative Learners, Analytics usually like a quiet atmosphere in which to work.

Analytic Learners have little trouble memorizing the fifty Bible verses and winning that free trip to camp. They thrive on competition.

These learners are skilled at creating concepts and models. They find the "right" answers.

Analytics' minds are their most valued possession. A's are important to them because those grades help them define who they are. Analytics need to be seen as good thinkers, thorough and industrious. Words they would use to describe themselves include *theoretical*, *intellectual*, and *knowledge-oriented*.

When they make mistakes, teachers shouldn't make light of them or call public attention to them.

Let's suppose a teacher asks Rick, an Analytic fifth grader, to name Jesus' twelve disciples. The child's mind goes blank and he can't think of a single name. In desperation he asks, "Was Jacob one of them?" The class and teacher laugh and the teacher says, "You need to move up a Testament." The child is hurt because the teacher has just made fun of his most valued possession.

Replay this scenario with an Imaginative Learner and that learner would laugh right along with the class and think, *Great! The teacher must like me. She just made a joke.* Learning style researcher Rita Dunn's quip, "There is nothing worse than equal treatment of unequals" rings true. In the situation just described, that Analytic fifth grader may tune out for the rest of the class period. The teacher has lost him. If this happens often enough, the church may lose him, too.

The Flip Side

Flip the Analytic Learners' strengths on their other side and you may find weaknesses in children, teens, and maturing adult Christians. Analytics rely more on thinking than on their feelings to make right decisions. This means that their thought processes tend to be limited to what is logical, analytical, critical, and generally impersonal.

Chuck Snyder illustrated the Analytic's mind-set and this weakness when he wrote:

> I approach TV shows different [from my wife] because I'm not as relationship-oriented as Barb. Take for instance the show "North and South" that ran a few years ago on TV. It was about the Civil War, one of my areas of interest. . . . I videotaped it for later viewing. As I was viewing it on the tape, I saw a couple grab their blanket and head for the lake. I knew I was in for twenty minutes of talking and sharing, so I used my remote and fast-forwarded the tape to the next battle scene. No use wasting my time watching people in a private conversation.[2]

Because they are more knowledge-oriented than people-oriented, they can often appear to be picky, stuffy, and critical. They have little tolerance for sharing of feeling-generated ideas and will tend to be moralistic, untempered with self-doubt or tolerance.

Meet Two Analytic Learners

Smart Kid: A Student's Story

I kept my mouth shut about Mr. Divet, my history teacher. Every other kid in my class hated him, but I thought he was sort of neat. He was my first male teacher, and he lectured and expected us seventh graders to take notes. I was impressed by how much he knew and how organized he was—just like a talking book. I had this mental picture of him rushing home, digging through musty old books, and coming up with just the right stuff to tell us the next day. In my mind's eye, he didn't have a wife or family or any life outside the classroom, and I liked the sense of ownership in him that that gave me.

He was exacting. His rule was that a misspelled word was a totally wrong answer. It's been several years since I was in his class, and I can still pull back my feelings about a C– that I got on an important test because I misspelled *hieroglyphics* in five different sections. I'd never gotten a grade that low before, and it meant I got a B on my report card. My mother was so upset—because my answers were really right, just misspelled—that she went to talk to him. He wouldn't change my grade. He said that a rule was a rule. My mother thought he was awful, and for a few weeks, so did I. But I was also glad that he had rules and stuck to them.

Math isn't my favorite subject, but I did have one great math teacher. After every test, she arranged us in a seating order according to our grades. I looked forward to every test because I wanted to move up. For a few weeks, I was in the first seat. That was one of the proudest moments of my life. Some of the kids hated her for this, and I didn't understand that. I like competing with my mind. There's always a good chance I'll win. Competition makes me work to get better. People who are afraid of competition just don't want to work their hardest.

People who are afraid of competition don't want to work their hardest.

People take advantage of me because I'm smart. Part of me doesn't mind, but the other part doesn't think it's fair. At school when we work on team projects, all the kids want me because they know I'll work hard. When I work for that good grade, they all get good grades. I'm not into group work or group grading. Why should anyone except me get credit for what I do?

True/false tests aren't my favorite either. I actually flunked one, and the teacher was so surprised she called me to her desk to see what was wrong. I went over every question with her and showed her why I had made the choices I did. When you think those true/false questions through, the simplest answer isn't always right. That teacher didn't think far enough. She changed my grade to an A–.

Teachers who really know their subjects aren't easy to find. Mr. Divet was my first, and my second was in Sunday school. I was just beginning to ask questions when I got to Mrs. Jackson's class. She knew where to look for answers. "How do we know there really is a God?" I'd ask. Or, "What proof is there that what we believe is really true?" "Why do so many intelligent people believe in evolution without God? Are you sure we aren't missing something?" And, Mrs. Jackson would come up with answers.

She didn't answer me personally, but she seemed to know exactly what I wanted to ask. She'd tell us what she was going to talk about, and I'd think, Yeah! I can hardly wait to hear what she has to say about that. I'd sit and take notes.

Once she brought in a tract that was written to convince people that Christianity is the one true religion. It would have been fun to have people of different faiths come to class and debate what we each believed. I'll bet I could have talked them into becoming Christians.

I enjoy a good debate. I can't understand people who hear reasonable explanations and aren't willing to change because of them.

As far as I know, Mrs. Jackson didn't have any favorites in her class. She never tried to be buddy-buddy. Never once did she hug me. That's the way a teacher ought to be. The best teachers are different from friends. I've had a few huggers in my day, and I suspect it's just easier for them to be friendly than to do the real work of teaching a good class.

I can contrast Mrs. Jackson with a youth leader who was never prepared. He would come to the meetings and ask us kids what we wanted to talk about. Some of the kids liked this approach, but I hated it. He's the teacher, so he should have decided what we needed. If he just wanted to share experiences, he should have given the youth group to someone who wanted to be a real teacher.

Recently some of us kids agreed to take on a service project. I chose to teach a third grader in our church to read better. I came up with this neat plan of reading the book to him, and then he would read it back to me. I thought I was getting somewhere until I realized he was memorizing most of the words when I read, and reciting the words back to me. This was supposed to be a quarterly project, so I couldn't quit. And, I certainly wasn't going to fail. I came up with another idea. This boy liked cars better than anything else in the world. I went to the car dealers in my town and got brochures from them. Then he and I made a book of pictures with the words under them. He was willing to work harder because he liked knowing about cars. He's probably the only poor reader in town who knows the word *carburetor* better than the word *apple*. When we reported on our projects, everyone was impressed with what I had done. I wish we had gotten grades because mine would have been an A.

I'm the smart kid in our family, and I like that label. When someone catches me at not being smart, I'm embarrassed. I remember I was just starting to read Shakespeare. A guest in our home asked me if I liked him. I said, "Sure, Shakespeare is great." I said that because I know that's how smart people are supposed to feel about Shakespeare. Then the guy came over and saw that I was only on page 4. I was embarrassed.

My favorite way to teach, and to be taught, is through lecture.

I like reading to find hidden meanings—stories on top of stories. For example, I enjoyed the Narnia series by C. S. Lewis. His symbols helped me look at the attributes of Christ in an all-new way. I never thought Christian writers were all that smart before I started reading Lewis. The stuff I've read seems too simple, but Lewis is different. Maybe I'll become a writer, although I wouldn't want to try anything that I might not be good at.

I'd like to get a weekend job, but my folks don't want me working on Sunday. I don't mind too much because I enjoy church. I like to listen to the sermons and try to guess the point the pastor will be making before he makes it. I also try to find jumps in his logic or conclusions he comes to that he really hasn't proven from Scripture. Occasionally we have a really boring sermon. I pass the time by trying to diagram sentences in my father's King James Version of the Bible.

I don't do drugs or drink. Part of the reason is because I'm a Christian and my church friends would have fits. But the real reason is that I don't want to wreck my mind. My mind is the favorite part of my body. I would never do anything to hurt my ability to think through problems.

As I look forward to the future, I want to be known as a wise adult. I want to be able to share my knowledge with others. A couple of people like Mr. Divet and Mrs. Jackson were mentors to me. They helped me develop my mind. As I grow older, I want to share my wisdom with others, too.

Will to Love: A Teacher's Story

Last Sunday a student asked me if I loved Jesus. Funny question and out of context, so I've been thinking about it all week. Yes, I do. But it's not a feeling kind of love. It's a mind love. I *will* to believe in Christ, and I *will* to love Him. I can share the facts and reasons for my faith, but my final commitment was a jump in reason. That was hard for me because I want everything to make sense. My mind tells me it is reasonable to love, so I make the Christ-choice rather than any other.

My favorite way to teach, and to be taught, is through lecture. When the superintendent asked me to teach the fifth grade Sunday school class, I said no. I couldn't lecture to kids who were ten and eleven. But when I prayed about it, I reasoned that it is during the elementary and middle school years that faith is formed. If that formation doesn't have a strong base, it may not hold during the difficult teen years. So here I am in the elementary division.

I like kids. It's fun to see them make discoveries. Their faces light up. I like their lack of sophistication. I like their assumption that a teacher is special. They are eager to learn.

When I took this job, the superintendent handed me a teacher's guide. I enjoyed studying the Bible part of the lesson in that guide and doing some of my own research on the background of the passage. But I didn't enjoy the games and projects and those activities that got kids talking about the way they felt. I wanted my kids to know the Bible, so that's where I decided to put all my efforts and all the class time. I worried that if my kids had to take Bible SAT tests to get into Sunday school, most would flunk.

I try to be sensitive to kids' special problems.

My solution was to not do any of the extras and get right down to the Bible facts. One Sunday I got out my maps and charts and showed the kids how to read them and what they could learn about the Bible story from them. My enthusiasm carried the day. After class many of the children came up to look more closely at the maps. They'd never had a class like that before.

Now I follow this pattern every week. I start by telling a Bible story or by talking about the main point of the story. Then the kids read it for themselves in their Bibles. Sometimes we read around the circle so everyone has a chance to talk. Finally I ask questions or have them work on a worksheet so they can keep a record of what they've learned. We end with prayer. Everyone is encouraged to add sentence prayers.

I try to be sensitive to kids' special problems. For example, a cult group was handing out cute cartoons about their beliefs to my children at school. The cartoons and the group's after-school activities were appealing to youngsters, and some of the children had even attended a few. I was sick when I heard about it.

I immediately started to do research on this group and told the kids that we would spend the next couple of Sundays talking about it. I attacked this like I would a term paper. I got books from my church library and bought others at the Christian bookstore. All were written at the high school or adult levels, so I had to age-grade my material. But if these people were going to hit on little kids, I would give those kids what they needed to survive those hits.

In class we studied what Christians and the cults believe about God, Jesus, people, and sin. I let the kids compare Christianity to the cults because I knew if they came to their own conclusions, it would mean more than if I told them what to believe.

I work, and I have my own family, so I don't do much with my kids outside class. (I do put their birthdays on my calendar so that I remember to send cards.) I ought to do better here. That's one thing I learned from the cult experience. Those people were willing to spend hours and hours doing kid stuff so that kids would trust them and what they taught. A Sunday school teacher should be just as willing. So I'm planning to go to the fun fair at the elementary school my kids attend. I just don't take naturally to games and unorganized play. This isn't just because I'm an adult. I felt the same way when I was a kid. My husband says I never learned to play. Maybe not, but I sure got a lot done in the time others were playing.

I'm in the process of setting long-range goals for my teaching. I'm spending a lot of time on this because I want to know exactly why I'm teaching and what I hope to accomplish.

I'm going to continue teaching in the elementary area. I'm different from most of the other teachers because I really care about the facts. The kids need to know what I've spent my lifetime learning. I can do important things for God in this position.

As one of my short-term goals, I'm going to list the kids I don't think I'm reaching. I know there are a few in my class who come only because their parents force them to. They think my class is boring. How do I reach them without turning my classroom into fluff and silliness?

Some of my students, not all, are ready to make a commitment to Christ. I enjoy being a part of that life decision. I make the process difficult for them, so both of us are sure this is something they are doing because they want to. I don't believe in just having kids put their hands up to signify their interest. Living in this world as a Christian is hard, and we don't do anyone any favor by making its starting point easy. I stay in my room between Sunday school and church. The kids know that they can come to me during this time and talk about their faith. Last week Sarah came and said she wanted to be a real Christian. I quizzed her on her faith. "Why do you want to do this? What does this mean to you in terms of how you will live? What exactly is it you think you are doing? What is involved in this decision?" Sarah had good answers. She hadn't just come back for a friendly chat. I felt good. She's a product of the firm foundation that I'm helping these children lay. At this point in their spiritual journey, they know a lot about what they believe and why. I find that exhilarating.

Learning Style Worksheet

- What are the characteristics of the Analytic Learner?

- Of the above characteristics, which are:

  Most like me

  Least like me

- In my teaching (or parenting), which students (children) might be strongly Analytic Learners?

- Based on how I teach, which one of the following applies to me?
  - ___ I capture these students' strengths weekly.
  - ___ I capture these students' strengths occasionally.
  - ___ I hardly ever capture these students' strengths.

Analytic Learners

Following is an incomplete list of characteristics that help define people who have a strongly Analytic learning style.

Analytic Learners often . . .

- Like information presented logically and sequentially
- Value facts, figures, and the theoretical
- Debate to logically prove the correct stance or answer
- Value smart and wise people
- Set long-range plans and see their consequences
- Are curious about ideas
- See themselves as intellectual
- Have a high tolerance for theory
- Think in terms of correct and incorrect answers
- Value being right
- Enjoy listening and taking notes
- Like teachers who are information givers
- Prefer a quiet learning situation
- Learn from traditional methodology
- Dislike situations and methods where no one wins
- Define themselves by how smart they are
- Enjoy reading the Bible for concepts and principles
- Need competition
- Are impersonal
- Prefer to work alone

NOTES

1. John Trent, Ph.D., in a seminar on "Team-Building Tools for Blending Differences" (PACE Convention, October 1, 1992), quipped about learners with Analytic characteristics, "It takes them a good two weeks to do anything spontaneous!"

2. Chuck and Barb Snyder, *Incompatibility: Grounds for a Great Marriage* (Sisters, Ore.: Questar Publishers, Inc., 1988), p. 56.

5

The Common Sense Learner

The words "work" and "worship" come from the same root word in Hebrew. There is something potentially sacred in our every act and in every moment of every day.
—Harold John Ockenga

Common Sense Learners like to start out with ideas and conduct experiments to test them. They like to think about problems logically, breaking them down into parts and putting them together again so they work. Their great delight is in making something usable. They value strategic thinking above all else—especially above what they might define as fuzzy thinking (theological or philosophical thinking). Action and doing are strategies for learning.

Two characteristics of Common Sense Learners often put them at risk in both the school and Christian education systems.

The first is their need to tie everything to the "now." They live in the here and now. Everything must make sense now or students will have difficulty wrapping their minds around it. Their strength is the practical application of ideas, and if what is being presented seems too "pie in the sky," something for which they can see no conceivable use, they will dismiss the information as unimportant. They may be willing to flunk a course if the need for the subject matter is not clear to them.

If students don't see its value of Christian education, they will write off Christianity. "Why," they might ask, "should we learn all of the rivers in Israel if we're not going to take a raft trip?" "Why," they want to know, "are we just talking about sharing our faith and making no plans to take what we have studied out into this neighborhood?" They should wear drip-dry shirts embroidered with the word, *Practical.*

The second characteristic is their need to move as part of the learning process. Testing things out requires action. Tests can't be done totally in their heads. Their minds aren't fully activated unless their hands, or some other part of their bodies, are moving too. This unique group of learners can work within three dimensions at once: spatially, kinesthetically, and intellectually.

Movement in a class setting is great if you happen to be in preschool or in the very early elementary classes. But as classes begin to get more and more traditional, these realistic, practical, matter-of-fact students may be lost. They prefer actions to words and involvement to theory. Not only do they prefer it, they demand it. They will fail in many of our traditional classrooms.

One father wrote about his son . . .

> "[Tim] escaped high school with a 1.9 grade point average, and looked at his diploma as a pardon. Since he could take the motor out of his car every afternoon, dust it off, and make it run again, we decided to encourage him to go to a diesel mechanics school. He signed up and began to get straight A's. He hated math in school, but now he was bringing home fractions and decimal problems. I mentioned to him that his homework looked a lot like math. He said it wasn't math, it was piston ratios and valve clearances."[1]

It is possible that the world-renowned actor who breathes life into Shakespearian drama, Brian Bedford, is a Common Sense Learner. As an actor, he exemplifies someone who must work spatially, kinesthetically, and intellectually all at the same time. He says, "I left school at fifteen because I was a terrible dunce. In point of fact, I wasn't such a terrible dunce but I couldn't connect with it. I got insanely low grades. I took a geometry, algebra, and arithmetic exam and averaged four percent. Four percent! It's weird, isn't it? It seems to be impossible, but I achieved the impossible. Anyway, they kicked me out of school when I was fifteen and I was very glad about that."[2]

They should wear drip-dry shirts embroidered, *Practical.*

Dr. Cliff Schimmels talks about his appreciation for a fellow student who sounds like a Common Sense Learner: "I am fortunate to have Roger for a lab partner. He is really good with his hands. Although the experiments so far have been fairly simple, he has the ability to set up the equipment and to arrange everything with the precision a truly scientific experiment requires. We are a good team. He can't read very well, but he can work with his hands. I can read all right, but I'm not good with my hands. Between us, we are discovering some interesting facts."[3]

Common Sense Learners may not enjoy reading, perhaps because it involves so much sitting still. Also, so much of what children read holds no immediate interest for them.[4]

One mother told about her son who had been asked to write an ending to the sentence "I like to read about . . ." Most of the children in her son's class had written typical third grade responses: "I like to read about . . . dinosaurs, sports, adventure." Her son had written, "I like to read about . . . one page."

Many Common Sense children are more active then their counterparts in other quadrants. Their hands and bodies move constantly because they use all of themselves in the learning process. A Common Sense child takes a $14.95 toy apart just to see how it works. The unaware parent might feel this is destructive. On the contrary, this child needs to see the pieces in order to know how the whole is put together. Taking things apart is an educational process for Common Sense Learners.

They strive to make things work—to make them "right." As they develop in spiritual maturity, many of them will become interested in righting society, making it work more effectively.[5] Their interest may be in justice for all, because justice makes such good sense. They become the just men and women of our congregations.

The Flip Side

Flip the strengths, and again you find the weaknesses. Common Sense Learners are more concerned about the logical consequences of what they do than they are in personal feelings. Relationships may get lost as they work on meeting deadlines and making projects work.

A Common Sense manager talked about this weakness in her own leadership. "We work with schedules, and when one project is off schedule, the whole process backs up. One of my staff reported late and explained that his wife was sick and he'd had to do all her jobs as well as his before the kids could get off to school. I genuinely felt for this man, and I knew he was telling the truth, not just making up an excuse for sleeping in. 'I'm sorry,' I said. 'Does this mean that you'll not be able to meet today's deadline?' He blew up and told me that I was a lousy Christian who cared more about creating Christian products than I did about the real people who would use them. I was stung by the truth of his statement."

Common Sense Learners can appear to others as harsh, severe, pushy, and often dominating. They will do anything to get the job done.

Meet Two Common Sense Learners

Hands-On Expert: A Student's Story

My mother has this rule that I have to spend time studying every night for a full hour. I have to just sit there watching the clock even if there is nothing I really have to do. Or, I watch my book and turn pages every once in a while. My mother often asks me, "Don't you care about school? Why don't you care?" The truth is, I don't. It's not important to me because I don't learn anything there that I can use. I can't see what difference all those dates and references and formulas make.

My life is outside, working on the old car my folks let me keep behind the garage. I'll be old enough to drive next year. Under that car, I can control the universe. I understand what makes it work. I'm successful. When I finish all the improvements I've got in mind for that car, it will be the fastest on the road.

My parents are a big problem. I resent my mother's nagging about what's important—important to her. She tries to understand what's going on in my mind, but she never will. She understands my sister who believes grades are important in the grand scheme of things. Not likely. And my sister has a fast mouth. I'd rather *do* than talk about doing.

I ignore my father. He's a bookworm. All he cares about is his books and his writing. How can a person sit in front of a typewriter and go on and on for hours? I want to say to him, "Why don't you just get out and do something?" One night I tried to get the whole family to go bowling. "It's not expensive. It's fun." But my father had some writing to do so we couldn't go. He just doesn't understand how different I am from him. I can fix things that he would just throw away, but that doesn't seem important to him. I wish he would try a little harder to understand me. If I ever have a son, I'm going to do the things he's interested in instead of making him feel like he's adopted because he's so different from everyone else in the family.

My hero lives a few blocks from our house. He runs a garage, and he's always interested in what I'm doing to my car. He talks my language. I know he likes me and he's never once asked me about my report card.

My mother doesn't like me hanging around that garage. She thinks it's a neighborhood eyesore. She tells me not to spend so much time with the mechanic, but I ignore her. He understands me, and my folks don't.

I've always hated school. My mother tells me I cried the whole way to school the very first day of first grade. My teacher reported that I would just sit with my head on my desk and quietly sob. I hated being cooped up in a place where nothing was happening.

I used to drop my pencil just hoping the point would break so I could get up and sharpen it.

I'm a Christian, but I think going to church is almost as bad as going to school. The teacher has all these discussions on what our problems are and how the Bible has answers for those problems. I'm not a great talker, so I just sit there and pass the time. What's worse is that we never get around to talking about why we're talking! So we have problems. So the Bible has answers. But how do we use those answers with our problems? Beats me, and I suspect it beats the teachers too. The whole process is so unpractical.

I'd rather spend Sunday morning working at the garage on a new alarm system. That alarm is a problem I've been working on for a long time—in my mind and on paper. How can I fit it around the windows and not blow every fuse in the place the minute it's turned on? I couldn't tell you one word my Sunday school teacher said last week because I was working on that problem in my head. I can't wait until I'm old enough not to sit just because my folks say God wants me to sit.

I would probably be good at sports, but I've never gone out for them. I like working by myself instead of in a group. Then I can make decisions and make them work. I have a paper route after school to earn money. I use most of it on parts for my car. No way is my mother going to give me money for stuff that she calls junk.

Project Conscious: A Teacher's Story

I agreed to teach the junior class because the pastor caught me in a weak moment, but I can get those kids off their duffs and doing something worthwhile for Christ. Christianity is more than facts and figures. I honestly don't care if they can name the disciples in the order in which they were chosen backwards. I care that they know how to put legs on their discipleship.

I don't think I'm an exciting teacher, but that doesn't mean I'm not a good one. I go step-by-step through the material that the kids need to know. I follow my teacher's guide, and in that way I'm a traditional teacher. But then I set students loose to work on projects to see if they really learned anything. If kids don't know how to live their faith, what good is Christianity? I find projects that get the whole group involved. I supply materials. I get them started and let them jump in and solve some of the problems themselves.

I find projects that get the whole group involved.

One of the projects I enjoyed was building a tabernacle to scale. I'd been talking about the tabernacle for a couple of weeks, and to be perfectly honest, I wasn't so excited about the unit. Who cares about a tent in the middle of the desert? But the more I got into it, the more I realized that those people were learning about worship. They were excited about what was going on between them and God. The tabernacle story was filled with all sorts of clues about God and His plan for us. It was fun for me to discover them as I was getting my lesson prepared.

I thought my kids would like that same discovery feeling. So I brought in Bibles, pictures, Bible encyclopedias, and boxes of wood and cloth. The assignment was to create a replica of the Tabernacle.

What surprised me was who the smart ones in the class were. People who never led before suddenly were leading. I had one kid who never read out loud. In fact, I wasn't sure he could read. But there he was reading the Bible—the really difficult sections in Exodus to find out how many poles went on each side to hold up the curtain around the courtyard. Another girl did some beautiful coloring for the actual curtains. I didn't even know she was artistic. But on the down side, several students I thought would enjoy this type of Bible study didn't. One boy kept asking me when we were going to get back to the lesson. He didn't understand that this was the lesson.

After the project was finished, we invited parents and friends to see it. Most were amazed that kids had pulled off this wonderful model. Some said it was the first time they had been able to visualize what the Tabernacle looked like.

It was interesting. The student who wanted to know when we were going to get back to the lesson explained things to the adults. He even memorized some verses that included God's conversation with Moses. Good.

That's something I never thought about doing. I hate memorizing, and I wouldn't ask my kids to do any more than absolutely necessary.

Sure, memorizing Scripture is important. Everyone says so. But I think when God told us to write His Word on our hearts, He meant that we are supposed to put what is written into action. Saying the words in their correct order isn't nearly as important as living them.

I have some unusual adult helpers for my projects, people who have never agreed to help in our Christian education program before. They don't want to teach, but they have some special gift for "doing" and they enjoy the action of our class.

One of my students, Bryon, came up with a great idea for quizzing. He wanted to develop electric cushions that were connected with a light panel. I would ask questions and kids would jump off the chairs if they knew the right answer. A light would tell me who had jumped first. My first thought was that my kids were going to be electrified from the bottom up, but Bryon was so sure he could make the chairs. He was awful at quizzing so I figured making the chairs at home would keep him coming. It sure did. He didn't miss a Sunday. He never did answer questions, but his chairs made him part of the class.

I'm big into community outreach. One time I taught four lessons on showing God's love in this community. We talked about projects that would show that love.

Everyone got involved. Some worked on individual projects and others enjoyed working with their friends.

One boy printed a flyer with information about our church that he thought people in the neighborhood would enjoy knowing. He got others to draw cartoons.

A group worked with their parents to put on a walk to Jerusalem in our parking lot on a Saturday. We invited our neighbors to join us to try Jewish food and traditional Hebrew games. Everyone who came also got an invitation to the church.

A group made a video of the life of Joseph. They invited their parents to see the finished production. About half the parents had never come to church before, but they came this time to see their kids in the movies.

One Sunday we planned a loving-hands car wash as a follow-up to studying Dorcas's life. Everyone who stopped by got his or her car washed free. When people asked why, the kids would say, "Because we want you to smile when you think of our church. Come visit us next Sunday." We gave out little folders that told about us. One lady tried to give a boy a five dollar tip. When he refused, she suggested he could put it in the offering plate. He said, "Why don't you come and do it yourself?" The next couple weeks, the students all showed up at the worship service—even those who hated sitting—to see if anyone they had invited showed up.

We spend a lot of time learning the technical side of our projects—operating the video camera so the picture doesn't jump all over everywhere or learning which pictures will photocopy in our news flyer. I know some of the other teachers see this as a waste of time. With only a few hours a week to teach Christian principles, why spend time on mechanical education? I've thought through that challenge, and I think I know the answer. When kids work on projects, they remember everything, not just the facts. They remember how it feels to work with people, even those they don't like much. They learn that Christ can be communicated in film, on paper, and through crazy projects in the church parking lot. With each project, they carry Christianity out into the world. This kind of Christian education makes sense to me. I like it better than isolating the learning in a classroom with a teacher telling kids what's what and then hoping that what is learned will eventually lead to action. Why can't the two mix?

I love these kids, but I don't always know how to let them know that. I plan one project after another. "If we do this and this, then this will happen," I tell the kids. It usually does. I affirm the kids when they meet these goals, but I wish I could be more comfortable telling them how proud I am of them. It's almost like they are my best friends.

I don't always know how to let these kids know that I love them.

Even so, one girl asked me, "Why don't you like me?" I was appalled. "You never say you love us." I pointed out how many hours I spent in and out of class with her. "That's not enough," she said. "You have to say it, too." So that's my challenge. I'm not a natural hugger.

I think back to my Sunday school experience. I remember nothing. Nothing. But I remember a church service when I was eight. A missionary talked about earthquakes in Greece and how cold the kids were. I understood that, and I could do something about it. I got out my little red wagon and went to the homes near ours collecting warm clothing. My family eventually joined in the collection. The missionary wrote me a letter thanking me. That was four decades ago and I still remember it. I want my class to put little wagon wheels on its Christianity and make it work.

This may be a good place to stop working through the various learning styles to think how wonderfully God made us—each different and each special. It's all too easy to overlook or underestimate the contributions of those who think differently than we do. Tony Campolo told the story of a tuba player who cut his lip and was unable to play his horn. For the first time in years, he was in the audience listening to the music while another player took his place on stage. After the concert someone asked him what it was like being a listener instead of a performer. He answered, "It was wonderful! I had forgotten that the whole band wasn't playing 'oom-pah-pah!' "[6]

Learning Style Worksheet

- What are the characteristics of the Common Sense Learner?

- Of the above characteristics, which are:
  Most like me

  Least like me

- In my teaching (or parenting), which students (children) might be strongly Common Sense Learners?

- Based on how I teach, which one of the following applies to me?
  ___ I capture these students' strengths weekly.
  ___ I capture these students' strengths occasionally.
  ___ I hardly ever capture these students' strengths.

Common Sense Learners

Following is an incomplete list of characteristics that help define people who have a strongly Common Sense learning style.

Common Sense Learners often . . .

- Move during the learning process
- Value action, product development, "how-to"
- Are realistic and practical
- Deal with logical consequences
- Are goal-oriented
- See skills as knowledge
- Value instruction managers
- Prefer to work alone
- Are impersonal
- Do not enjoy lecture
- Value strategic thinking
- Restrict judgment to concrete things
- Grade success by how well projects work
- Resent being given answers
- Excel in problem solving
- Enjoy "how-to" reading
- See Christianity in terms of action
- Read the Bible to get hands-on information
- Dislike sitting quietly in a learning setting
- Teach and learn through demonstration
- Can be mechanically and computer literate

Assignment

The ad on the following page ran in *Newsweek,* July 26, 1993.[7] Common Sense Learners would be attracted to "muscular Christianity." Brainstorm what kind of advertisements your church could put in the local paper that might attract the unchurched Common Sense Learners in your community. Unchurched Imaginatives? Unchurched Analytics?

Muscular Christianity

In the Mennonite Church some of our most satisfying work-outs take place not in gyms but in the yards of hurricane victims and the homes of the poor.

Satisfaction happens when you put Christian faith into action by choosing a life of giving, instead of a life of merely getting.

This Sunday, check out a church that will challenge you to sweat . . . to work out your faith in ways that make a difference.

The Mennonite Churches

Our Family Can Be Your Family

Notes

1. Chuck and Barb Snyder, *Incompatibility: Grounds for a Great Marriage* (Sisters, Ore.: Questar Publishers, Inc., 1988), p. 216.

2. Norman De Bono, "Hollywood's Loss Is Stratford's Gain," *The Beacon Herald*, Festival Edition, 1990, p. 16.

3. Dr. Cliff Schimmels, *Notes from the World's Oldest Freshman* (Elgin, Ill.: Chariot Books, 1989), p. 123.

4. Teacher Nora T. O'Neill told about her success with a second-grade boy who needed to move in order to learn. "Gregory began working with the cards for our Floor Game. He was so delighted with his success that he reached into his pocket and pulled out a quarter to pay me for allowing him to learn this way. I told him that my pay would be a hug and the satisfaction that he got to see how smart he is when he uses his kinesthetic learning style,"—reported in the 1993 *Learning Styles Network Newsletter*, cosponsored by National Association of Secondary School Principals and St. John's University, New York.

5. Wise churches find creative ways to use their hands-on people. *The National Christian Reporter*, March 19, 1993, told about Messiah Baptist Church, Nashville, Tennessee, where the members offered free haircuts and manicures to their low-income neighbors. "The manicure idea is special because we meet people who've never had one," the pastor said. "It'll do more for their self-esteem than for their hands." In this case, the church might find people coming to Christ by their fingernails!

6. *Leadership with a Human Touch*, May 11, 1993, p. 1.

7. Used by permission of Mennonite Media Ministries, Harrisonburg, Virginia.

6

The Dynamic Learner

Not only did we build a better mousetrap, we built a better mouse.
—Michael Eisner of Walt Disney Company

Dynamic Learners look at everything in terms of the future—what can this become? They love new ideas, but they have no difficulty moving from idea to idea if one doesn't work. The fun of learning is often its variety, not in carrying a single idea from its birth through maturity. *Flexibility* is a word that defines them.

Every committee needs a Dynamic Learner. (For that matter, every committee needs at least one person from each of the four styles.) This person comes up with fifteen ideas while the rest of the group is trying to think of one. Not all the ideas are winners, but hidden among the off-the-wall suggestions just may be the beginning of an idea that will change the world. Ideas come easily to Dynamic Learners, so they may value numbers of ideas more highly than a fully developed plan.

Humorist Jonathan Winters quipped, "I couldn't wait for success . . . so I went ahead without it." Dynamic Learners understand his mind-set. They have project after project started and nothing finished. They enjoy exploring each new idea so much that they lose interest in the old ones.

The Dynamic Learners might be called the "soloists" of the church. They are willing to do things alone, to take risks. They have little fear of failure, perhaps because they know if their latest idea doesn't work, they can come up with a dozen others. Note how different this is from their learning style opposite, the Analytic Learner. The Analytic will not make a move until he or she is certain that the answer or concept is right.

In class, the Dynamic Learner will often run ahead of the teacher or want to do something totally different from what the teacher has planned. These learners don't want to do less; they want to do "different." They are often defined by the word *but*.

The pastor comes into the third grade classroom and explains that he's going to be preaching on the 23rd Psalm for the next few weeks. "I'd like this class to do a Scripture choral reading on that Psalm each Sunday." The class is delighted. They can read their scripts and their parents will be so proud. But no sooner has the class bell rung than a student comes up to the teacher and says, "Teacher, great idea to have a choral reading! *But*"—there's the problem word that signals an idea is coming that diverges from the teacher's and pastor's plan—"what would you think if I got my mother to drive me to the homes of people in this congregation and I'll take pictures of them acting out the 23rd Psalm? And, I've been taking guitar lessons for three weeks. I could write an original piece and . . ." Unless the teacher guards against it, she or he is tempted to squelch this highly creative, imaginative dreamer. It's easier when everyone fits into a traditional mold. It's easier when the teacher remains in control.

The Dynamic Learner has a curiosity about new ideas and a tolerance for ambiguity. These students will often make decisions and judgments based on intuition rather than senses. Many Dynamic Learners value artistic expression.

In school they like to be tested on fluency of expression and the originality of their responses.

As they grow toward spiritual maturity, many Dynamics become the courageous people of the congregation, those willing to champion a new concept or get excited about something no one else believes in. This takes courage. This courage was expressed in the inaugural address by R. Judson Carlberg at Gordon College, Massachusetts.

> As evangelical Christians we have too long vacillated between being critics or copies. Neither is free to strike out with new expressions of joyous creativity.
>
> Those given gifts in music, drama and dance, or the visual arts are beginning to find freedom to express them. Gordon should be home to those who want to use their gifts. As the English dramatist Nigel Goodwin said recently, "It should be a place where Christians can swing from the chandeliers to the glory of God."
>
> And to my son, I say, "Remember, Chad, we're talking metaphor here."[1] [Chad was a junior at Gordon at the time.]

Dynamic Learners are often leaders, not because of their well-thought-out plans but because of the strength of their personalities and personal enthusiasm. They get so excited about new ideas that their excitement is picked up by others who follow them. They can talk their peers into almost anything.

You might be watching a budding Dynamic when you see little children playing in the backyard. Everyone wants to play cowboys except one child. That child wants to play hospital. And, sure enough, the whole group ends up playing hospital.

If you identify a Dynamic Learner in your class, follow Paul's example with Timothy. Spend extra time "Timothy-ing" this person because he or she will be a class leader. In fact the tone of the class is often set by Dynamic Learners. If you have a youth choir where a Dynamic Learner is sold out to Jesus Christ, you may find the group arriving at church at 7 A.M. to walk around the church and pray that God will bless the service that morning.

The Dynamic Learners lead because of their enthusiasm.

The Flip Side

On the other hand, if you have a Dynamic Learner who thinks youth choir is something she puts up with so she can go out after practice and have "real" fun, you may find the youth group lining up behind her idea to go down to the shopping center for a treasure hunt.

Dynamic Learners can be egotistical. After all, they have all these creative, insightful ideas. They can see the possibilities beyond what is present, obvious, and known—and many of their peers can't. They are good at hypothesizing and synthesizing. They enjoy divergent thinking and may have difficulty giving credit to people who think more analytically and traditionally.

They tend to be excitable and undisciplined. One project after another gets started, but they need the partnership of their peers to help them carry out their grand plans.

They lead people; untempered, this ability allows them to be manipulative.

Meet Two Dynamic Learners

Anything Different: A Student's Story

The hardest thing for me is doing what I've been told to do in exactly the way I'm supposed to do it. I don't want to break the rules just to break them, but if they are silly or if there is a better way, I'm for trying it. For example, why do we always have to put our names at the upper right-hand corner of our math papers? What's the big deal? Or sit in assigned seats? What kind of rationale is there for that—like maybe we're supposed to be building friendships with our chairs?

I like to do things with flair, something to separate me from the rest of the kids. We used to have to write our spelling words in sentences. Boring. So I decided to write mine in a story. I kept waiting for the teacher to read one of these in class or at least tell me what a clever idea I'd had. But she never did. I finally realized that she didn't even read our papers. It made me so mad, I stopped liking her.

In fifth grade a substitute teacher was asked by the principal to send some kids to the library to straighten books. When I found a box of books that were falling apart, I got the kids to tape and glue them together. We worked all day, and I think the sub thought that was what we were supposed to do. She never found out that I had added to the instructions, and the other kids didn't tell. Actually, I was proud of myself. We didn't miss much in class and we did get all those books fixed. Going beyond where anyone else would think of going is my idea of fun.

Teachers who let me be different are my favorite.

I've always thought I should be selected as a hall monitor, but the teachers never appoint me. I finally asked why. "Because I'm never sure what you're going to do," a teacher said. I think that's silly and I resent not getting the job. I would have been best at it. Kids pay attention to me and almost always do what I want them to do. Well, eventually!

I'm good at heading things up, but I don't always get to be part of the group. It's hard to explain, but I never feel as if I'm one of them.

Teachers who let me be different are my favorite. We had to memorize a poem and I picked a long one—about five minutes long. It was rhyming couplets, and told a story, so I figured I wouldn't have any trouble with it. Unfortunately, I forgot when it was supposed to be memorized and was almost—but not quite—ready. When I forgot a little bit in the middle I just made up some new couplets that continued the story. It didn't hurt the story and in my opinion, it made it a little more exciting. The kids said my poem was best, but when the principal came to hear some of them, my teacher didn't pick me. I suspect she was afraid I would forget and make up lines, and the principal wouldn't think the teacher was so great.

I'm a good salesperson. When our school sells candy and Christmas cards, I sell more than the others. I like talking to people about the reasons they ought to buy. They often say, "Well, you talked me into it."

Once a Sunday school teacher said I had a fast mouth. I was insulted, but I also liked it. I can make the rest of the kids laugh in class, and most teachers don't think that's funny. Once this teacher had us write what we could discover about the disciples in the book of Mark. I added the color of their hair and a big section on polyester togas. The teacher got mad and said I was ruining the study for the rest of the kids. I wasn't. I don't think it hurts anyone to laugh a little. Pardon me, Lady. My mistake.

I don't like Sunday school this year. My teacher is too sweet. She's always trying to hug us and tell us how much she loves us and prays for us. Makes me itchy.

Church isn't so bad. I discovered the concordance in the back of my Bible. I use it to make up crossword puzzles. Since I have my Bible open, no one bothers me. The Bible contains some pretty strange words.

I try hard to be different. It's more fun than being like everyone else. My father says things like, "Why do you always have to be different? Why can't you be like everyone else?" He'd be upset if he knew how I felt about those speeches. I like them. They prove I really am special.[2]

I had the part of Miriam, Moses' sister, in a church play. It was a short part, but I could actually believe that I was down by the Nile holding that little basket. It was scary when the queen found my baby brother. The whole part was over too quickly. I wish I could do it over again. After the play, I went back to the platform and stood there for a minute even though there weren't any people. I think I would like to be someone else once in a while. Not Miriam because I know about her leprosy. But Queen Esther would be nice.

Sometimes I wonder if I'm really a Christian. Other kids talk about how they feel Jesus in their lives. I don't. I once used clay to sculpt a picture of Jesus in my life. It was fun to do, but after it was done, I couldn't find anyone to show it to. It didn't seem like God was there anymore. So I crushed it into a ball, and put the clay back in the box.

Another time a teacher had us tear paper into a picture of us—not really our faces or anything like that—but something that showed our feelings. Some of the smarter kids who know all the answers couldn't do it at all. They just tore their initials. I did a good job. My teacher said I'd gotten my whole personality into the tearing.

I like teachers who don't have all the right answers, teachers who are open. I like it when we discuss those "What if . . ." questions. What if Jesus really didn't rise from the dead? What if Christianity isn't true? These discussions sure beat fill-in-the-blanks. I wonder what Jesus would have done in our Sunday school class. I'll bet He would get tired of blanks, too. Maybe He would throw spitballs or find a way to make stories from the clouds that float by the window. My mother's got a saying, "Boredom as a recruiter of energy is unbelievable." I guess she's right.

Idea Maker: A Teacher's Story

I agreed to teach because I got tired of people telling me how boring Sunday school was. I like being with teens and they like me. Probably the main reason we relate is my ability to talk to them as if they are real people! When I was considering being a teacher, I noticed how many people talk down to teens. A few talk over their heads or even at them. But it's hard to find adults who will talk with them and listen and wait for their side of the conversation.

Young teens are my favorite group. They are never the same people twice. I try to be their adult friend. I figure they have enough friends their own age, and I'm not there to fill that job. They don't need a parent since they all have one, two, or even three. I just want to be an adult friend.

I worried a little about parents being jealous of the relationships I was building with their children. But most are thrilled to have a nonrelated Christian man interested in their kids.

I try not to pick favorites, but of course I have them. I like the kids who are creative. I challenge them to ask, "What can I become? How can I enlarge my thinking? What are my potentials?"

One boy in particular is very bright, but not always nice. He's almost too smart. He can talk himself out of any situation, even when he's obviously wrong. I don't know yet if I'll make a difference in his life, but I'm going to try. He may never know it, but my goal is to have him be someone better, for Christ's sake, than he would have been if I hadn't been in his life.

Most of my kids like me, and I work hard for that. There are a few, particularly the shy and studious ones, who may feel bowled over by my enthusiasm and the numbers of ideas that dash through the class hour.

Some kids just don't think like me. They want easy answers and straight lines. I'm sorry that I'm missing those kids, but to be honest, I find it difficult to relate to them. Through the years other Sunday school teachers and school teachers have picked them as favorites.

I like the kids who follow that different drummer.

I like the kids who follow that different drummer.

I value imagination. I love it when a kid connects in ways I would never have thought of. For example, one kid loves science fiction. In class he asked how I thought a popular sci-fi film would have been different if a Christian were in the script. Interesting question. We raced off discussing that and whether a Christian ought to be writing science fiction. That wasn't the lesson I had planned, but it was a lot more interesting and growth-producing for the kids than anything I came up with.

When I first started teaching, I could never have allowed a class to take off without my knowing exactly where it was going, even though I enjoyed teachers who did that. I just wasn't secure enough in my teaching skills. But I know my Bible better now, and I'm also off my big ego trip. I no longer feel that a good teacher must know all the answers and wrap things up with a string by the end of the class period.

The first time I let go of a class I was scared to death. Even though I knew it was the way I liked to learn, I wasn't sure anyone else was like me. I announced the week before that I wasn't going to prepare any lesson. The kids could ask any questions and we would talk about them. I also told them that I didn't have all the answers, so this wasn't going to be a stump-the-teacher hour. They were to bring things to class that really bothered them, things they questioned. I wanted them to take the whole process seriously, and it turned out just that way.

They wanted to talk about what happens after death. They wanted to know what happens to soldiers who die for their country but didn't know Christ. They wanted to talk about what was fair and what the Bible taught and what our church believed. From that time on, I tried this free-for-all about twice a year. It wouldn't work week after week. Anything gets old through repetition, but when I do it infrequently, it's very effective.

I like contests, but not the facts-and-figures kind. Once I gave a prize for the best painting to illustrate John 3:16. In another contest I had kids come up with new games for a class retreat and the craziest got the award. These are the kinds of contests I could have won when I was a kid, and it's also the type of stuff no one else rewards. Over the years, I've developed the courage to follow my own instincts.

Not everything I try works. Big deal. There's always another idea. Even failures teach the kids something. I'm willing to drop a few bombs in order to get the great stuff. For example, I once asked kids to do something, anything they wanted, to show what their assigned Psalm had to say to kids their own age. I got a weaving, painting, and even a cartoon of God Almighty on His throne dressed in blue jeans. I put the cartoon on the bulletin board, and that was a big mistake. Two parents were very upset with the cartoon. They especially mentioned the rope belt that was holding up the jeans. They took their child out of my class, and put her into a more traditional one. I was sick about it, and it made me examine my creative methods to make certain I wasn't out of the bounds set for teachers.

Some of the methods I've used have bombed. For example, once I planned an original mime production for the teens' part of the Christmas program. It didn't work. The kids didn't understand mime and I wasn't skilled enough to teach them. When the fiasco was over, one of the guys said, "I'll bet we won't have to do that again." I was almost ready to agree with him when my true feelings surfaced. "Wrong," I told him. "Next time we'll be better. Next time I'll get someone who knows something about this art form to teach you. I failed. You still don't know yet if you failed."

I like to change things. If they have always been done one way, I want change for change's sake. Sometimes the new way is better and sometimes it's not. But let's just dare to find out.

I joined the worship planning committee at our church because my kids refused to come to sermons they labeled boring. I'm not against sermons, but I don't think they are the only way to present truth or lead people to worship. The pastor was open to change so one Sunday the congregation broke into buzz groups to discuss the Scripture readings.

I remember another time at Easter. We had all the windows covered and the lights turned low. The congregation entered to funeral music. We sang slow, sad songs. Then in the middle of one song, a child ran in and yelled at the top of her lungs, "He is risen. He is risen." The lights went on and shades went up and all the little Sunday school kids walked in carrying flowers. Talk about effective! People who had been in church every Easter since they were born and couldn't remember one service from another still talk about this service.

I like coming to worship God and not knowing exactly how that service will unfold. I like the delight of being surprised by finding Christ in the service. I treasure what I learn through these surprises. That's what I want my young people to feel when I'm teaching. I want my teaching to communicate to them: "Pay attention! You never know what surprises will be around the next corner. This hour just might change your life."

Learning Style Worksheet

- What are the characteristics of the Dynamic Learner?

- Of the above characteristics, which are:
  Most like me

Least like me

- In my teaching (or parenting), which students (children) might be strongly Dynamic Learners?

- Based on how I teach, which one of the following applies to me?
  ___ I capture these students' strengths weekly.
  ___ I capture these students' strengths occasionally.
  ___ I hardly ever capture these students' strengths.

Dynamic Learners

Following is an incomplete list of characteristics that help define people who have a strongly Dynamic learning Style.

Dynamic Learners often . . .

- Lead
- Have experimental attitudes and behaviors
- Cultivate a well-developed sense of humor
- Demand flexibility
- Take a long time to complete an assignment
- Need options
- Like student-directed classrooms
- Are curious and insightful
- Enjoy teachers who facilitate and stimulate creativity
- Are future directed
- Want to do anything that is different or breaks the mold
- Make decisions based on hunches
- Enjoy people
- Communicate with great skill
- Enjoy dramatics, or any art form that allows them to assert individuality
- Are unpredictable and willing to take chances
- Value creativity
- Have strong intuition
- Can see numerous ways of approaching a situation or problem
- Work to make things better or different

In the last four chapters, you have met students and teachers whose learning styles are very different. These styles or learning patterns are deep in each person's psychological makeup. Learning styles provide one more clue into the nature of how our brains work. It is just one part, and as research continues, more and more will be discovered. Of course, each discovery may make teaching more challenging, and the exciting part is that each discovery can also make teaching more effective.

Consider the infant in a good home. Input flows into the brain, not in some well-planned sequence as with an orderly, articulated curriculum.

Rather, the infant in the beginning hears vocabulary totally beyond its experience and observes activities that initially have no meaning.

Amazingly, the brain sorts it out, learning some five- to ten-thousand words by age five, not one of which was looked up in a dictionary or learned with a worksheet. By five, the child recognizes thousands of objects and hundreds of relationships. The child formulates theories of how something works on a computer.

If only school learning could proceed so rapidly and joyously! It will . . . when we design schools that attend to the brain's functioning and the child's preferences in environment and learning styles.[3]

The brain learns five- to ten-thousand words by age five.

Assignment

Read the following illustration of two teachers[4] both teaching their students Robert Frost's poem, "The Road Not Taken," and observe their two different approaches.

I shall be telling this with a sigh
Somewhere ages and ages hence;
Two roads diverged in a wood, and I
I took the one less traveled by—
and that has made all the difference.

Miss Tolbert is reading this well-known poem to her English class. When she finishes, she encourages the students to discuss what it means to them.

Some of the children are very eager to share their ideas and experiences. Others, however, are drifting off; they seem distracted and begin to fidget and look at the clock. After a few more minutes, Miss Tolbert gives the children a homework assignment to memorize the poem. The next day some of the children enthusiastically want to recite the poem, while others are sullen, nervous, or disinterested.

In another school, Mr. Kerner is also using Frost's poem.

Before he introduces the poem, he asks for some volunteers to act out a situation where a decision has to be made. After several such short scenarios followed by a brief discussion about making decisions, he passes out paper and crayons and asks the students to draw something about making a choice. He then reads the poem aloud to the class. For a second reading he uses an overhead transparency with the poem written on it and asks the class to follow along. Finally he asks the students how their skits and drawings might relate to the poem they have just been reading. A lively discussion ensues in which most of the class participates. In a little while he brings the discussion to a close and gives the assignment for the next day. Written on the board, it includes several choices, among which are memorizing the poem, illustrating it with a drawing, or acting out an example of its message. The next day the students return, anxious to share the projects they have chosen to do.[5]

Now suggest how a Sunday school teacher with Mr. Kerner's attention to the different ways students learn might encourage tenth graders in all four learning style quadrants to demonstrate that they know I John 1:1-4.

NOTES

1. "Welcome Home," inaugural address by R. Judson Carlberg, Gordon College, March 5, 1993, reported in *Stillpoint*, Summer 1993, p. 14.

2. Educator Kathleen Butler, panel member on the 1989 ASCD tape, "The At-Risk Students: A Global Understanding of Learning Styles," told the story of a third grader who was aware of the different ways people learn. He gave a science report about carrots by talking about his life as a carrot. Understanding that everyone in the class wouldn't learn about carrots from his creative presentation, he ended up by holding up a chart on how carrots grow and announcing, "For those of you who didn't get it my way, here's the information."

3. Wayne B. Jennings, Ph.D., "Brain Based Principles in Action," *The Networker*, Spring 1994, p. 5.

4. Pat Burke Guild and Stephen Garger, *Marching to Different Drummers* (Alexandria, Vir.: ASCD, 1985), pp. 60, 61.

5. Ibid.

Part III

Learning Styles and Curriculum

A student's learning style is his or her favorite place on the cycle. In that place the student can say, "Here I am smartest. Here I can contribute best."
—Bernice McCarthy

As we saw in Chapter 1, the four learning styles fit into a learning cycle: "If the teacher follows the four steps in the cycle, every student will have an opportunity to learn and share his or her contributions with the whole class" (page 21).

A Danish proverb suggests that a good example is like a bell that calls many to church. The next two chapters contain examples of lessons built around learning styles. Hopefully, they will call each of us to more effective teaching—teaching that affirms every person in the class.

Chapters 7 and 8 show how the four learning styles work in elementary, youth, and adult Sunday school and Bible camp. All students participate in every part of each lesson. However students will find it easiest to excel in one or two quadrants. Success within their strength area will encourage them to try more difficult tasks, both within and without their "home" quadrants.

The illustrative curriculums will follow this pattern:

Step 1: Imaginative Learner. This step will answer the question: "Why do I need to know this? Why is it important to me?"

Step 2: Analytic Learner. This step will answer the question: "What do I need to know—the facts, stories, concepts?"

Step 3: Common Sense Learner. This step will answer the question: "How does this work? How can I use this?"

Step 4: Dynamic Learner. This step will answer the question: "What can this become? How can I put what I've learned into practice this week?"

A Brief Review of the Learning Style Cycle

1. *Imaginative Learner*—Students start with what they already know, sharing from previous experience. This will become the foundation on which the rest of the lesson is built. The Imaginative Learner helps the whole class see why the lesson is important to everyone. Skip this step in the learning cycle and the rest of the teaching time may be just so many wasted minutes.

2. *Analytic Learner*—When students know how what they are studying fits into their worldview, they are ready to move a step further. Many Analytic Learners will find this search for new knowledge most exciting.

3. *Common Sense*—In the third part of the lesson, students apply what they have learned to their own lives. Common Sense Learners will be able to show the practicality of what they have studied. As a preparation for real life, they test whether what they have learned works in the classroom.

4. *Dynamic*—The final section in any Christian teaching should not be a period, but a comma. Dynamic Learners come up with creative ways to move what has been learned from Sunday to Monday. They lead by coming up with creative ideas for going beyond what the teacher has taught.

Curriculum built around the four quadrants makes sense. It's a learning cycle. Christian educators will not find the pattern totally new. Educator Dr. Larry Richards popularized the same cycle when he taught this pattern:

- Hook—(Imaginative) Why study this lesson?
- Book—(Analytic) What do I need to know?
- Look—(Common Sense) How does this apply to me?
- Took—(Dynamic) What am I willing to invest in what I have learned?

The four-quadrant pattern is also used in the Bible-in-Life and Wesley curriculums, and the African-American Literature, *Echoes—Teaching God's Resounding Word,* all three produced by David C. Cook Church Ministries.

- Life Need—(Imaginative) Why study this topic? What personal need will it meet?
- Bible Learning—(Analytic) What do I need to know from Scripture to meet my need?
- Bible Application—(Common Sense) How does what I learned work in meeting my need today?
- Life Response—(Dynamic) How can I creatively respond on Monday to what I have learned and tested on Sunday?

No matter what curriculum is used, a wise teacher will examine each lesson in light of learning style information.

7

Learning Styles Sample Lessons for Children

Teacher: *What are you drawing?*
Child: *I'm drawing God.*
Teacher: *But no one knows what He looks like.*
Child: *They will when I'm finished.*

Chapters 7 and 8 illustrate how a teaching plan moves through the four learning style quadrants to complete the Learning Style Cycle. On the following pages, the left-hand column provides the content in a typical lesson. The right-hand column comments on the learning style function that is happening. By comparing content with function, you will see how every student, no matter what his or her learning style preference, is needed and important to the whole group.

Each lesson also uses a variety of methods. These use students' hearing (auditory), seeing (visual) and moving (tactile/kinesthetic) senses.

Chapters 9—13 will explore the importance of using methods that appeal to these three senses (or modalities).

Sunday School Curriculum for Children Ages Eight and Nine

The early years in school see children identifying themselves as separate entities, similar to others but unique. They are becoming aware of their special characteristics and abilities. They are working at overcoming feelings of inferiority. They are learning right from wrong and may be motivated to right actions by a fear of getting caught and a desire to avoid punishment by those in authority.[1]

Jesus' Birthday at My House

Bible Basis: Angels celebrate Jesus' coming by praising God for His Christmas gift. Luke 2:1-20. ("Suddenly a great company of heavenly host appeared with the angel, praising God and saying, 'Glory to God in the highest, and on earth peace to men on whom his favor rests'"—vss. 13, 14.)

Lesson Aim: Students will celebrate Jesus' birthday and start a family tradition in their homes.

Step 1

Before class, fill the classroom with secular Christmas items: Santas, wrapping paper showing candy canes, advertisements for Christmas toys, etc. In the corner of the floor set up a creche. As class starts, hand children large pieces of brown paper. Have them tape over or cover everything that doesn't have anything to do with the celebration of Jesus' birthday, the real reason for Christmas. When secular Christmas is covered, ask students to work in small groups to come up with some things that point to Christ's birth that they might put in place of the world's Christmas decorations.

Discuss as a group: If you covered the Christmas decorations in our community that celebrate winter and the holiday, but not Jesus' birth, what would you cover? Why do you think we have so many beautiful decorations that don't tell us anything about the real Christmas? What Christmas decorations do you have in your home that remind you of Jesus' birthday? What does our church do to remember Jesus' birthday? What does your family do? Why is it easier for many people to celebrate Christmas without Jesus than with Jesus?

(Imaginative Learners)

This section answers the question, "Why do I need to know this? Why is it important to me?" By encouraging students to cover the secular celebration of Christmas, you have created an experience that the whole class can share. The class also reflects on that experience, allowing the Imaginative Learners to tell the stories of their Christmases. No new information is presented to the students. Instead, what they already know is rearranged to allow them to think about Christmas in a new way.

Methods used:

Student demonstration
Brainstorming
Group discussion

Step 2

Write identifications of people, angels, and animals in the Christmas story on slips of paper. Example: Angel, manger, Mary, sheep, shepherd. Turn the slips upside down and have each student take one. Also make pipecleaners available. As you tell the Bible

(Analytic Learners)

This section answers the question, "What do I need to know?" It takes the children into God's Word and encour-

story, ask each person to twist pipecleaners into the shape of the item on the slip. Explain that they can twist as they listen to the story. Then you will read the story a second time, this time directly from the Bible (or paraphrase). When the story is finished, bring out a cookie tray that you have filled with a thin layer of clay.

(In a complete teacher's guide, many questions would be provided. What follows are illustrative.)

Ask the following questions of the children, identifying them by the pipecleaner piece they have developed. When they answer, they can stick their figure into the clay. If a student doesn't know the answer, he or she should insert the pipecleaner figure and ask for a volunteer to answer the question. When all figures have been added, you will have a manger scene.

Mary: A friend asks why you are going to Bethlehem, especially now, when you are almost ready to have a baby. What do you say? If you were planning a birthday decoration for your baby to put in this room, what would you add?

Angel: Why do you think God sent you to poor shepherds instead of rich kings with your birth announcement? What kind of decorations would you add to this room?

Shepherd: The Bible says that after the angels left, the shepherds talked over what had happened. Why do you think they talked it over before they rushed to see the baby?

Sheep: Where did the shepherds go after the angels had sung? What might they have said to people on the road who asked, "What's the big rush?"

When the questions have been asked, walk in a circle around the manger scene and sing songs of Christmas praise as they are suggested by the children. Or, develop a

ages them to develop concepts about Christmas that may be new to them. Students answer a mixture of content and analytic questions.

Methods used:
Pipecleaner art
Storytelling
Singing, choreography
Content and analytic discussion

Note how much movement has been going on in this classroom.

simple choreography. The children might walk in a circle and every five steps skip twice. They could repeat this pattern throughout the song. Emphasize biblical content by talking after each song about what things in the song are really from the Bible and what things were added.

Step 3

Explain that even though we probably won't hear angels sing over our homes this Christmas, God still wants us to celebrate their message. In fact, some people in this church may be so busy this Christmas that they have forgotten the real message. Let's remind them. Provide a long sheet of shelf or butcher paper. Have students suggest what message they want to share about Christmas with the whole congregation. Then have them write their message in huge letters on the paper and color or decorate those letters. Be as creative as time allows with glitter, aluminum foil, and Christmas paper. Each student should write his or her name on the sign. The class should take the sign to the church foyer or some other place where it will be seen and hang it.

When the class returns, allow time for volunteers to ask God to use their sign to point people to Jesus—maybe in the same way God used the angels to point the shepherds toward Him.

(Common Sense Learners)

The Common Sense student excels at seeing the relevance of the issues studied. He or she needs to ask and answer, "How does this work today? What difference does this make?" Students practice what they have learned and begin to plan how it might be useful to them.

Methods used:

Writing (full body motion used for drawing large letters)
Project
Volunteer prayer

Step 4

Brainstorm ideas students could use in their own families to point directly to the importance of Jesus' birth. Give them a few ideas to get started: read the Christmas story before opening presents on Christmas; hang only Christmas cards that have biblical messages on them; earn money to buy a manger scene for their homes; put on a Christmas play with their friends for their parents.

Encourage students to pick one idea and

(Dynamic Learners)

Students are now ready to add something of themselves to the lesson, creatively taking the idea provided by the teacher and personalizing it. They answer, "What can this become in my life? How can I put what I've learned into really do it. Send each student a Christmas card during the week encouraging him or her to follow through with an idea. Next week begin class by talking about what each person did and how each felt about the celebration.

practice this week?" In the personalizing, they actually become teachers. The adage states, "No one learns as much as the teacher." In so doing, we are providing them with the ultimate training.

Method used:
Brainstorming

Sunday School Curriculum for Children Ages Ten and Eleven

Children in fifth and sixth grade are beginning to question their beliefs, and as they find answers, some are ready to make the decision to live for Christ. (They may reaffirm their decisions in their teenage years as their facility to reason more fully develops.) Juniors are limited to concrete categories of thought—things they have seen, heard, and felt. They can manipulate their thoughts to make plans, determine cause and effect, solve problems, and classify and organize. They are working on four primary tasks—learning social cooperation, self-evaluation, skills, and team play. They have a good handle on the difference between right and wrong and can make deliberate choices regarding their actions.

RUNNING SCARED

Bible Basis: Even though they had a lot to be scared about, Joshua and Caleb trusted God. Numbers 13:1—14:35.

Lesson Aim: Students will learn to picture Jesus being with them when they are running scared.

Step 1

Each student picks a color crayon that illustrates how he or she felt in a frightening situation. Ask students to draw how they felt in that scary situation by setting the crayon on the paper and drawing their feelings without lifting the crayon from the paper.

When students are finished, divide them into pairs to share what feelings they were illustrating and why they chose the color they did. Ask volunteers to share why it's easy to be scared even when they know that

(Imaginative Learners)

Students will create an experience that is their own. They will then discuss that experience with the whole group.

Methods used:
Emotion drawing
Pair Sharing
Large group discussion

Jesus is with them. Have them respond: Do you think that knowing Jesus will ever completely take away your fear?

Step 2

Divide the Scripture into small chunks and give one section to each student to read. Beginning with the first student, have each briefly tell his or her part of the story. Then have students sit in a circle on the floor. Place lots of different colored blocks (one-inch squares) in the center. Go through the story a second time, adding details the students may have missed. Stop at several significant spots and have students pick a color block that illustrates how they think Joshua and Caleb were feeling at that point in their experience. For example, you could stop at Joshua 13:16: Moses sent the twelve men to explore Canaan.

Divide the class into study groups. Make certain each group has at least one Bible. Give groups several minutes to write one sentence that expresses what children their age might learn from this story.

(Analytic Learners)
This Bible story may be new to many Sunday school students. The approximately 30 percent who are analytic learners will want to understand the facts of the story first and later look for the concepts that they feel have relevancy in their lives.

Methods used:
Scripture reading
Student stories using color symbols
Group reasoning

Step 3

In groups of three, develop a pantomime that shows a situation where a kid might use what he or she learned from this story. For example, the group might have written, "Even when we're afraid, God expects us to follow Him." The triad could pantomime a kid saying no to drugs, even when the others are laughing at her or him. After all groups have done their short pantomimes, students should individually think of something that scares them a lot.

(Common Sense Learners)

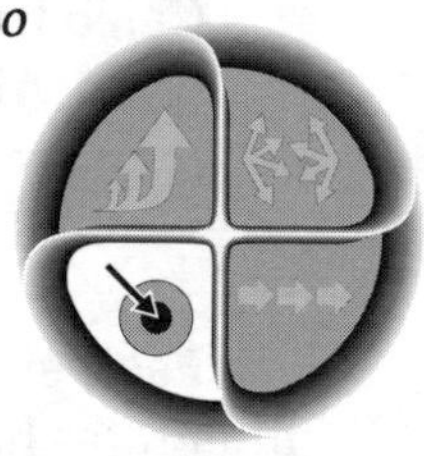

"It's been fun, but so what?" Common Sense learners will benefit by reviewing what has been covered and applying it to their own situation by answering, "Does this work? How can I use this?"

Methods used:
Triad pantomime

Step 4

Each student should pick two color blocks the same color that will remind him or her of that scary thing or situation. Stu-

(Dynamic Learners)
Dynamic students enjoy the unusual and different. They are bored by the same thing Sunday

dents should take one color block home and put it some place where they see it regularly. It will help them remember that when hard times come—and they will—God is with them. (The teacher may want to give his or her phone number for students to write on the block. Kids this age are often faced with giants every bit as scary as those Joshua and Caleb faced, and they may need an adult Christian to help them.)

The second block is to give to someone who needs the same reminder this week. When they give the block, they should retell the story they learned in Sunday school and what God wants kids to learn from it.

after Sunday and their interest and creativity are often captured by surprise. They enjoyed the color block earlier in the lesson and will benefit from personalizing it.

Methods used:
Color block as life response

Camp Curriculum for Children Ages Nine through Eleven[2]

When a child goes to camp, his or her whole body gets involved—hearing, seeing, feeling, tasting, smelling, thinking, touching. The involvement of these senses (called modalities) enrich the experience and can be the stimulus to life-changing experiences.[3]

Growing Christians Are in Top Spiritual Shape

Scripture: I Samuel 23:13-28 (The story of David and his men hiding from Saul who was determined to kill David).

Eye Opener—Morning Devotions

Clear a spot of ground and find a sharp stick. Write your answers with the stick. What are three things someone your age could do if that person were in top physical shape? Circle the things you can do. What grade would you give yourself on your physical fitness? Before you go on, touch your toes twenty-five times and do five push-ups.

Wipe out your ground tablet, and write new answers to these questions. What three things would show that someone your age was in top spiritual shape? Circle the things you do. What grade would you give your-

(Imaginative Learners)

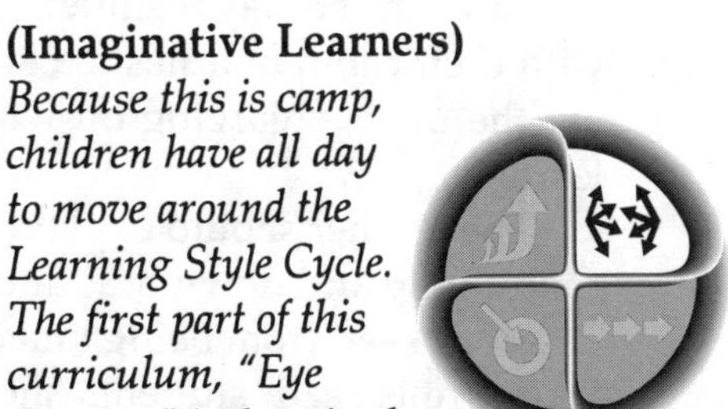

Because this is camp, children have all day to move around the Learning Style Cycle. The first part of this curriculum, "Eye Opener," is done in the morning as campers begin their day alone with God. Imaginative Learners usually prefer to work with other students; however the day will be filled with group activity. This section of the lesson appeals to

self on your spiritual fitness? Erase your ground tablet.

Pick the sentence that is true of you and say it out loud.

1. I am in better shape physically than spiritually.
2. I am in better spiritual shape than physical shape.

the Imaginative's need to put what they will do into a personal context.

Methods used:
Ground writing
Reading
Exercise

Morning Devotions (Continued)

Read I Samuel 23:13-18. Every time you come to something that shows that David is in good physical shape, put a line on the ground. Every time you come to something that shows he was in excellent spiritual shape, draw a circle. Later today, check with a friend and see how many lines and how many circles he or she drew. If your numbers don't agree, review what you drew. Think to yourself, How did Jonathan help David stay in spiritual shape? (The verses don't tell you, but they do give you clues. Think of how your Christian friends help you stay in good spiritual shape.) Tell Jesus how you feel about your physical shape and your spiritual shape.

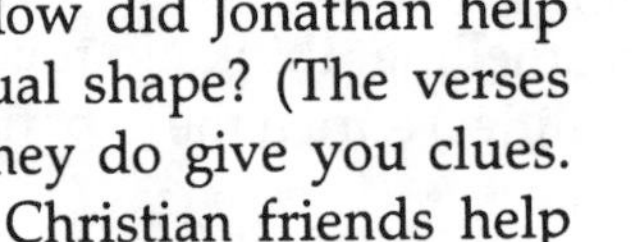

(Analytic Learners)
At this point in the "Eye Opener," the questions begin to appeal to the Analytic student.

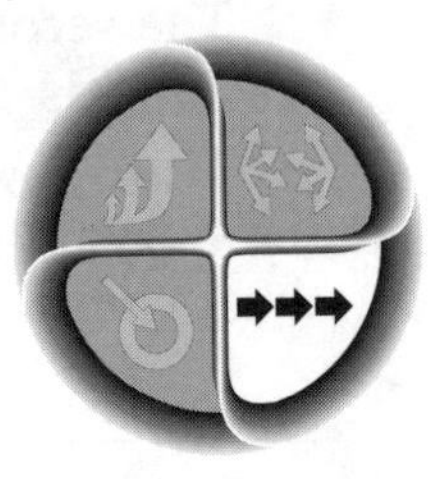

Methods used:
Inductive study
Self-evaluation
Prayer

Cabin Bible Study

Later in the day, campers meet outside with their cabin buddies to continue studying the Bible, enlarging on what they have learned.

The teacher should explain that David is running up and down hills and through the desert to keep from being killed by Saul. As Scripture is read, students should run quietly in place.

David often had to hide to keep from being killed. Sometimes kids need to hide from things that would hurt their spiritual growth. Encourage campers to share things they think kids should hide from.

Use some of the following questions to encourage sharing: What physical exercise

(Common Sense Learners)
This section is answering the question, "What can I, as a camper, do with all the information I've been learning about David?" ("How does this work?")

Methods used:
Bible reading
Group discussion
Pair Prayer
Physical exercise

is hardest for you to do? What spiritual exercise is hardest? (For three minutes have kids do a physical exercise that's hard for them—but do it with their eyes closed. In their mind's eye, they should picture themselves doing the spiritual exercise. For example, if reading the Bible is hard, they should visualize themselves reading God's Word as they run or do push-ups.) No matter what happens to us, God is there to help. David did a good job of taking care of himself.

But what do you think would have happened if the message hadn't come telling Saul that the Philistines were raiding the land? What's the real reason David wasn't caught by Saul?

Everyone should lie on the ground and quietly look up at the sky for three minutes. Think about ways God keeps you safe. After reflection, pairs should sit together and answer the following prayer-starter sentences. (Remember that David and Jonathan encouraged each other to grow closer to God.)

- "Jesus, the exercise I enjoy most is . . ."
- "The spiritual exercise I enjoy most is . . ."
- "The area where I could use more spiritual exercise is . . ."
- "A Christian I know who is in good spiritual shape is . . ."
- "Thank you for this person because . . ."
- "I know my friend here is loved by you because . . ."
- "I know I am loved by you because . . ." Amen.

Cabin Bible Study (Continued)

Close the Cabin Bible Study by giving campers the following challenge: To be physically fit, you need to exercise. To be spiritually fit, you also need to exercise. Try doing both at once. Start running and at the same time recite all the Bible verses you can remember. When you run out of Bible verses, try singing aloud songs that talk about God.

(Dynamic Learners)

Dynamic Learners will enjoy seeing how what they have studied carries over into the future and can be expanded by them.

Run until you run out of physical energy or spiritual energy—whichever comes first.

Pick up something from nature near the place where you stop running. Put it in your pocket and carry it all week to remind you to work at being both physically and spiritually fit. Every morning of this week of camp, you will have an opportunity to share what you have done to increase your fitness and how you have helped others to do the same.

Methods used:
Physical exercise
Symbolic visual aid

Notes

1. Characteristics overview for age levels in this chapter and Chapter 9 are from *Nurturing My Students* by Lawrence O. Richards and Marlene D. LeFever (Elgin, Ill.: David C. Cook Publishing Co., 1982).

2. Portions of this section were taken from *Survival Kit for Growing Christians* and *God's Special Creation—Me!* by Marlene LeFever (Carol Stream, Ill.: Harold Shaw Publishers' Bible Discovery Guides for Junior Campers, 1988).

3. An overview of camping and learning styles is provided in "Adapting Camp Bible Studies to Individual Learning Styles" by Marlene LeFever (*Journal of Christian Camping*, January/February 1988).

8

Learning Styles Sample Lessons for Youth and Adults

I touch the future. I teach.
—Christa McAuliffe

Teens who have reached formal reasoning are able to think independently, critically, logically, and inductively. Adolescence is the time for identity formation, a process that begins in the early teen years or before and usually is not completed until the early twenties. Teens are moving away from those they have been emotionally dependent upon, processing who they are and what they believe.

Youth Group Curriculum

Teens are dealing with their emerging sexuality—his identification with his manhood; her identification with her womanhood.

Sexuality—It's Good, But It's Not Everything

Bible Basis: Genesis 1:27, 28, 31; 2:21-25

Lesson Aim: Students will correctly use their sexuality as a treasured gift from God.

Step 1

Ask the teens not to think about the walls in this room for the next ninety seconds. Keep track of time.

Then guide group discussion by asking questions like these: How might this experiment relate to the whole area of sexuality? How important is sexuality to kids your age and how does that importance reflect itself in the way kids think, talk, act? If you were to develop a short list of the most important topics for kids your age, what topics would be on that list? Why?

Pair students with friends. Ask them to prioritize these lists in terms of importance.

List 1: Getting my picture in the school paper. Dating a good-looking person. Getting straight A's.

List 2: Going to college. Winning a million in a sweepstakes. Being a virgin.

List 3: Being elected to student government. Having others think of me as sexy. Learning to speak another language.

Add other lists as they apply to your kids. Then pull the groups together to discuss, using questions like these: Was it hard to put these items in order? Why or why not? How did you decide which were most important to you? Do you think your answers might change in a few years? Explain.

(Imaginative Learners)

Set the tone for what will follow by encouraging discussion on what is already known and felt. While all youth will be interested in the topic, the Imaginative Learners may find it easier to talk about the issue than teens who have other learning style preferences. Because this is definitely a "Hot Topic,"[1] students may need less affirmation in their preferred style. The more difficult or boring the students perceive the topic to be, the more important being affirmed in their own style becomes.

Methods used:

Demonstration
Pair discussion
Prioritizing activity
Full group discussion

Step 2

Students return to pairs and read Genesis 1:27, 28, 31 and 2:21-25 aloud together. Give each student four small paper clips and explain that everyone is to answer each question you ask by doing a paper clip sculpture and then sharing with the partner what the symbolic twisting means. Give directions like these: Twist a clip to show what God thinks of our sexuality. Twist a clip to show how the secular world views sexuality. Twist a clip to illustrate the ideal way for

(Analytic Learners)

The Analytic Learner will usually enjoy the Bible study portion of this study more than the manipulation of the paper clip. However, since everyone participates in every section of the lesson and the Bible study is the core of what is learned in

Christian teens to view their sexuality. Finally, twist a clip to illustrate how you think many of your Christian friends really do view their sexuality.

youth group, the paper clip activity will be helpful to the Common Sense and Dynamic Learners. In this lesson, the paper clip serves another function. The Analytic Learner may be hesitant about sharing feelings. Psychologically, he or she can hide behind the clip. The student becomes freer to share what he or she really meant.

Methods used:
- *Pair discussion*
- *Paper clip sculpture*
- *Bible reading*

Step 3

This guy is about to take a stroll on the "hot coals" of sexual immorality. But he's going to get burned. After reading Proverbs 6:20, 27-29 and Hebrews 13:4, write on each coal the possible results of going against God's perspective on sex.

When students have completed the worksheet above, discuss questions like these: If you took a survey at school on the reactions to these verses, what do you think most kids would say? How do TV and movie attitudes compare with the assertions?

(Common Sense Learners)
The reason for this study has been obvious to teens from the start, so the Common Sense Learner has been involved. However the accompanying worksheet will underscore the sense of this lesson for this learner, as well as for the whole youth group. The Common Sense Learner will enjoy working alone. This lesson has had quite a bit of group participation.

Methods used:
- *Worksheet*
- *Discussion*

Step 4

Dump enough small boxes in the center of the group so that each student will have one. Provide beautiful wrapping paper and ribbon. Reaffirm that our sexuality, correctly used, is a gift from God. Ask each student to consider the box a symbolic representation of his or her sexuality. Each student should move to an area in the room where he or she can be alone, and take along a pencil, paper, and enough wrapping paper and ribbon to wrap the box. Ask students to write a prayer thanking God for this gift to them, asking Him to give them the strength to use it properly. They should then wrap the boxes. Suggest they take the boxes home and place them where they will be a reminder of the beautiful gift God intended for each of us.

(Dynamic Learners)

Dynamic teens will feel the lesson is complete only after they have added something to it, answering for themselves, "What can this become?" This lesson gives them that option. Although most would rather do this activity with a group than alone, Dynamics need to learn to reflectively consider their actions.

Methods used:

Prayer writing
Symbolic project

Adult Women's Bible Study

Maturing people must be capable of continued change. Their choices might be limited by their past, but their ability to change within their limitations is rich. They must develop self-determination. They are able to make Christ-like choices and live with the implications of those choices. They develop wisdom. This means they know the facts and they know how to apply those facts. Maturing people are comfortable with the reality of their lives and themselves. They are pleased God made them the way they are. They are still growing, and they are positive about the "becoming" process. Maturing people get along with others and respect them. They are examining their values in light of their growing understanding.

This study was developed for women who are seekers, moderately interested in finding out more about Christianity.

Little Stresses: Straws-on-Camel's-Back Situation[2]

Bible Basis: Luke 10:38-42 (the story of Martha and Mary)

Lesson Aim: Women will begin to minimize stress in their lives and spend time nurturing their souls.

Step 1

Ask the women to sit in a circle, and beginning with yourself, have each person

(Imaginative Learners)

This lesson starts with an overview of stress, giving

name an everyday stress. If someone can't think of a stress, she should say "pass." If she thinks of one by the next time her turn comes around, she should join right in. After the group has gone around the circle four or five times, discuss questions like these: Why is it that the little stresses are the ones that so often do us in? What's the worse thing to you about everyday stress? If you had to rate your small-stress level from one to ten—with ten being, "I can't take it any more!"—what would your number be?

women an opportunity to create an experience that will give them a common starting place and an opportunity to begin reflecting on everyday stress.

Method used:
Discussion

Step 2

Ask someone to read Luke 10:38-42. Discuss the text. Why do you think the story of Mary and Martha was important to include in the Bible? Jesus didn't tell Martha that her work wasn't important, just not most important. What did Jesus consider to be the most important thing for Martha to do? Make some guesses about the internal qualities of Martha's life. Of Mary's. Join one other woman and discuss and decide if you are more like Martha or more like Mary. Why? Together, write one or two principles from these verses that you think Jesus wanted the sisters to grasp.

(Analytic Learners)
In this content section, many seekers may be unfamiliar with the story. Analytic Learners who have not been raised knowing Bible stories may come up with insights that amaze long-time Christians!

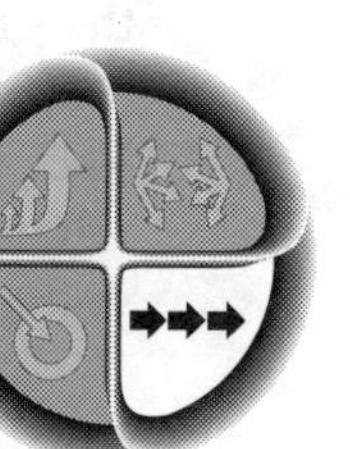

Methods used:
Bible reading
Group discussion
Pair discussion

Step 3

Give each woman a large piece of shelf or butcher paper and a crayon. Have everyone work on the floor. Ask each woman to draw a large circle. Explain, "The circle represents your day. Now divide it into pie-shaped wedges to show which parts of your normal day are filled with the most stress. Perhaps breakfast is a big high-stress wedge since this is the time a woman is getting her family, and often herself, off to work and school. A dozen little irritations can cause tempers to flare.

(Common Sense Learners)
The next section of the lesson moves the women from Mary and Martha into their own lives. It makes sense to take the principles that have been isolated and see if they apply today. The activity on the floor using large hand movements will appeal to the Common Sense Learner's preference

Explain your diagram to a friend. Discuss questions like these: If Mary could look at your stress circle, what things would she tell you to take away? Why? What things might she tell you to add? Explain. If Jesus looked at your life, how do you think He would finish these lines: "You spend too much time worrying about . . ." "You could be less busy, less frantic, if you cut . . ."

for moving during the learning cycle. We don't outgrow this preference. This valuable learning experience would not seem childish to adult women.

Methods used:
Personal pie graph
Pair discussion

Step 4

How do we slow down and listen to the Lord, nurturing the person inside us? Get the group thinking about some slow-down-and-nurture ideas. Invite brainstorming. Idea starters: Call a friend and talk about what's on your mind. Daydream about who you are, the potential you have.

If women don't come up with slow-down activities that foster spiritual growth, have someone read Psalm 46:10; Psalm 37:4, 34; and Isaiah 40:31 and share how these verses might apply to women's lives today. Give each woman an assignment to complete before next week's study. *Assignment:* In a modern translation Bible read the chapter listed below and ask God to help you understand what you read.

Monday: Read John 1.
Tuesday: Read John 2.
Wednesday: Read John 3.
Thursday: Read John 4.
Friday: Read John 5.

(Dynamic Learners)
The brainstorming activity is where the Dynamic Learner shines.

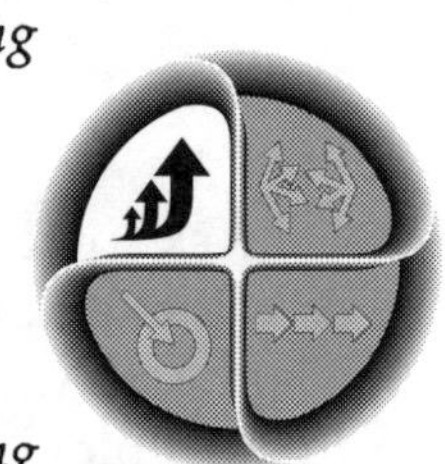

Methods used:
Brainstorming
Homework devotions

NOTES

1. This lesson was edited from the youth elective series Hot Topics, *Doubts, Male and Female, and School* (Elgin, Ill.: David C. Cook Publishing Co., 1989), John Duckworth, editor. The lesson, "A Sure Way for Scorched Feet," was written by Sandy Larsen. Used with permission.

2. This lesson was edited from the Questions Women Ask series book, *Is Your To-Do List About To Do You In?* by Marlene LeFever (Colorado Springs: NavPress, 1991).

Part IV

Seeing, Hearing, Moving Methods

The only bad method is the one that you use every *week.*
—Anonymous

Every lesson has a goal or an aim, a place where the teacher wants the students to end up at the end of the lesson. Every good Christian education goal is designed to push the student out of the classroom and into real life. The teacher reaches the goal by moving around the Learning Style Cycle using a variety of methods.

I've done a lot of teacher training sessions where I demonstrate a variety of methods. All too often, a teacher will say, "That was fun! I'm going to use that method in my Sunday school class this week." Wrong—unless it furthers the lesson aim. Lesson aims determine what methods should be used, not the other way around. It is all too easy to chase an aim with a clever method instead of asking, "Does this method accomplish the content goal? Does it forward the aim? Within the parts of the lesson, does it help my students answer one of the primary learning style questions?"

1. Why study this topic? (Imaginative)
2. What do I need to know about this topic? (Analytic)
3. How useful is what I learned to me today? (Common Sense)
4. What can what I've learned become? (Dynamic)

No method fits with just one learning style preference, although in Chapters 10—13, each method is written to show how it would work within one of the four places on the Learning Style Cycle. Methods are flexible. Depending on how they are used, they can fit in two, three, or even four different sections of the lesson. Be creative with the methods suggested in this section, and find ways to expand their application. (Practice adjusting them when you complete the do-it-yourself lesson in Chapter 14.)[1]

Methods also span age levels. In Chapters 10—13, age levels for each method are suggested, but most methods can be structured to fit a wide age range.

Hearing, Seeing, Moving

Good teaching methods make use of our senses, especially our ability to learn by hearing, seeing, and moving. Many methods make use of more than one of these three senses. For example, people who participate in a roleplay will use all three of these senses—hearing what is said, moving around to make the roleplay more realistic, and watching the other person's expression and responding to what is seen there.

These senses are called "modalities," an educational term referring to our main avenues of sensation. Those who learn best by seeing are called *visual learners*. Visual learners may learn best through words or through pictures. Those who learn best by hearing are called *auditory learners*. Those who need to move around in order to learn are called *tactile/kinesthetic learners*, T/K for short. Tactile refers to a sense of touch. Kinesthetic refers to large body movement such as dancing or miming.

There are people in every learning style quadrant who really enjoy seeing what they are learning. There are people in every quadrant who enjoy methods that require movement. Others in every quadrant learn best when they hear what is to be learned. In the Learning Style Cycle that we have been exploring, we can assume that there are more T/K learners who are Common Sense Learners, but there will be T/K learners in other quadrants as well.

In Chapter 9 you will learn more about these modalities. Then, in the four chapters that follow, you will find examples of methods that use combinations of seeing, hearing, and moving in all four Learning Style quadrants.

In Chapter 14, the rubber meets the road! You'll have an opportunity to put everything you've read into practice. The Do-It-Yourself Lesson Plan will be fun, and also a kind of test in which you will answer the Common Sense question, "How does all this work in my own teaching situation?"

METHODS OVERVIEW: CHAPTERS 10—13

Abbreviations: C—Children Y—Youth A—Adult

IMAGINATIVE LEARNERS (See Chapter 10)

Age Level	Modality	Method
C, Y, A	Auditory	Tape Thanks
Y, A	Auditory	Christian Music
C, Y, A	Auditory	Questions
C, Y, A	Auditory	Acrostic Speak
C	Auditory	Bible Reading
C, Y	Auditory	Paired Reading
C, Y, A	Visual	Video Clips
C, Y, A	Visual	Show and Tell
C, Y, A	Visual	Picture Watching
C, Y, A	Visual	Students As Artists
Y, A	T/K	Tangrams
C	T/K	Action Songs
C	T/K	Squeeze Art
C, Y, A	T/K	Roleplay
C, Y, A	T/K	Scriptural Choral Reading

ANALYTIC LEARNERS (See Chapter 11)

Age Level	Modality	Method
C, Y, A	Auditory	Content Circle
Y, A	Auditory	Dictionary
C, Y, A	Auditory	Spin Discussion
Y	Auditory	Riddles
Y, A	Auditory	Sharing Questions
C, Y, A	Auditory	Audio-Guest Learning
C, Y, A	Auditory	Silence
C, Y	Auditory	Score the Performance
C, Y, A	Visual	Draw a Bible Study
C, Y, A	Visual	Cross the Message
Y, A	Visual	Question the Passage
C, Y	Visual	Thinking in Sets
C, Y, A	Visual	Picture Storytelling
C, Y, A	Visual	Story Stops
C, Y, A	Visual	Overheads and Flip Charts
C, Y	T/K	Do-It-Yourself Content Board Game
C	T/K	Relief Map
C, Y, A	T/K	Content Boards
Y, A	T/K	Yes/No Debate

COMMON SENSE LEARNERS (See Chapter 12)

Age Level	Modality	Method
C, Y	Auditory	Triad Think
C, Y, A	Auditory	Illustrations
Y, A	Auditory	Survival Kit
A	Auditory	Bible Reading
C, Y	Visual	No-Word Story
Y, A	Visual	Worksheet
C	Visual	Shadow Drama
A	Visual	Visual Aids
C	T/K	Foot Game
C, Y	T/K	Computer Possibilities
Y	T/K	Do-It-Yourself Game
C, Y	T/K	String Thing Project Review
C, Y, A	T/K	Charting
C, Y, A	T/K	Pipe Cleaner Progress
C, Y, A	T/K	Food As a Learning Tool

DYNAMIC LEARNERS (See Chapter 13)

Age Level	Modality	Method
Y, A	Auditory	Outcome Sentences
C	Auditory	Worship Celebration
Y, A	Auditory	Parables
Y, A	Auditory	Metaphor
C, Y, A	Auditory	Interview
C, Y	Auditory	Sentence Sets
C, Y, A	Auditory	Brainstorming
C, Y	Visual	Stick-Figure Bible Praise
C, Y, A	Visual	Free Visuals
C, Y, A	Visual	Faces
Y, A	Visual	Godly Graffiti
C, Y	Visual	Puppets
C, Y, A	Visual	Picture This
Y, A	Visual	Color Blocks
C	T/K	Clay in Class
C, Y	T/K	Alternative . . . Verse Memorization
Y	T/K	Video Creativity
C, Y, A	T/K	Theological Miming
Y	T/K	Strobe Theater

NOTE

1. For additional how-to information on methods (drama, roleplay, mime, simulation, storytelling, discussion, case study, creative writing, music, and art), see *Creative Teaching Methods* by Marlene LeFever (Elgin, Ill.: David C. Cook Publishing Co., 1985).

9

Do You Learn Best by Hearing, Seeing, or Moving?

Sunday school is a building that has four walls with tomorrow inside.
—a teacher

I was vacationing on a beach in Mexico when a group of Indian children arrived with their parents for a picnic. We exchanged smiles, and within minutes the children and I were "talking" without knowing a word of each other's language. With body motions, they told me that this was the spot where fishermen brought in lobsters. The children lived thirty minutes away. This day was a school holiday. They loved to swim, but not at this spot because the coral would cut their feet. They had cake that their mother baked, and she wanted me to have some. Yes, they would love some of the candy I had brought. Great communication on a beach was done with only body movements and facial expressions.

All young children are body-language smart. They learn by moving. They are tactile-kinesthetic learners. If we are to teach young children effectively, we must move around the Learning Style Cycle using methods that require large body movements.

In the early years of schooling, some children switch from a preference for methods that require moving to a preference for seeing. They become visual learners.

Around ages ten through twelve, some children switch their preference to hearing. They learn best when they hear what is being taught to them. They are auditory learners.

Research varies on how many students from ages ten through adult have each preference. One research base[1] suggests that in a group of ten students, two would prefer auditory methods. Many more girls than boys learn best through methods that involve hearing.[2] Four would learn best with visual methods. Four would learn best with methods that require movement. They are tactile/kinesthetic learners. Many more males than females learn best by methods that require movement. Yet, these are the hardest types of activities to fit into lessons for young people and adults. Perhaps our lack of tactile/kinesthetic methods explains in part why many boys drop out of Sunday school.[3]

About 30 percent of these students would not have a strong preference. Their interest in a subject would determine their enthusiasm for the methods incorporated into the lesson.

When students are taught with methods that use their preferred strength and are reinforced through their second preference, they learn more and enjoy learning more. When methods do not fit students' learning styles, our teaching is not as effective as it should be.[4]

These preferences show remarkable resistance to change. Cinda Gorman, while in the Doctor of Ministry program at Fuller Seminary, found that even at that educational level, her classmates' preference for auditory, visual, or tactile/kinesthetic learning was still predominant and matched their behavior in class. The visual learners took copious notes and drew charts and diagrams. The auditory learners placed tape recorders on their desks and listened to the tapes as they drove home. "One of the kinesthetic learners had amazed me for days," Gorman wrote. "Rarely had he taken a note, but he contributed thoughtfully to the class discussion. While he had appeared not to be participating, he'd absorbed a great deal of material. He'd also completed a rather complicated needlepoint project! Obviously, his fingers were helping him learn."[5]

Most adults already know what types of methods they enjoy most. For example, if you are a visual learner, you may remember a sermon better when the pastor uses an overhead. Or when Scripture is read aloud, you may need to follow along in your Bible to really take in what is being said. But just in case you are wondering about your preference, take the follow predictive test. It will tell you your number one preference and your secondary preference as well.

Find Your Strength—
Visual, Auditory, or Tactile/Kinesthetic[6]

Directions: Complete the sentence by marking the letter on the right of the statement that is most typical of you. Then count the number of checks in each column. This will give you a rough idea of your strength in each area.

	A	B	C
1. My emotions can often be interpreted from my: (A) Facial expressions (B) Voice quality (C) General body tone	❑	❑	❑
2. I keep up with current events by: (A) Reading the newspaper (B) Listening to the radio (C) Quickly reading the paper or spending a few minutes watching TV news	❑	❑	❑
3. If I have business to conduct with another person, I prefer: (A) Face-to-face meetings or writing letters (B) The telephone; it saves time (C) Conversing while walking, jogging, or doing something physical	❑	❑	❑
4. When I'm angry, I usually: (A) Clam up and give others the silent treatment (B) Am quick to let others know why I am angry (C) Clench my fists or storm off	❑	❑	❑
5. When I'm driving, I: (A) Frequently check the rear view mirror and watch the road carefully (B) Turn on the radio as soon as I enter the car (C) Can't get comfortable and continually shift position	❑	❑	❑
6. I consider myself: (A) A neat dresser (B) A sensible dresser (C) A comfortable dresser	❑	❑	❑
7. At a meeting, I: (A) Come prepared with notes and displays (B) Enjoy discussing issues (C) Would rather be somewhere else	❑	❑	❑
8. In my spare time, I would rather: (A) Watch TV, go to a movie, attend the theater or read (B) Listen to the radio or stereo, attend a concert or play an instrument (C) Engage in a physical activity of some kind	❑	❑	❑

Continued on next page

[Find Your Strength, Cont.]	**A**	**B**	**C**
9. The best approach to discipline is to: (A) Isolate the student from the peer group (B) Reason with the student (C) Use acceptable forms of punishment	❑	❑	❑
10. The most effective way of rewarding students is: (A) Positive written notes or awards others can see (B) Oral praise to the student in front of peers (C) A pat on the back, hug	❑	❑	❑
Total the number of checks in each column	A__	B__	C__

A = Visual
B = Auditory
C = Tactile-Kinesthetic

The caution for teachers in "Find Your Strength" is the same one that the Learning Style Cycle provides. It is easier to spend the most time teaching in the place in the cycle where we as teachers are most comfortable. It is easier to use the types of methods that match our modality strengths. But we can't do this! We teach not to meet our own learning needs. We teach to our students who may have similar preferences or who may be very, very different.

Now, let's take a closer look at students who have a strong auditory, visual, or tactile/kinesthetic preference in methodology.

Students Who Prefer Auditory Methods

One Sunday an adult teacher left his easy-going speaking patterns and suddenly started talking very, very fast. Finally someone asked him why he had begun to sound like an auctioneer. "Well," the teacher explained, "I learned that students only remember about 10 percent of what they hear, so I decided to talk faster. If I say more, what is covered in the 10 percent is larger, too."[7]

Auditory Learners will remember much more than 10 percent. Visual and Tactile/Kinesthetic Learners may remember much less than 10 percent of what they hear.

Some Auditory Learners cannot take notes, because it distracts them from hearing. They are so in tune with sounds that they need to pay total attention to what the teacher is saying. Often when they read silently, they move their lips. They are mentally making the sound that helps their minds to respond.

Auditory Learners often learn very well in groups. Most will benefit from "cooperative learning."[8]

Students who Prefer Visual Methods[9]

Visual Learners need words and/or pictures in order to learn. In an auditory teaching situation, they may stop and stare into space, giving their minds time to visualize what is being said. We have little trouble with the person who needs to see the words in order to learn. But in today's learning environment, many of our visual learners are more picture literate than word literate.

Albert Einstein was a Visual Learner. He had a marked disability with auditory learning and the use of language. Yet he had an extraordinary ability to construct complex card houses, use building blocks, and manipulate geometrical diagrams. These skills suggest that he had a specialized mental ability for visual-spatial (space) perception, visual reasoning, and visual memory.[10] If he were evaluated in the traditional way, he would be labeled learning disabled.

A child with Einstein's learning style would never win Bible quizzes or be called on to read Scripture in front of the congregation, or serve as the youth representative on a church board. Without visual stimuli that allows him or her to shine, a child with the potential of Einstein may drop out of our church program. That would be a great loss for both the child and the church.

We need to find ways to combine pictures and words. In fifty-five secular experiments using pictures (performed by different educators), test results showed that when picture and text went together, learning was higher and what was learned was remembered longer.[11]

In one study, sixth grade children were shown drawings that reinforced the main ideas of a story they had read. The control group just read the story. When tested, children who had seen the words and pictures did 24 percent better than those who had seen only words.

In some cultures, the need for visual stimuli may be higher than it is for others. For example, the majority of Native Americans learn more easily when observation, artistic and spatial skills, and physical activity are emphasized.[12] They would do better in classrooms where picture literacy and tactile/kinesthetic methods are used.

Poor readers make even greater use of pictures than average and good readers. Poor readers in the fifth grade were tested on what they remembered when pictures were part of the text. They did 35 percent better than poor readers who had not seen pictures. When tested for recall, poor readers did 133 percent better than their picture-less peers. Poor or non-readers represent sixty million Americans, one-third of the adult population. Forty-five percent of all adults do not even read the daily newspaper—10 percent by choice, the rest cannot.[13]

There is overwhelming evidence that we should be using pictures with every lesson we teach. In no test among the fifty-five studies was text without pictures better in terms of the grades students got or what they remembered.

[Cont.]

An adult attending a Christian education convention in Harrisburg, Pennsylvania, said to me, "If my teachers had taught me in pictures, I wouldn't have dropped out of high school. I have trouble remembering words, but show me a picture and I suddenly become a lot smarter. My memory kicks in! Tell me a Bible story without a picture, and it just won't register. Show me a picture and I'll remember the story and what God wants to teach me through the story."[14]

Consider the feelings of this visually literate child in a traditional Sunday school classroom.[15]

He always wanted to say things. But no one understood.
He always wanted to explain things. But no one cared.
So he drew.

Sometimes he would just draw and it wasn't anything.
Sometimes he would lie in the grass and look at the sky and see pictures that needed saying to God.
Then one day he drew THE picture. It was a beautiful picture.
He loved it.

He took it to Sunday school. Not to show anyone. But just to have it with him as a friend.

It was funny about Sunday school.
He sat on a hard brown chair like all the other hard brown chairs, and he thought his should be red.
His room was a square brown room. And it was tight and close.
And stiff.

He hated to hold the pencil and work in his book. He hated his feet on the floor, stiff.

The teacher came and spoke to him. She asked him to consider wearing a tie like all the other boys. He said he didn't like them, and she said it didn't matter because people dressed up in God's house.

After that they drew. And he drew all yellow. It was the way he felt about the morning. And it was beautiful.

The teacher came and smiled at him.
"What's this?" she said. "Why don't you draw something like Ken's drawing? Don't you like all the colors? Can you see what it is? Isn't it beautiful?"
She was all questions without waiting for answers.

After that his mother bought him a tie, and he drew the Garden of

Eden and the animals on the ark like everyone else. He threw the old picture away.

And when he lay out alone looking at the sky, it was big and blue and all of everything, but he wasn't anymore. He had nothing to draw for God.

He was square inside and brown, and his hands were stiff and he was like everyone else. And the thing inside him that needed saying didn't need saying any more.

It had stopped pushing. It was crushed.
Stiff.
Like everything else.

Students Who Prefer Tactile/Kinesthetic Methods

The T/K learner needs movement in order to learn.[16] He or she may have low visual and auditory skills and may fail if taught in any other way. This learner cannot sit still, especially if he or she is engaged in an activity that does not include manipulating materials. (Writing does not constitute an active process for T/K learners. They need methods that involve things they can touch, feel, and manipulate. They need methods that allow them to move.)

If this student is not actively involved in what is going on, the teacher may lose him or her. When students' learning styles and the instructional methods used are mismatched, children can become tense and even physically ill. "Frustration and stress often lead to unacceptable conduct," says Marie Carbo, director of research and staff development, Learning Research Associates.[17]

As an indication of how this child is feeling, the teacher should look beyond facial expression to the general body posture. The whole body is an index of emotion.

The Apostle John's Use of the Senses in Teaching

In I John, the apostle is so excited about his discovery of who Jesus is that he wants to share that excitement with everyone. If his learners need to hear in order to learn, he'll tell the story. If his listeners need to see in order to learn, he's got a resurrection picture to share. If a person needs to touch and move in order to learn, he'll teach that way, too. He's not going to miss anyone. Notice how he uses seeing, hearing, and moving in his celebration paragraph, I John 1:1-4.

> *That which was from the beginning, which we have heard* [auditory],
> *which we have seen with our eyes, which we have looked at* [visual]
> *and our hands have touched*—[tactile/kinesthetic]

[*Cont.*]

this we proclaim concerning the Word of life.
The life appeared; we have seen it [visual]
and testify to it, and we proclaim to you the eternal life,
which was with the Father [auditory]
and has appeared to us [visual].
We proclaim to you what we have seen and heard,
so that you also may have fellowship with us.
And our fellowship is with the Father and with his Son, Jesus Christ. We write this to make our joy complete.

NOTES

1. See Chapter 19 highlighting the work of Dr. Rita Dunn, St. Johns University, Jamaica, New York.

2. "After wiring a playground for sound, researchers found that 100 percent of the sounds coming from girls' mouths were audible, recognizable words. As for little boys, only 69 percent of their sounds were understandable words! The remaining 31 percent were either one-syllable sounds like *uh* and *mmm* or sound effects like *Varoooom! Yaaaah!* and *Zoooom!"* From Gary Smalley and John Trent, "Why Can't My Spouse Understand What I Say?" *Focus on the Family*, November 1988, p. 3.

3. Women keep their hearing longer than men. According to medical notes presented in *Reader's Digest*, May 1993, "Ears Looking at You," even though there is "no established explanation, data from an ongoing study show that hearing declines approximately twice as fast in men as in women."

4. Our modality preferences make a difference no matter if we are ten or eighty-six. Michael W. Galbraith and Waynne B. James, "Assessment of Dominant Perceptual Learning Styles of Older Adults," *Educational Gerontology*, Vol. 10, No. 6 (1984), p. 455, point out that "since learning styles impact the amount of information processed and retained, knowledge and utilization of an older learner's most effective learning style will enhance learning."

5. Cinda Gorman, "Preaching for the Senses," *Leadership*, Vol. 11, No. 2, Spring 1990, pp. 112, 113.

6. "Find Your Perceptual Strength—Visual, Auditory, or Tactual-Kinesthetic," *Instructor* (January 1980). From Zaner-Bloser, Inc., Columbus, Ohio (1980). Used with permission.

7. Wes Willis, "Editorial Perspective," *Christian Education Journal* (Spring 1989), p. 6.

8. For a brief overview of cooperative learning, see Chapter 19. Also see "Cooperative Learning," *Educational Leadership*, Vol. 47, No. 4 (December 1989/January 1990), pp. 4-66.

9. If you are a visual learner, you will benefit from the "Teaching to Learning

Styles" video. Write ASCD, 1250 N. Pitt St., Alexandria, VA 22314. Phone: 703-549-9110.

10. Bernard M. Patten, "Visually Mediated Thinking: A Report of the Case of Albert Einstein," *Journal of Learning Disabilities*, August-September 1973, No. 7.

11. W. Howard Levie and Richard Lentz, "Effects of Text Illustrations: A Review of Research," *Educational Communication and Technology: A Journal of Theory, Research, and Development*, N.d., pp. 198-232.

12. Genevieve Cuny, O.S.F., "Teaching Native Americans," *Religion Teacher's Journal*, March 1992, p. 11.

13. Roger Palms, "Illiteracy—A Major EPA Problem in the 1990s," *Evangelical Press Association Liaison*, January-February 1990, p. 1.

14. Andrew Windham, quoted by the author in *Teacher Touch*, Fall 1994, a publication of David C. Cook Church Ministries. For an excellent resource on the effects of pictures with children, college students, and adults, see *Picture Books for Gifted Programs* by Nancy Polette (Metuchen, N.J., and London: Scarecrow, 1981).

15. This Sunday school version of this verse was created from the original secular one that was found in the files of the National Defense Education Act Institute on Counseling and Guidance of Purdue University.

16. *Communication Briefings*, Vol. 8, No. 4, reported on research at the University of Southern California that indicates that people digest complex facts better—absorbing information 40 percent faster—and make quicker decisions when standing. It would be interesting to test the participants in this study for T/K preference. Youth leaders might build on this study by conducting a Bible study with teens standing. Rate the participation of those students who are strongly T/K.

17. Marie Carbo, "Matching Reading Styles: Correcting Ineffective Instruction," *Educational Leadership*, October 1987, p. 57.

10

METHODS: IMAGINATIVE LEARNERS

The Lord is not compelled to use theologians. He can take snakes, sticks, or anything else, and use them for the advancement of His cause.
—*Billy Sunday*

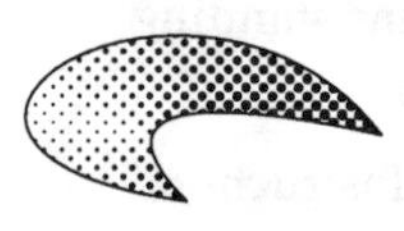

Imaginative Learners respond most positively to content presented through methods involving observation and reflection, group interaction, artistic interpretation, roleplay, creative listening, group singing, storytelling, drama, and arts and crafts projects.

The following methods are illustrative of those many Imaginative Learners will enjoy.

AUDITORY

Tape Thanks
(Older children, youth, adults)

Provide an overview of the church in action by having volunteers tell thank-you stories about people in your church who have helped them in their Christian lives this year. Tape their stories.

You may want to duplicate the tape and encourage each participant to give his or her story to the person who was thanked.

Christian Music
(Youth, although adaptable for all ages, including adult)

All students, not just Imaginative Learners, enjoy listening to music.

Contemporary Christian musicians often bring up issues that can lead directly into Bible study.

Amy Grant, for example, sang a song titled, "You're Not Alone" in her album, "Heart in Motion" (1991). In her song she talks about how lonely it feels when love ends and how very much it hurts.

There is a natural bridge from her song into Bible study. You can say, "Yes, I've been unhappy, too, but how do I know I'm not alone in this world?"

Insightful questions would help all students discuss the song, with Imaginative Learners taking the lead.[1] One could ask . . .

- How could a person be "burned" by love?
- If you've ever broken up with a boyfriend or girlfriend, how did you feel? Did you want help or to be left alone?
- When the singer says, "You're not alone," is she referring to human companionship, Jesus' presence, both, or something else? Explain.

At this point in this lesson, the focus shifts to new information and the Analytic Learner's interest is piqued. "What do I need to know in order to deal with loneliness?"

- Read Matthew 5:4. How might this apply in the case of a breakup?
- Read I Timothy 5:5 and discuss: How is a widow like a person who has just broken up with a boyfriend or girlfriend? How might their feelings be similar?
- If we're "not alone," as the song says, why does the verse describe a widow as "left all alone"?
- If a person has just ended a relationship, what might he or she be tempted to "hope" in? What could it mean for that person to "hope in God"?

In a full lesson plan, the lesson would now move into the Common Sense Learner's territory to discover how students could apply the information from the song and Bible study.

Questions

(For adult students, but questions are appropriate at all levels.)

"Why" questions are those that draw upon past knowledge to broaden the group's base of knowledge or feeling. The "why" expects the student to defend the answer, perhaps with fact, but more frequently with opinion based on personal experience.

Acrostic Speak

(For older children, youth, and adults. Adults may be more comfortable writing their lines and then reading them.)

Pick a short word that serves as a pivotal word for today's lesson and ask

[Cont.]

pairs to mind-write an acrostic. Nothing is written on paper, but the pair comes up with an acrostic that it can share with the whole group. In an acrostic, the first letter of each line spells the key word. So, for example, depending on the direction of the lesson, the groups might write acrostics based on words like SIN, JOY, MIND, WIN. For example:

M Minds are gifts from God.
I I'm proud of mine.
N No one thinks just like I think.
D Don't doubt what I can do.

Bible Reading

(Children, and adaptable for all levels)

When Bible reading is used in the very early part of a lesson, it must be tied to the question, "Why should I study this?" In the following illustration, the script from John 4:47-52 could be performed in preparation for students to share some of the things God did that totally surprised them.

Part 1: When this man heard that Jesus had arrived in Galilee from Judea, he went to Him and begged Him to come and heal his son, who was close to death.
Part 2: "Unless you people see miraculous signs and wonders," Jesus told him, "you will never believe." The royal official said,
Part 1: "Sir, come down before my child dies."
Part 2: Jesus replied, "You may go. Your son will live."
Part 1: The man took Jesus at His word and departed. While he was still on the way, his servants met him with the news that his boy was living. When he inquired as to the time when his son got better, they said to him,
Part 3: "The fever left him yesterday at the seventh hour."
Part 1: Then the father realized that this was the exact time at which Jesus had said to him,
Part 2: "Your son will live."

Visual learners might enjoy listening to the script with their eyes closed; this way they will "see" what they're hearing.

Paired Reading

(Older children and teens)

Pair students and have them take turns reading to each other a life-related story that will pull them into the Bible study. They enjoy it, get practice reading, and are much more involved than they are when a teacher asks students to read a paragraph each.

One leader[2] suggested that teachers give directions for what students are to do when they have completed the reading. For instance:

- Talk over the reading and see what you think about it.
- Each person write in your journal . . .
- Talk about some things you liked or found interesting. Be ready to share at least one thing.

Visual

Video Clips

(All ages)

Use very short video clips to illustrate a truth or to get students involved in a topic.

Don't rule out secular videos. For example, the football coach's pep talk to Rudy in the movie of the same name might introduce a lesson on how we encourage each other to live the Christian life.

A three-minute segment of the mother's dedication and refusal to give up on her son's life in the movie "Lorenzo's Oil" might help students see how important it is not to give up praying for someone who has been sick for a long time.

Show and Tell

(All ages)

Bring items to class for show and tell, even if you teach older students. For example, a puzzle with one piece missing could illustrate the flaw in the life of a Christian who willfully refuses Christ's control of one part of her life.

One teacher brought a baby pig to class and allowed youngsters to hold it. They informally talked about all the things they could know about pigs just from watching this piglet. This became an introduction to a story on our wonderful Creator.

Picture Watching

(Middle elementary through adults)

This activity can be done with any Bible story picture and is designed to equalize the knowledge of all students before they are given new knowledge. Pictures can be used, of course, in the actual Bible study, but here, they whet students' appetites for the content study that will correct or validate what they say.[3]

Look at this picture for a full minute. In your group discuss the following questions:

[Cont.]

- How does your eye travel around this picture? Where does it go first? Second? What do you think the artist wished to communicate by this?
- Do you like or dislike this art? Support your choice.
- If you had painted this picture, what changes might you have made? Why?
- If you didn't know what was happening in this picture, what would you guess was happening? Read the expressions on the people's faces.
- Has the picture told you anything about the story you didn't already know, anything you'd like to check with the text?

Picture-watching exercises can be done with almost every picture. On the one showing the widow, questions centered on the content of the picture and story. On this one of the prodigal son, students will approach the picture as art.[4]

These three categories of questions can be used with any picture.

1. *Content*
   - What part of this picture carries the message?
   - What is the picture's point of view—where is the camera?
   - What is the mood of this picture?
2. *Form* (having to do with colors and shapes)
   - Why do you think the artist used the colors he did?
   - What do the colors tell you about the people in the picture?
   - What impact do the two upraised hands have on the message of the picture?
3. *Interpretive questions* (combining form and content)
   - What is the picture's personality?
   - Knowing what you know about this picture, what real emotions are hidden by the smiles on these faces?
   - If this picture had depicted the son's homecoming, what things would be changed? How might the artist have used color and positioning on the canvas to show these changes?

Students As Artists

(Older elementary through adult)

There are a limited number of resources that give older students an opportunity to draw as part of the learning process. Notice that both of the following ideas give the students structure. For some this may be restraining, but most will find it makes their efforts look more successful.[5]

Draw your answer to the question, "What is sin?"

[*Cont.*]

The above figure of the seated person could be used in a number of ways.

- Color how you feel inside when you think about something that doesn't please God.
- Doodle how you think (Samuel, Moses, Jonah, Esther) might have felt if he or she had been in your shoes at (school, home, work) today.
- If a completely colored-in figure represented a person totally sold out to Jesus, color in the portion of this figure that represents how sold out you think people in this (church, class, denomination) are.

Of course, students could simply give their answers to these questions without drawing them, but the graphing makes the answer weightier. It's also helpful to put answers into unique forms to help us see things from different perspectives.

Students should share what they have done with at least one other person. This debriefing is more important than the actual drawing or coloring.

Tactile/Kinesthetic

Tangrams

(Teens and adults)

A tangram is a square that has been cut into these seven geometric shapes. The shapes can be arranged in any configuration.

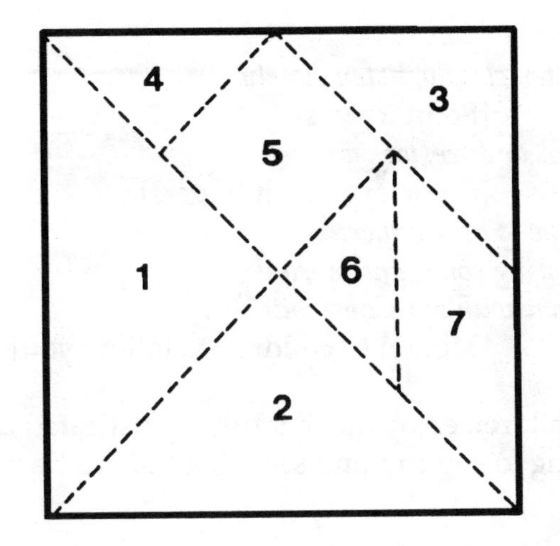

Possible tangram groupings:

- Each person can work alone on his or her tangram.
- Small groups can do a single tangram, perhaps as they sit on the floor and use the rug as their canvas.
- Small groups can show their designs to the class by placing the pieces on the overhead projector.
- In a camping or out-of-doors setting, the tangram pieces can be replaced by sticks or stones of various sizes.

With an activity like this, students who thought they had nothing to share, often because they are not gifted verbally, will provide unique insights.

Ideas for tangram assignments:

- Symbolically show what Christmas means to people in this town.
- Illustrate the most important principle you found in your Bible study this past week.
- Use a tangram to show someone what this church is really like.
- Use a tangram to illustrate how important regularly practicing the disciplines of your faith is to you.
- Show how it feels to be a student in a new school.
- Show how your group feels about sharing its faith aloud.
- Illustrate how people in this church respond to world hunger . . . hunger in this community.

Action Songs
(Preschool and young elementary)[6]

Sing to the tune of "Are You Sleeping?"

[Cont.]

Listen closely, listen closely.
[Point to ears]
Look and see, look and see.
[Circle eyes with fingers]
Time to be together,
Sharing songs and stories.
Come with me. Come with me.
[Motion to children to follow you]

Elementary children enjoy much more sophisticated choreography. Give the idea and a song to a group and see what they come up with.

Squeeze Art[7]
(Children)

Children will use aluminum foil to build shapes that encourage them to focus on the topic of the lesson. For example, if the lesson is going to be about God's family, children might squeeze shapes of their family. If the lesson is about praise, children might squeeze scenes of people in various praise situations.

Directions for squeezing the family: Tear twelve-inch pieces of foil off a roll of aluminum foil. Use a piece for each "person" being squeezed. Wad a paper towel for the head and place it in the center of the foil. Wrap the remaining foil around this wad and squeeze it at the neck (A). Form arms on the sides (B), and cut the foil to separate arms from the lower body (C). Place figures on a cardboard base and glue them in place (D).

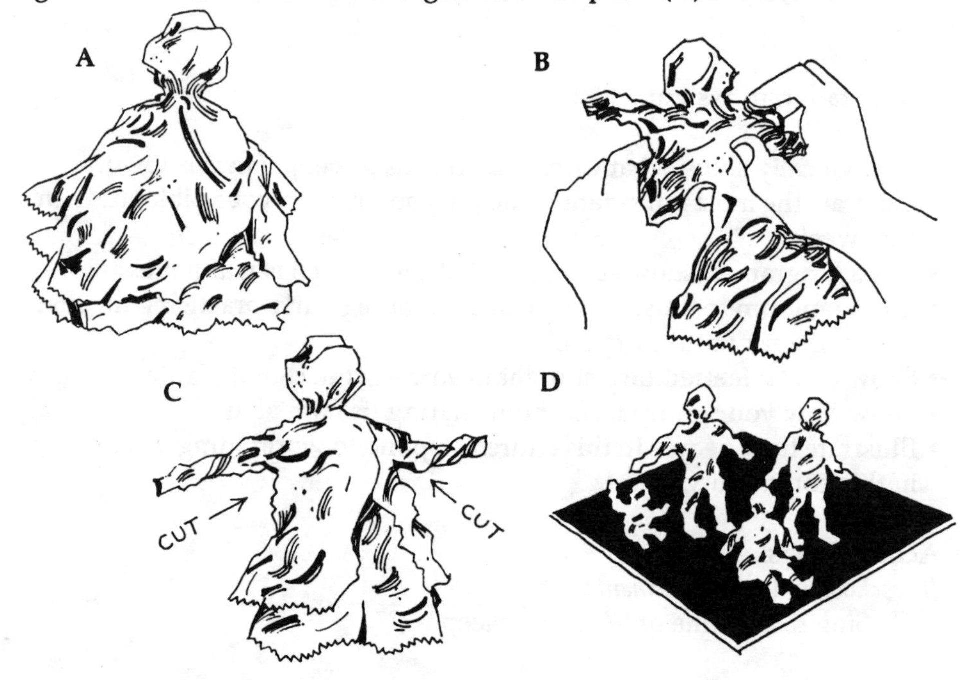

Roleplay

(Adult example. Roleplay can be used from elementary levels through adult.)

Roleplay is a powerful tool in the hands of a skilled teacher. In it, the teacher assigns group members roles of people who are involved in real or hypothetical situations. The students talk back and forth, looking for solutions to problems or setting up situations that can be discussed by the group. Roleplays help people explore the feelings of people whose roles they have assumed, learning to articulate how their faith informs real-life situations.

Consider these benefits of role play:[8]

- Roleplay stimulates inductive learning.
- By evaluating what students say in their roleplays, the leader is able to determine where students are and concentrate his or her teaching in the areas of greatest need.
- Through roleplay and the discussion that follows it, students may learn how to solve their own problems.
- Roleplay gives people a chance to experience new, unusual, or problem situations in a protected, caring environment.
- Roleplays allow anonymity, dealing with problems group members have not dared to mention.
- When students place themselves in roles of other people, they learn to identify with them and gain information about why others behave the way they do.
- Participating in roleplays allows Imaginative Learners to use their intellectual potential more fully and gain the respect of their classmates.
- Roleplay can guide students into Scripture. Roleplay helps the entire class answer the question, "Why do I need to know this?"

Scriptural Choral Reading

(Older elementary through adult)

This method is an example of how difficult it is to put a method into a box—it will appeal to visual and T/K learners.

In a choral reading use the same groupings that a choir would—soloists, duets, trios—but students talk instead of sing. They should not change the wording of Scripture, but they can repeat words and phrases for emphasis.

The tactile/kinesthetic part of the method comes when the leader asks the group to add something other than words to the choral reading. If this is the start of the lesson, the teacher may ask that each group find some way to illustrate through actions why this section of Scripture is important to study today. What the group adds will depend on the group's imagination.

Notes

1. Curriculum ideas are excerpted from the music-based youth curriculum series Spectrum, *Tough Times* (Elgin, Ill.: David C. Cook Publishing Co., 1992), written by John Duckworth.

2. Merrill Harmin, *"Inspiring Active Learning—A Handbook for Teachers"* (Alexandria, Vir.: Association for Supervision and Curriculum Development, 1994) p. 102.

3. This picture is one from the Spanish/English picture kit "Scripture Pictures" (Elgin, Ill.: David C. Cook Publishing Co., 1993).

4. Ibid.

5. Marlene LeFever and Kathleen Weyna, *Creative Kids Book* (Elgin, Ill.: Chariot Books, 1984).

6. Most young children will enjoy action songs no matter what their learning style preference. These two illustrations are take from *100 More Action Songs!* (Elgin, Ill.: David C. Cook Publishing Co., 1991). Used by permission.

7. Marlene LeFever, *62 Activities for Kids* (Elgin, Ill.: Chariot Books, 1984).

8. For a more complete elaboration on roleplay, see *Creative Teaching Methods* by Marlene LeFever (Elgin, Ill.: David C. Cook Publishing Co., 1985), pp. 94-96.

11

Methods: Analytic Learners

I remember praying . . . "Lord, take my life but don't touch one neuron of my beautiful brain." . . . It was painful to realize that my adult relationship with God was grounded very firmly in my intellectual apprehension and half-brained spirituality. . . . What if my world-class left brain was permanently out of commission? Where did this leave my understanding of a relationship with God?
—Diane M. Komp, professor of Pediatrics, Yale

Analytic Learners respond most positively to content presented through methods involving commands, programmed instruction, lecture, competition, demonstrations, gaming, self-study, and targeted class discussions (focus on content).

Auditory

Content Circle (Circle of Knowledge)
(All ages)

With this method, students hear something said three or four times. Some auditory learners will memorize the content through this repetition.

The method is best used as a review: reviewing books of the Bible, names of Old Testament leaders, names of people who spoke with Jesus, Church history leaders, names of Christian martyrs, countries where people are struggling to survive, etc. Here the illustration uses a review of memorized Bible verses. The process would be the same with any topic.

[Cont.]

Bible Memory Illustration:

Divide the class into small groups of three to five. Each group picks a leader. Explain that when you say, "Go!" that leader should recite a Bible verse. Moving clockwise, the next person should recite a Bible verse. Move around the circle until you say, "Time!"

As the verses are recited, the leader records the verse reference.

If a team member doesn't know a verse to recite, he or she just says, "Pass," and the next person in the circle recites.

When time is up (three to five minutes) canvas the different groups, having each one in turn recite one of the verses from its list. After a person from a group recites it, the leader should recite it back. (Every student will hear the verse three times in this process.) If any other group has that verse on its list, it must cross off the reference. They lose it. Only the group that first recited it to the whole class keeps it on its list.

Groups say verses until one group runs out. The group with the most verses remaining on its list wins.

Dictionary

(Teens and adults)

Often we use Christian vocabulary easily and correctly in context without really understanding what the words mean. As a review activity, ask students to talk through working definitions of the "Christian" words that were part of the study. For example, one unit might require students to define sin, salvation, redemption, joy. By labeling the definitions "working definitions" students are freed from being too technical.

Students may feel most comfortable working on this assignment in pairs. Have one pair combine with another to share what they have done and come up with a single definition. Combine again until the group has agreed on one definition. Discuss the process.

Spin Discussion

(All ages)

Draw circles and divide them into four or six parts and number the parts. Attach a cardboard arrow onto each circle's center with a brad so that when you flip the arrow with your finger, it spins to a different number.

Divide the participants into groups, and give each group a spinner. The size of each group should match the divisions on the spinners. Everyone in the group is given a number that corresponds to a number on the spinner.

Ask a question and have the group leaders spin. The person in each group who has the number that is the same as the one on the spinner must answer.

The activity is especially effective for very large classes where the teacher wants to stimulate a lot of participation.

Alternatively, make one spinner on an overhead transparency by attaching the arrow to a hole punched through the center of the transparency. Spin the arrow, and the person in each group whose number comes up must answer.

This activity works best when questions have a variety of possible answers. For instance:

- Based on what you know about Moses' life, how would you describe his leadership style?
- God chose the timing of Christ's birth. What made His choice so excellent?
- If you could only have one book of the Bible in your possession, which would you pick and why?

Riddles
(Youth)

Challenge teens to come up with couplets that are riddles. Build a contest around this idea. Collect riddles for a month. Then at a youth meeting, read the riddles and see who can solve them. Award silly prizes. For instance:

> *I'm big, strong, and hairy.*
> *Don't cut my hair—that would be scary!* [Samson]

Sharing Questions
(Older teens and adults)

"Sharing questions are a useful tool for helping persons bring to consciousness some of the important preunderstandings that they bring to a particular text," says Ernest Hess.[1] He continues . . .

> Some ask for previous understanding of the text:
> - What has this text meant to you?
> - What is your earliest memory of this text?
> - How has your understanding of this text changed during your life?
>
> Others try to elicit a holistic response to the text:
> - Whom do you identify with in this text?
> - What bothers you about this text?
> - What questions do you bring to this text?
> - Who or what comes to mind as you listen to this text?
>
> It is important that the personal thrust of these questions be emphasized. Personal honesty rather than objective truth about *the* meaning of the text is what we are after. . . . There must be an acceptance of diversity and a recognition that there are no "right" or "wrong" answers to these questions. Care must be taken by both leaders and participants not to evaluate and judge the answers given at this time.

Audio-Guest Learning
(Older children through adult)

Use a speaker phone to bring guests into your teaching setting. Equipment is inexpensive, from $40 to $100.

With a good phone, more than thirty students can speak back and forth to an audio-guest. Students should prepare questions for the audio-guest,

[Cont.]

and the list of guests is limited only by imagination:

- An expert in the subject you are studying. Few classes can afford to have these people visit, but with this method, the phone bill may be the only expense involved. (For most guests you invite, this idea will be unique enough to get them to say yes, even if their ministry schedule is quite full.)
- A missionary who has taught this subject in a different culture.[2]
- A teen who faces a difficult problem—drug abuse, AIDS, unwanted baby, etc.—and is willing to talk to peers, but not face to face.

Silence

(All ages)

A wise teacher agrees, "There is no substitute for brains, but in some cases silence does pretty well." Learn to use silence effectively.

Ask a question and tell students they are to think about their answers for thirty seconds before anyone answers.

When people are asked to pray aloud, give them permission to take thirty seconds to think about what they will say.

Score the Performance

(Older elementary and young teens)

Students will give sports' scores as answers to questions, encouraging their maturing thinking processes. They must give reasons for their answers. *Examples:*

- If the effort you put into Bible study were your bowling score, what would that score be?
- If Moses' obedience to God were a hockey score, what would it be?
- If the disciples' service to Jesus were a basketball team, what player would be high scorer?

Visual

Draw a Bible Study

(All ages)

Using art as part of a Bible study is not preferred by many Analytic Learners. Even though the method helps them answer, "What do we need to know?" they would rather the process be less adventuresome, and more easily measured. They shouldn't have to complain too often; there are all too few methods that use art in the content-gathering process.

That's too bad. Elliot Eisner, professor of education and art at Stanford University, "suggests that art offers students an alternative to the 'one right answer' approach so characteristic of some . . . subject areas. . . . In art, 'there's an opportunity for youngsters to recognize that there are multiple solutions to problems, that they can affix their own individuality onto their work. . . . That is a very important lesson.' . . .

Moreover, Eisner and others point out that all cultures have used the visual arts to create and share meaning. All of the art forms, Eisner says, allow humans to say things that they could not say in other ways.[3]

An Example: Thomas Heads[4]

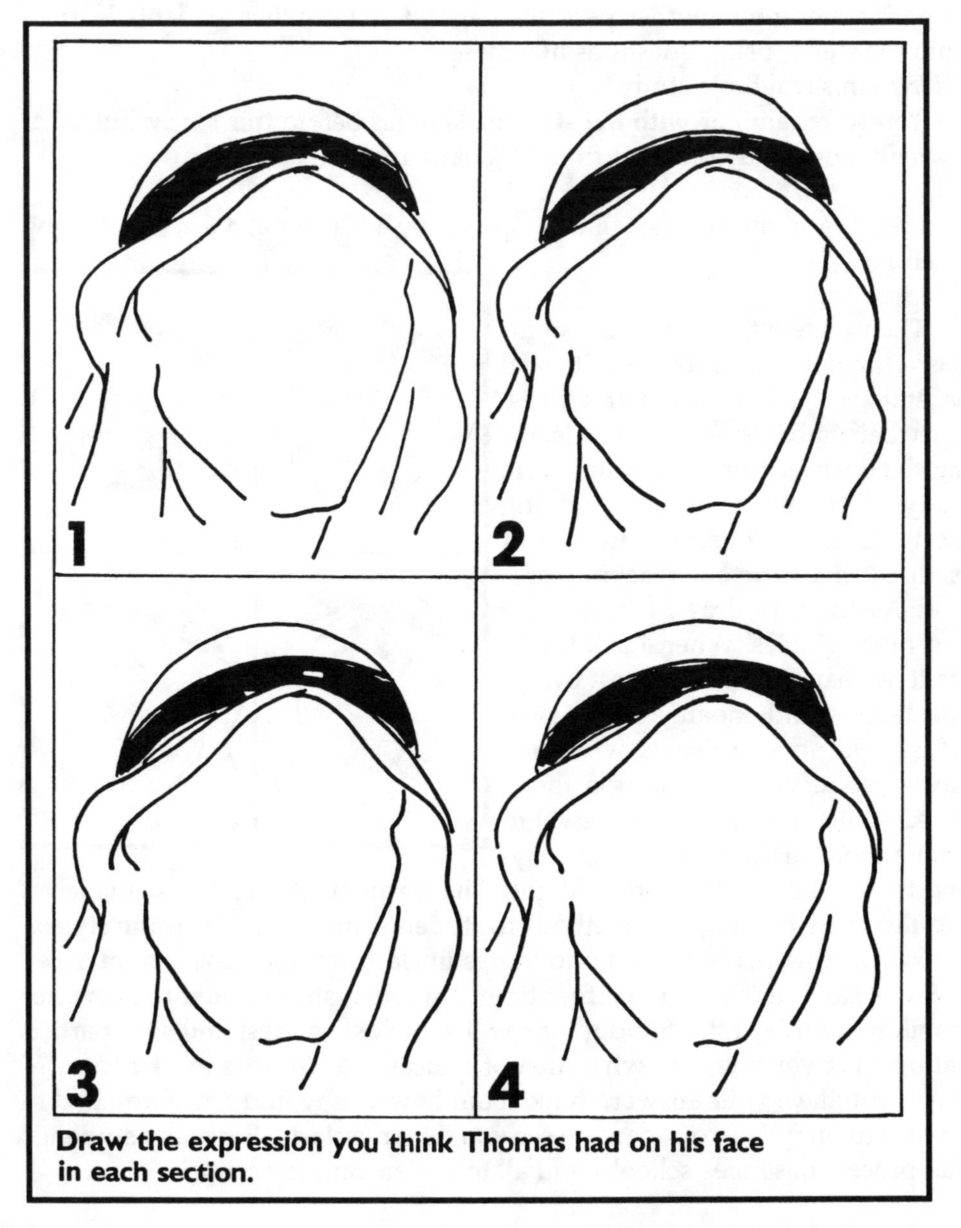

Draw the expression you think Thomas had on his face in each section.

[Cont.]

Directions: Each student should have a copy of the "Thomas Heads." The teacher should read the story of Thomas directly from Scripture, pausing four times in the reading to ask the students to draw Thomas's expression, showing what he was feeling at that point.

1. John 20:24, 25
2. John 20:26
3. John 20:27, 28
4. John 20:29

Ask students to exchange papers with someone who hasn't seen what they have drawn. Go through the reading a second time with students following along on another person's paper. Discuss what students learned from the study, using questions like these:

- Was this real Bible study?
- You were familiar with the story of Thomas before this study, but what new things did you learn from this participation?[5]

Here is a sample of a set of faces drawn by a teacher at a teacher training meeting:

The first few times they try an in-class drawing, teens and adults will be embarrassed about their efforts. Turn their embarrassment into a learning experience. I often use the Bible study of Thomas in teacher training meetings to demonstrate the use of pictures in the actual teaching process. As teachers draw, I hear more and more giggles. When I ask teachers to exchange papers almost everyone laughs and moans. Some even refuse to let anyone else see what they have drawn. When I question them, the same answer always surfaces, "I'm such a lousy artist. I don't want anyone to see me at my worst." Right! The participants have just made an excellent case for adapting methods to students' individual learning styles.

When Amanda is asked to do things in class at which she cannot excel, she may think it is funny the first time, but when she is asked to show her inabilities Sunday after Sunday, she will soon lose interest and stop participating. Ask yourself, "In what area of educational process am I poorest?" When you have your answer, think about how you would feel if you had to invite a room full of your peers to see you do it regularly. For many students, that process describes school—and all too often, Sunday school.

Cross the Message

(Older elementary through adult)

To cross a message, students should fill in blocks with words to create phrases that have meaning when read across or down. (The words do not necessarily have to create complete sentences.) Students are given a grid like the empty one below and, working alone or in pairs, they create two-directional messages.

When the grid is finished, shade in the unused blocks. Below is a sample.

Jesus	died	for	my	sin
took		me		
place	of	Son	was	Heaven
of		of		given
lamb	of	God		to
Sacrifice		died	for	world

Question the Passage

(Youth and adult)

[*Cont.*] Work in small groups to study a passage and develop three questions that could be asked about the passage. These should be questions that require higher-level thinking, rather than simple content answers. Ideas:

One question for a seeker.
One dealing with how this section fits with the redemption story.
One that is life related.

One question on the context of the passage.
One on the specific theme of this section.
One on implications of specific word choices.

When questions are finished, groups work together to discover answers.

Thinking in Sets

(Older elementary and teens)

Ask students to pull words together in sets of three and explain the reasons for their choices. This activity makes a good review. Add some words that do not logically follow a sequence, and listen to students' thinking as they work with the difficult "fits."

For example: Put the following words together in five sets of three. Not all the words will be used.

Father	Abraham	son
Peter	Andrew	grandson
Mark	Jacob	Holy Spirit
Isaac	John	James
Luke	Sarah	Hannah
priest	Esther	temple

Picture Storytelling

(All levels)

Sunday school regulars know the story. The teacher will hold their attention with new details, a new perspective on the story, and his or her expressive excitement about the story.

If you want to become a better storyteller, practice telling the story to a tape recorder. Then listen to yourself two days later. Waiting will help you hear yourself more objectively. Then ask yourself:

- Did I capture the feeling of the story? When things were funny, did my voice sparkle with fun? When things were sad, did my voice reflect it?
- Did I vary my speaking pace? I should speed up and slow down, just as I do in normal conversation.

- Did I vary my expression so listeners could tell which character was speaking?
- Did my pauses build suspense?
- If I told the story again, what would I do to make it more effective?

Expression in your voice should match the expression on your face. If something terrible just happened to the prophet Amos, you should not be smiling. Let your face show the larger categories of emotions—rather than the nuances of emotions an actor or actress would try to capture.

Keep the story short with adults and teens, perhaps no more than three or four minutes. You are reviewing the story and getting everyone ready to do something with it.

Use pictures, even when you are reading or telling a story to teens or adults. A picture sets the stage. For Visual Learners, the picture will make your story come alive.

If you must hold the picture, hold it so the class, not you, can see it. Establish eye contact with your students, not with the picture.

Transparencies:

If your picture is small and the class is large, consider having the picture made into a color transparency at a local instant print facility with a color photocopier. If class lighting can be dimmed, inexpensive duplicating will be adequate; if you have windows in the classroom, you will need a more expensive process requiring a Kodak machine. Costs range from $1 to $11.

Student Response:

Sometimes it is possible to use the picture as a vehicle for student response. For example, on the picture of Jesus sharing the truth about Himself with Nicodemus, students could pencil in initials of people who need that truth. Or, following a lesson on Christian responsibility for the earth, students might sign their names on a "Genesis picture" if they are willing to implement one new earth-saving idea.

Story Stops

(All ages)

Plan several pauses as you tell the Bible story. During the pauses, ask students to picture the scene. Encourage their creativity by asking questions about what the people in the story might have felt or seen. This activity can bring a familiar story alive for regular Sunday school attendees.

Examples:

- What did the air smell like on the first Easter morning? Describe the garden by standing outside the tomb and looking around. Picture the way the women walked as they came to the garden tomb.
- What did the lion's den smell like? How might smell have contributed

to Daniel's fear? If the den were totally dark, what might Daniel's hands have felt during his long, safe night there?

[*Cont.*] **Overheads and Flip Charts**
(Older children through adults)

Professional looking overheads are easy to make with computers and photocopying. You can show content outlines, charts and graphs, or enlargements of Scripture sections that you want the whole class to study. For more attractive overheads, use computer and print clip art.

Have several color transparency pens available to do doodling and diagraming while you teach.

A pen or laser pointer will help people focus.

An overhead projector can also be used for small group work. Give each group an assignment and a transparency. Students should prepare a transparency that illustrates what they want to share with the entire class.

If you have no overhead projector and no money for the investment, use a flip chart. Individual flip chart pages can be torn off and taped to the walls.

TACTILE/KINESTHETIC

Do-It-Yourself Content Board Game
(Elementary and young teens)

Students can do all the development work on this game.

Draw blocks around the four outsides edges of a large sheet of paper. In some blocks write penalties like these: "Take two steps back"; "Start over"; "Lose a turn."

Cut about fifty small paper blocks. On some write numbers from 1 to 3. On most of the blocks write questions about the topic of the lesson. For example:

A. Laws of our country
(Sample questions)
- What should you do if you witness a traffic accident in which there are injuries?
- What does a blinking red light mean?
- What happens if a person doesn't pay owed taxes to the government?
- What traffic signs must a person on a bicycle obey?
- What does the law say you should do if you find something valuable?

B. Old Testament characters
C. Facts about our church and its history and what we believe
D. Facts about leaders in our church
E. Bible facts

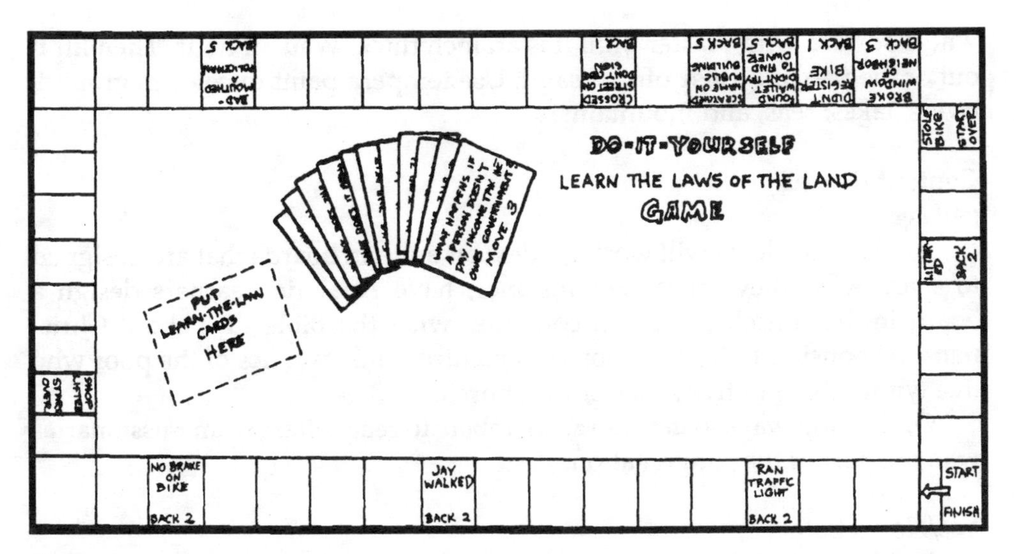

Rules:
(Students should add their own rules to the following. Dynamic Learners will come up with ideas to make this content game very interesting.)

1. Take turns moving your marker around the board.
2. Each player draws a card. If it has a question on it, and the player can answer correctly, he or she moves. If the player can't answer, the marker stays where it is. If the card has a number from 1 to 3 on it, the player moves that number of spaces.
3. If two players land on the same block, the last player to land on the block can either send the first person back four spaces or draw another card and do what it says.
4. The first person (or team) around the board wins.

Relief Map

(Elementary)

Children will enjoy doing research on maps that make the biblical content more understandable. The whole class will be involved, but the Analytic Learners will take the lead, because without careful research, the project cannot be successful.

Map ideas: Contemporary Israel; the route Moses led the Israelites; ancient Jerusalem; the areas mentioned in the life of Joseph.

Directions: Pour several inches of sand into a baking pan, remembering that the landscape will be only as high as the sand is deep.

Dampen sand. Then make holes for places where mountains will be, and rounded mounds for seas and lakes (just the reverse of how the map will be). Mix plaster, using instructions on the package. Do not stir or you will have lumps. Instead vibrate water with a spoon, and the water will slowly seep into the plaster. When the plaster looks like a milk shake, it is ready.

Spoon plaster onto the sand. Fill up the holes first and then cover the

[*Cont.*]

whole surface with plaster until it is an inch thick. Wait an hour. Then lift it out of the pan and rinse off the sand. Use tempera paint to color in ground, rivers, lakes, seas, and mountains.

Content Boards
(All ages)

Analytic students will work hardest on bulletin boards that are designed to share what they know. For instance, have Analytic Learners design a board in the church foyer that combines what the Bible says about Christians' responsibility for the poor with pictures and statistics of the poor who live within three to five miles of the church.

Or develop ways to get church members to read letters from missionaries who are part of the congregation.

Yes/No Debate
(Older teens and adults)

Most Analytic Learners thrive on traditional classroom settings, so those who have a tactile/kinesthetic modality preference are at a disadvantage. By asking students to walk from one side of the room to the other, the T/K's preference is accommodated.

Pick a question on which there are two legitimate sides. Ask students to go to one side of the room if they think the answer is yes, to the other side if they think no is the answer.

Examples:

- All Christians should fast at least one meal a week.
- Fasting is necessary if we want to gain God's favor.

Give sides a set number of minutes to prepare defenses for their positions before they share with the rest of the class.

Notes

1. "Practical Biblical Interpretation" by Ernest Hess, *Religious Education Journal*, Vol. 88, No. 2, Spring 1993, pp. 198, 199.

2. Bilingual (English and Spanish) teacher, Gilda Keefe, teaches fourth grade students. She uses this method in her schoolroom. "Keefe sees many benefits to teaching with telecommunications. For one thing, by allowing her students to carry on conversations with Spanish-speaking children in another country, such projects give her own students an important sense of validation and self-worth. And, of course, they show that distant countries are filled with living, breathing people." ("Making School Like Play," *Education Week*, January 12, 1994, p. 38.)

3. "Rethinking Visual Arts Programs for All Students," *ASCD Curriculum Update*, January 1994, p. 2.

4. Marlene LeFever and Kathleen Weyna, *Creative Kids Book* (Elgin, Ill.: Chariot Books, 1984). Reprinted with permission.

5. Students will be surprised at what their minds saw. For some visual learners, methods like this could open a whole new door for growth. Writer Saul Bellow was asked how he trained his eye to see so much. Bellow replied, "I don't know whether it was training at all. I think it was just spontaneous. I think that when I was a very small child it wasn't what people said, the contents of what they said, so much as the look of them and their gestures that spoke to me. That is, a nose was also a speaking member, and so were a pair of eyes. And so was the way your hair grew and the set of your ears, the condition of your teeth, the emanations of the body. All of that." From "Solid Bellow" by Mark Harris, in *Tribune Books, Chicago Tribune*, Sunday, April 10, 1994.

12

Methods: Common Sense Learners

Learning style is in itself neutral, therefore students of various learning styles should have an equal opportunity to do well.
—Bernice McCarthy

The Common Sense Learner is the most at-risk of our students.[1] This student needs to tie everything to how he or she can immediately use the information—why it is important to him or her today. The child prefers to make that connection through classroom methodologies that require movement.[2] The educator's challenge is to capture the intelligence and commitment of this student. As Dr. Howard Gardner and Julie Viens have said,

> For too long we have measured intelligence along one line, and we have based education on a model of remediating deficits: pulling children out of the classroom to work for long periods of time in areas of proven weakness. It is time to move from the deficits model of education to identifying children's strengths, be they intellectual or stylistic. The identification and nurturance of such information is obviously a challenge worth taking in our quest for more appropriate and effective education.[3]

This student responds most positively to content presented through methods involving inquiry, problem solving, independent study, logical problems, computer-generated games, projects, and learning activities.[4]

The methods that follow encourage movement as part of the actual learning process, but not just activities for activity's sake. Teaching for all students involves attempting to enable a learner to engage in the sort of activity that requires forming intentions, making decisions, drawing conclusions, and attributing meanings; in other words, activity that requires the application of critical and creative intelligence.[5]

AUDITORY

Triad Think

(Elementary and youth)

Divide the students into groups of three and ask them to lie on their backs with their heads together. They will be able to hear what they say in their triads, but they won't be able to see each other. Then guide their discussion by asking questions.

Example:

- What do you think an angel really looks like?
- What is the place of angels in kids' lives today?
- If you saw an angel, what do you think your response would be?
- Why do you think there is so much fascination with angels?
- What difference do they make?

Illustrations

(All ages)

Keep a story file of illustrations that help make the lesson aim clear. David G. Buttrick suggests three rules for choosing illustrations for sermons. The same rules are helpful to teachers.

> 1. There must be a clear analogy between the idea being presented and the illustration.
>
> 2. The structure of the content and the shape of the illustration should parallel each other. If the sermon's point is presented in an either/or form, so should the illustration be; or, if the sermon is making a dual point, there should be some sort of double in the illustration.
>
> 3. Illustrations should be appropriate to the content, honoring and not demeaning, not trite or overused.[6]

Survival Kit

(Youth and adult)

After studying a subject, students should put together individual survival kits to help them deal with the issues covered. The kits should be simple—envelopes and small slips of paper on which the items are identified. Then students should share what they put in their kits.

For example, if the lesson were on God's unconditional love, students might place items in their kits to help them remember His love when they are feeling totally alone and unloved. A person might write, "Call a good friend for a verbal hug." Encourage participants to be honest and practical.

Bible Reading
(Adult)

Reading the Bible makes "sense." Many sections are heavily "how-to."
[*Cont.*] Encourage adults to come up with ways to make sure the Bible reading is heard. Here are some ideas, and adults will come up with others.

- Ask people to listen to the reading from a different perspective—that of a teenager who is not as sure of his faith as he was several years ago. Or, as a child who may not understand vocabulary or difficult concepts.
- Read the same passage from two versions and two paraphrases such as *The Living Bible* and *The Message.*
- Sing or chant the passage.
- Read the passage in several different languages, or listen to people with different accents read the same verses.
- Between each verse, read the commentary about the verse.
- Read each verse and ask the class to repeat it.
- Play music that fits the tone of the passage while the verses are being read.
- Listen to a tape, perhaps from a professional audiotape series, of the passage being read.
- Ask students to close their eyes to shut out distractions while they listen to the Scripture.
- Burn incense or a scented candle during the reading, explaining that our active attention to His Word is a sweet savor to God.

VISUAL

No-Word Story
(Elementary and young teens)

Students make up a story that illustrates what they have learned in the Bible. Working individually or in pairs (most Common Sense Learners will enjoy working on their own, but Dynamic and Imaginative Learners will usually choose to work with friends), they draw symbols or clues for the words in their story. Using those clues, they "write" the story.
Example:

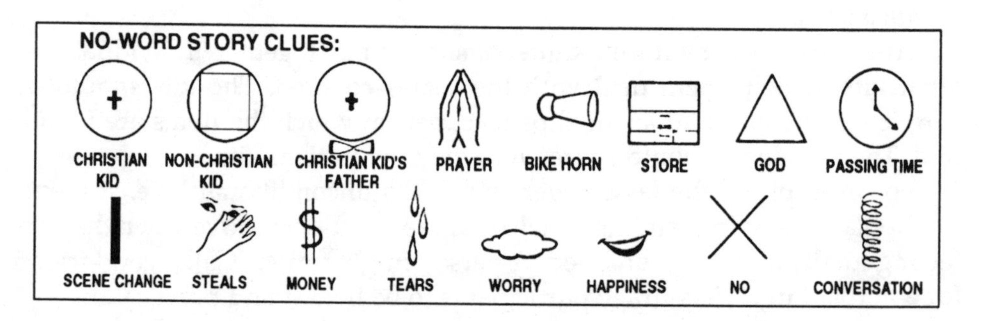

When stories are finished, class members exchange stories and discuss how each story shows the same truth as the Bible story. Here is a sample.

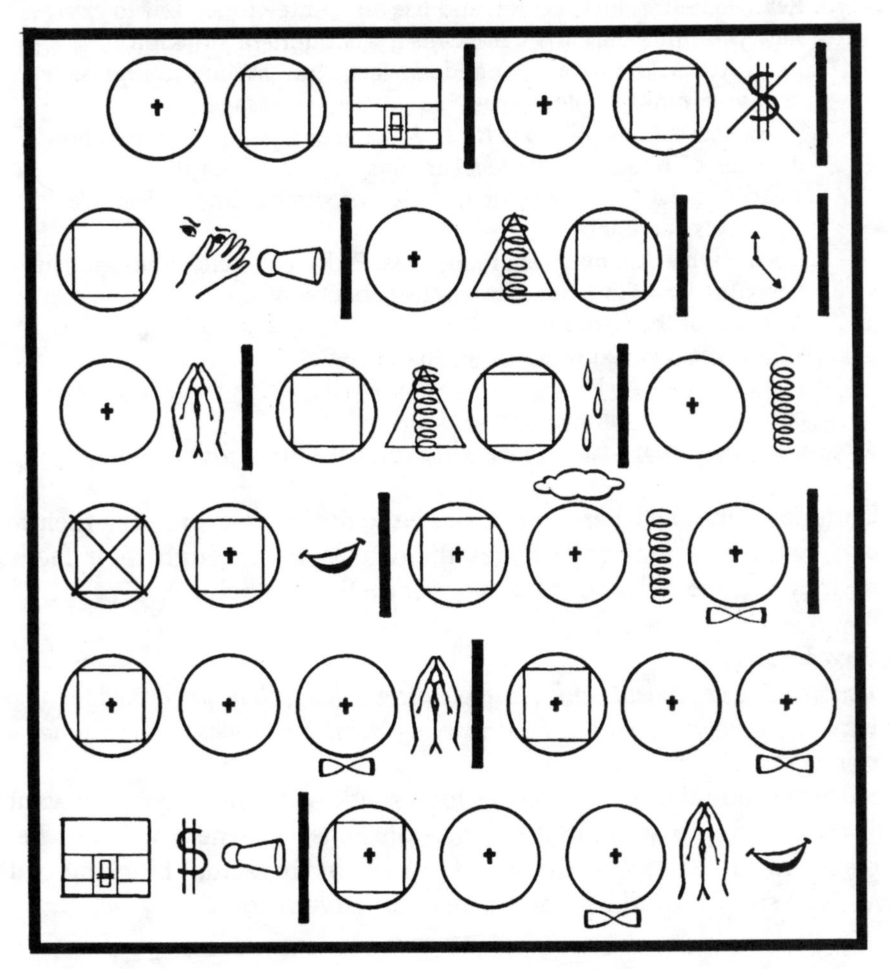

Worksheet

(Teen and adult)

Common Sense Learners enjoy worksheets and projects that allow them to demonstrate what they have learned. The further away these worksheets can be from traditional pencil-in-hand sheets the better. The following worksheet is an illustration of one that would appeal to Common Sense Learners more than a traditional sheet.

This following sample could also be adapted for different Scriptures.

Directions:

Each person should have seven small sheets of paper and access to a number of crayons.

1. Read Acts 4:32-37; 5:1-6 three times.
2. Draw your answers to the following seven questions, one answer on each of your seven sheets. Your color choices and the pattern or design

[*Cont.*]

you scribble should work together to express moods, emotions, and attitudes. Be ready to explain what you did by referring to Acts.

a. Read Acts 4:32. Pick a color, and use an uninterrupted line to express how you think the early Christians felt about their situation.
b. Read Acts 4:33. Pick a color and use four straight lines to express how you think people hearing the salvation message felt.
c. Read Acts 4:34-37. Pick a color and, using any pattern, express how you think Christians today feel about giving to the church.
d. Read Acts 5:1-6. Pick a color and use one straight line to describe Ananias's personality.
e. Decide what Ananias's sin really was. Pick a color and a design that describes how Christians should feel about that sin.
f. Pick a color that describes how you think Christians felt when God killed Ananias. Express that feeling in circles.
g. Read Acts 5:7-11. Pick a color and symbolic design that shows the correct way we should give to God.

3. Now comes the hard part. Share what you have done with another.

Common Sense Learners sometimes have difficulty expressing their feelings. A worksheet that encourages them to think through their feelings before they have to talk about them or act on them is helpful.

Shadow Drama

(Elementary. Older students enjoy shadow drama that will be performed for a large audience. This method makes a great starting point for all-church Christmas and Easter programs.)

Students should block out scenes for a shadow drama. They may want to write their own story, although Common Sense Learners will not be as interested in the writing activity as they are in the actual blocking of the scenes. The story should be read by an expressive reader.

As an alternative, review a passage and assign various verses to small groups who must illustrate them through a single shadow picture. As the passage is read, each group contributes its shadow.

Shadow directions:

Stretch a sheet tightly from the floor to the ceiling. Place a strong light (100 watts or more) on the floor behind the sheet. Players should stand between the lights and the sheet, and stand frozen during the whole time their picture is on stage. The light should be switched off while the scenes are changed.

Visual Aids

(Adults)

Look for aids that symbolically emphasize what is being taught.

Examples:

- *Play Money:* If the lesson is on tithing, give each person a play dollar. Ask students to tape it into their checkbooks as a reminder that our love for God demands our financial participation in His projects.
- *Stone:* If the lesson is on remembering those who participated in the history of this church, provide each person with a stone of remembrance to place by the grave of a church father or mother. This is a Jewish tradition.[7]
- *Toothpicks:* If the lesson is on bearing each other's burdens, provide each person with several wooden "burdens," perhaps toothpicks. Ask them to consider whose burden they might help carry.
- *Barn:* A lesson on the incarnation could be taught in a barn.
- *Flower:* Following a creation lesson, give each student a flower to study for at least three minutes. Students should then share what they have seen during their inductive flower study and how this relates to study of familiar Scripture passages.

Look for ways to bring the stuff of teaching into the classroom, no matter what age level you teach.

Tactile/Kinesthetic

Foot Game

(Elementary)

Each player should draw and cut from newspaper ten of his or her own footprints. The child then writes ten questions on the subject the class has been studying.

Rules:

1. Each player stands on one footprint and holds the other nine prints. Since the player has one print on the ground, he or she will have to stand on one foot. If a player loses balance, that player must start over.

2. The teacher, using a mix of all the students' questions, reads them to the players.

3. As soon as players think they know the answer, they should quickly place another footprint on the floor in front of themselves. The first player to put a print on the floor gets to answer the question. If the question is answered correctly, the player stands on the next footprint. If he or she misses, the player loses a turn and cannot answer the next question.

4. The first player to stand on the tenth footprint wins the game.

This game can be built around any topic. Common Sense Learners will enjoy the movement while they are reviewing.

For many of our students this type of kinesthetic learning is key to capturing their interest and intelligence. A public school teacher from Accord, New York, points out:

> It's not surprising at a joint teacher evaluation to find that the "problem child" for one teacher is a prized student for the kinesthetic teacher. It's much easier, after all, to channel disruptive energy into creative paths when a teacher is working with a physical language. Simply providing an opportunity to express pent-up physical energy often produces surprising amounts of concentration and focus.[8]

Jack Hayford, pastor of Church on the Way in Van Nuys, California, suggests taking kinesthetic movement out of the exclusive domain of the classroom and moving it into the worship service:

> The next step in worship is to engage people physically.
>
> The simplest way to do that is to get people to use their hands and arms. People can open their hands, simply facing palms upward in front of them—a simple symbol of openness to receive God's blessing.

The point is to get them to express their praise in some physical way. The liturgical churches (which encourage kneeling and crossing oneself, for example) have appreciated for centuries the value of movement in worship. Other churches may have people lift their arms in adoration. Our forms may be different, but not the substance of their meaning.[9]

Computer Possibilities

(Older elementary and youth)

Brainstorm ways a computer could be used in class. Affirm all ideas. Suggest that members may want to investigate those that seem most viable. Be ready for students to think of ideas that revolutionize the way a classroom works. Don't become your own brain police by telling yourself, "That would never work. I could never do that!" Don't let lack of finances limit dreaming. God has a way of handling those problems.[10] Open the door for the next generation who in not too many years will also be challenged to teach. Teacher, Crawford Kilian said,

> Talking to prisoners at a local penitentiary a couple of years ago, I naively expressed the desire that they get online. They laughingly told me the authorities would never grant them access to modems, probably because modems would make even the penitentiary walls a transparent technology. Indeed, someone would surely start robbing banks online while still doing time.
>
> Similarly, educators sense that kids with computers are likely to break out into that horizontal knowledge flow and escape teacher control. Some of us think such a breakout is the whole purpose of education, but most of us are still scared to death of the possibility. . . .
>
> Yes, computer technology can and will transform the schools. But it will be a process that many educators will resist bitterly because it also will transform their roles. As someone recently observed, the teacher will be not "the mentor at the center, but the guide on the side."[11]

One Common Sense Learner, Erik Johnson, drew the following illustration to explain how he saw himself—the plugged-in computer ready to conquer new worlds—with the way he felt others viewed his abilities—an unplugged computer.

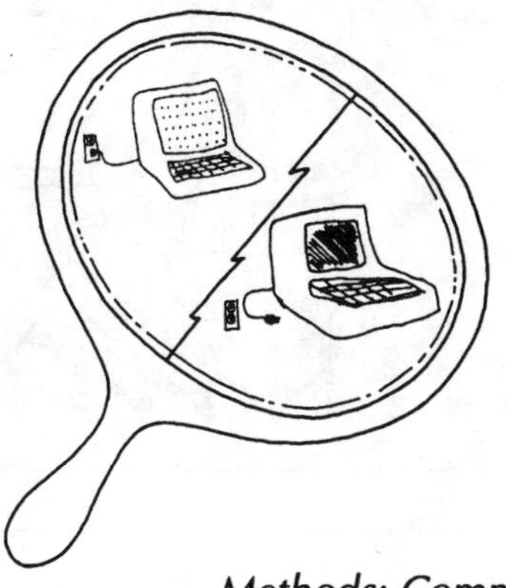

Do-It-Yourself Game
(Youth)

[*Cont.*] Divide the class into small groups and ask them to choose an existing game with existing rules—baseball, soccer, tennis, bowling. Groups develop a way to review the content (from the lesson or unit) by using the basic rules, and perhaps some of the skills, of the existing game. The challenge includes playing in the space where class is being held.

String Thing Project Review
(Older elementary, youth)

Students identify the pivotal principle of the lesson, and write that principle on a square of construction paper.

Additional materials needed for this project are a square board (plywood or scrap wood) about one inch thick, one-inch nails, string, hammer, ruler, pencil.

The pivotal principle should be fastened in the center of the board by hammering a nail in each corner of the paper.

Lightly draw an inch border around the wooden square, and use a ruler to mark half-inch spaces the whole way around the square border. At each half-inch space, hammer a one-inch nail halfway into the wood, making certain there are the same number of nails on each of the four sides.

Now wind a design. Tie the string to the center nail along any side. Go from that nail to the closest of the four nails holding the written principle. Then go back to the nail beside the nail where you started. As you wind, push the string to the base of each nail. Continue going back and forth to the corner nail, then continue till you reach the center nail along the next side. At this point one-fourth of all the nails will be connected with one of the nails in the middle.

Do the same thing on each of the four sides (corners).

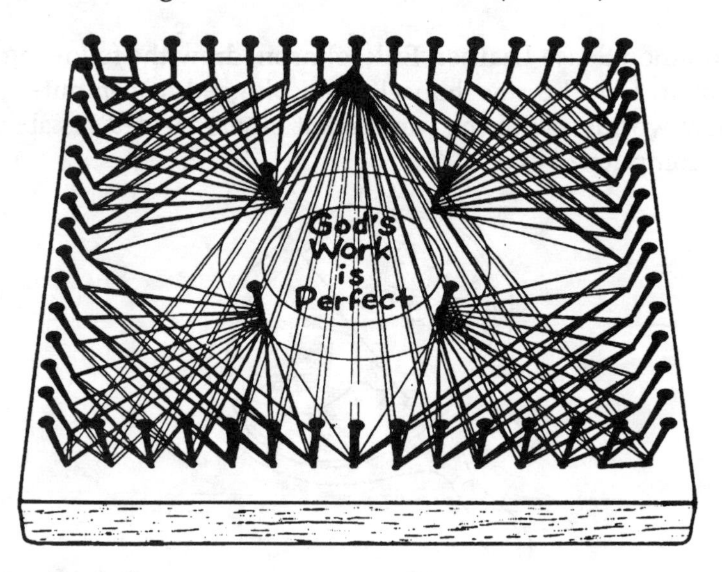

The finished products are reminders to all students of how what they learned should touch their lives.

Charting

(Middle elementary through adult)

In the example below, children chart how they handled temptation. They are learning to count on Jesus' power to help them overcome temptations that displease Him. By the end of the charted time, they will have a picture-record of how they pleased or disappointed Jesus in this aspect of the Christian life.[12]

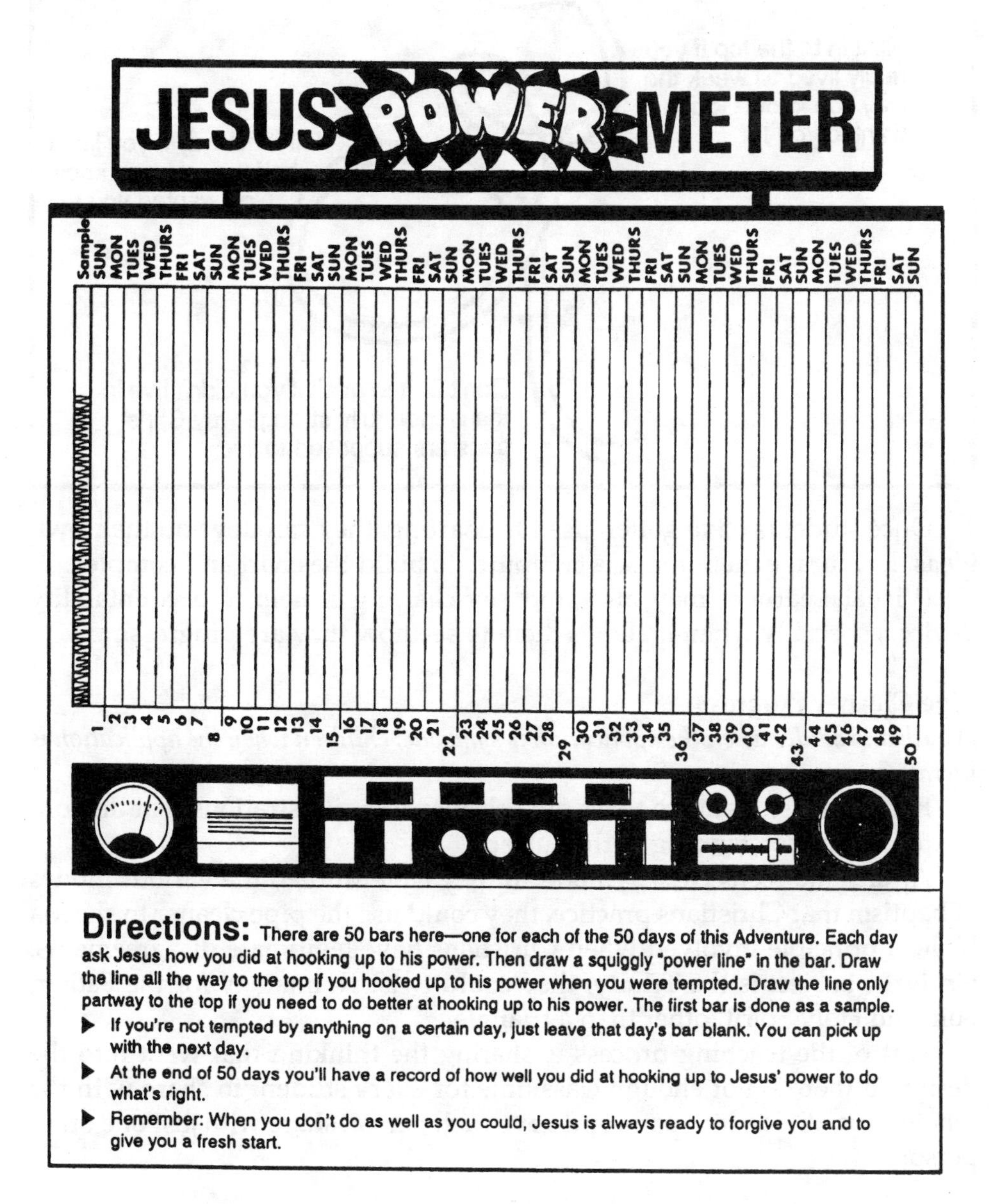

[Cont.] Here's another example of a chart that younger children can complete.[13]

Directions: Christians are wonderfully strange. They really believe that God wants them to do things that are totally unnatural, like being nice to people who are hateful back, or not hitting your sister when she smacked you first. Think back over your week before you fill in the wonderfully strange line.

Once students have gotten used to charting, they can develop their own ideas. Encourage them to use a computer to build the chart and complete it.

(Visual Learners may also find self-charting a helpful accountability device, especially when it allows them to see how they are progressing.)

Pipe Cleaner Progress

(Youth and adults when the application is symbolic; children when the application is literal)

Encourage students to twist pipe cleaners into illustrations that demonstrate their understanding of the subject.

Adults and teens twist symbols. If they have studied the various modes of baptism that Christians practice, they could use the pipe cleaner to show a biblical principle involved when Christians have legitimate disagreements. Or, if the subject is the Trinity, they could twist an analogy for the Father, Son, and Holy Spirit, other than a triangle.

Part of the teaching process is sharing the thinking that went into the design. If there is not enough class time for every student to share with the whole class, divide into pairs and have each person share with just one other person.

Children enjoy this activity, too, but their assignments need to be more literal. They might twist the pipe cleaner to show something they could do at school that would bring a smile to Jesus' face.

Food As a Learning Tool
(All ages)

Our sense of taste can also be a learning tool. Get Common Sense Learners involved in researching and making food that in some way ties in with the lesson.

- *Bible time meal:* Plan an everyday meal or a Seder or Passover, the celebration of Israel's deliverance from Egyptian slavery.[14] An everyday meal might include beef or lamb stew, bowls of raisins, apricots, or grapes, beans, unleavened bread.
- *Food and content:* Connect snacks directly with the foods mentioned in the Bible: Honey snacks when John the Baptist's life is studied; fish crackers for the feeding of the five thousand.
- *Memory puns:* When studying Revelation, ask people to bring bite-sized goodies that taste "heavenly." Or, have build-it-yourself ice cream sundaes (pyramids) while studying the Hebrews' life in Egypt.

NOTES

1. Many methods that encourage Common Sense Learners to learn can also be used to capture the interest of children with special learning disabilities. The information that follows centers on one disability, Attention Deficit Disorder (A.D.D.), but the strategies that teach A.D.D. children are often helpful to children dealing with other dysfunctions. Children with A.D.D. respond to movement in the teaching process and the systematic use of novelty.

Christian teachers will find that these students have their best chance of success when teachers use experimental methods, while maintaining control in the classroom. For this group teachers must allow movement during the learning process. They must make special concessions. For example, a child may need extra time to finish an assignment or may need directions delivered simply. Steven Forness and Hill Walker report in "Classroom Systems and Strategies for Attention Deficit Disorders," *Challenge* (Vol. 5, No. 4, July/August 1991) that "most children may talk themselves silently through new tasks as they initially encounter them. They quickly move beyond these subvocal means of regulating their behavior as their responses become more automatic. Children with A.D.D., on the other hand, often do not seem able to automatically generate these strategies on their own, since their inattention and impulsiveness often interfere. Teachers have begun to discover that such strategies that often seem natural or automatic in most children, have to be systematically taught to children with A.D.D."

Effective teachers with these children have good eye contact and a good sense of humor. These children need an easy-going teacher who is willing to share the stories of his or her life. Students need to know they are liked; however, many do not like to be cuddled or touched.

Successful teachers are not so rigid and strict that if these kids say something off the wall, the teacher will blow up. The teacher must be more loving than critical. A.D.D. children are sensitive to criticism. Confrontations don't work. A teacher who confronts in the traditional way will have lost the opportunity to teach the child.

The teacher must be high on reinforcement, focusing on the positive no matter how large the negative looms. If the child comes into class and sits down on the floor or chair when it's time to sit, that's worth celebrating.

The following twelve teacher tips for working with A.D.D. children were provided by H&R Educational Materials, Inc., 1988 (used by permission). These are designed for a school teacher but all can be applied to the Sunday school, club, or youth leader volunteer teacher.

1. Try to be brief and specific, with short and easily attainable goals.

2. Provide a working environment that will diminish distractions as much as possible (work corners, front row seats, etc.).

3. When giving assignments, break into short work segments so you can give frequent praise and encouragement.

4. Encourage the child to use a marker when reading and arrange his or her papers in columns and rows to help provide structure.

5. An A.D.D. child may be subtly rejected by peers. Set up circumstances to assure his or her involvement with other children.

6. If possible, seat the child next to a student who serves as a "special" helper.

7. Find an academic strength and use this in a way in which the A.D.D. child can act as a peer tutor for another student. This can boost self-esteem.

8. Find avenues to help channel excess energy in a positive way (office runner, student in charge of sharpening pencils, caretaker of classroom animals, etc.).

9. Keep in close communication with parents. Consider using daily or weekly behavior feedback reports.

10. Try maintaining a low-key, positive and non-threatening teaching approach. A.D.D. children can easily become frustrated and discouraged.

11. Try having the child verbalize softly to himself or herself when engaged in independent work tasks.

12. Have the child use assignment notebooks. Time charts can help with organization. These should then be closely supervised to help maintain consistency.

For additional information see the Attention Deficit Disorder chapter by Marlene LeFever in *The Christian Educator's Handbook on Family Life Education* (Wheaton, Ill.: Victor Books, 1995).

2. Thomas Armstrong, in his book, *Discovering and Encouraging Your Child's Personal Learning Style in Their Own Way* (Los Angeles: Jeremy P. Tarcher, Inc., 1987) suggests, "It is almost ironic that the youngsters who appear to be most suited to the new demands of information overload could well be the so-called learning disabled. 'Dyslexics are the wave of the future,' proclaims Charles Drake, headmaster of the Landmark School in Prides Crossing, Massachusetts. Drake points out that as the requirements of society become increasing complex, 'the world's going to demand people who can see relationships and who have problem-solving potential.' . . . So-called learning disabled kids possess superior creative and visualization abilities. . . .

We need citizens who have vision, integrity, intuition, flexibility, creativity, and wisdom—not just people who are good with numbers, words, and logic. Tragically, the schools may be writing off many children as school failures, underachievers, or disabled learners who possess these badly needed qualities" (pp. 170, 171).

3. Dr. Howard Gardner and Julie Viens, "Multiple Intelligence and Styles: Partners in Effective Education," *The Clearinghouse Bulletin*, Winter 1990, p. 5.

4. For additional idea-starters that could be adapted to your program see Edgar A. Falk's book, *1001 Ideas to Create Retail Excitement* (Englewood Cliffs, N.J.: Prentice Hall, 1994).

5. "Editorial: Teaching Religion," *Religious Education*, Vol. 89, No. 1, Winter 1994, p. 4.

6. Mark E. Yurs, "Using Illustrations," *The Christian Ministry*, January/February 1994, p. 23.

7. Consider playing the five-minute video clip from the movie "Shindler's List" where people who survived the Holocaust because of Shindler's actions pay tribute to him by placing stones on his tombstone.

8. Susan Griss, "Creative Movement: A Language for Learning," *Educational Leadership*, February 1994, p. 80.

9. Jack Hayford, "Expressive Worship with Reluctant People," *Leadership*, Spring 1994, p. 38.

10. At a Michigan Christian educators conference, I challenged participants to dream of what a computer might do to help them minister more effectively. Pastor Ron White wrote, "When you challenged us to think bigger and not be afraid of technology, I got excited about the possibility of getting a computer for our Sunday school. The following Monday morning I was back home working outside when a neighbor stopped and invited me to breakfast. He told me that he wanted to give his old computer system to the church and wondered if we could use it! I hadn't even started to pray for it yet, and God was already answering."

11. Crawford Kilian, "Education Unbound," *Teacher Magazine*, January 1994, pp. 38, 39.

12. Marlene LeFever, *50 Days to Welcome Jesus to My Church* (Wheaton, Ill.: Chapel of the Air, Inc., 1990), p. 7. Reprinted with permission.

13. Marlene LeFever, *50 Days to Love My Country with Jesus* (Wheaton, Ill.: Chapel of the Air, Inc., 1984). Reprinted with permission.

14. For complete directions, including recipes, for a Passover Easter Freedom Celebration see *Creative Hospitality* by Marlene LeFever (Wheaton, Ill.: Tyndale House Publishers, 1980), pp. 155-158.

13

Methods: Dynamic Learners

If you want to move a train, you don't need a new engine, or even ten engines—
you need to light a fire and get the steam up in the engine you now have.
—Charles Spurgeon

Dynamic Learners respond most positively to content presented through methods involving: moral dilemmas, student-led activities, case studies, guided imagery, creative imaging, unstructured drama (mime, roleplay), open-ended discussion, simulations, brainstorming, and interviews.[1]

Auditory

Outcome Sentences

(Young teen through adult)

Outcome sentences are something that teacher Merrill Harmin describes as "sentences students [speak or] write after reflecting on a lesson or experience, prompted by such phrases as I learned . . . , I'm beginning to wonder . . . , I was surprised . . . ."

> Purpose: To help students create meaningful learnings for themselves and to help them develop the habit of learning from experience.
>
> . . . After students have taken a few minutes to write their thoughts, the teacher might proceed in one of two ways:
>
> • He asks whether anyone is willing to read one of the outcome sen-

tences. The class listens to a few volunteers. Then the teacher asks students to pair up and share some of their "I learned" statements with each other. The two sharing processes help students see ideas in the lesson that they had not noticed.
- He starts going around the group, giving each student a turn either to read one outcome sentence to the whole class or to say "I pass."[2]

Worship Celebration

(Children)

This activity is placed under "auditory" but note how the author, Carl Heine, makes use of visual and tactile/kinesthetic as well.

Use these ideas for a planned or spontaneous worship experience. Provide some of the following ideas, representing different modalities, just to get the children thinking in nontraditional ways. Remember: the best idea is always the one the children think up!

Visual Worship Expressions

Red is a traditional color for the coming of the Holy Spirit at Pentecost.
- Wear red clothing.
- Hang red crepe paper.
- Blow up red balloons, putting a promise from the Bible in each one.
- Tie orange, yellow, and red ribbons to sticks and shake them to make the appearance of flames.

Auditory Worship Expressions
- Pop the balloons. Read the notes aloud.
- Give a cheer for God.
- Read a praise psalm. Then be silent for ten seconds.
- Tell a story that points to a reason to worship and have kids provide the sound effects. For example, with the story of the Spirit's coming, the kids might make sounds with ribbon sticks, rhythm instruments, or voices for wind sounds, fire sounds, etc.
- Recite together parts of your church's creed, interspersed with applause.
- Mouth a verse of a song; then sing the next verse loudly.
- Have students think of one or two words about how they feel toward God and shout them all at the same time. End with "Amen."

Tactile/Kinesthetic Worship Expressions
- Pass or throw a roll of red crepe paper around the group. The first person holds an end, and each person holds on when he or she receives it until the whole group is wrapped up. Each person who catches it says a phrase that praises God.
- Bat balloons around so none of them touches the ground. If a balloon touches the ground, the person responsible must freeze. That person can't move until the leader whispers a message about Jesus in their ear. For example, the leader might whisper, "Did you know that Jesus loves you lots and lots?"
- Throw confetti.

- Shake seven people's hands.
- Parade around singing while shaking ribbon sticks.[3]

[*Cont.*] **Parables**

(Teens and adults)

Teach in parables just as the Master Teacher did. Find parables in everyday situations.

If you've been to the beach and seen someone rescued from drowning, how would you relate this to a spiritual truth?

If your child is always wandering away from you at the shopping center and crying when she realizes she is lost, relate her situation to a struggling Christian's relationship to Christ.

Is there a parable-starter in a kite flying freely through the sky, trailing its broken string?

Finding parables is easy once you build the habit of looking for them.

Encourage your Dynamic Learners to help you find parables. If they know the next week's topic, they may live the perfect parable and be able to share it with the class. There is no better way to get students interested in Bible study than to start with their own life needs and life situations. Few teaching methods work better than parables.

Metaphor

(Teens and adults)

When people engage in thinking metaphorically, they bring knowledge to a situation they didn't know they had.

See how ideas like this expand the thinking of your students.

- Metaphorically, how does the neighborhood see this church? (First Church is like a ____________________, because ____________________.)
- Think in terms of a plant metaphor for who you are. Why did you pick the plant you did?
- Find a metaphor that describes to a non-Christian what being a follower of Jesus is like.
- Find a metaphor for raising a child to Christian maturity.

This type of thinking can be done in reverse. The teacher gives to students the metaphor and the students expand its possible connections.

- Explain how the Christian family is like an ecosystem.
- When Scripture uses the word *lamb* to describe Jesus, what does it mean? Don't stop with a single answer.

Interview

(Older elementary through adult)

Look for interview ideas that are creative and offbeat. Encourage students to find creative ways to present their findings to the class.

This sample assignment is for adults.

Assignment: Interview a teen in our church. Pick someone you don't know very well, perhaps someone who scares you just a little because he or she is so different from you in age, attitude, talk, or dress. Start with questions like these, but leave the "canned" questions when something more interesting surfaces.

- If you had to use three words or phrases to describe the adults in this church, what would they be?
- Pick one adult in this church with whom you might enjoy spending a day and tell me why you made that choice.
- What are some things you wish Christian adults knew about the kids who are involved in this church's Christian education program?

Sentence Sets

(Older elementary and teens)

Put together sets of words and ask student pairs to construct sentences using all the words. For example:

1. disciple, heart, money, time, significant, relate, failure
2. interest, prayer, church, window, youth, teacher, why

Brainstorming

(Middle elementary through adult)

Brainstorming is a freewheeling way of generating lots of ideas without making value judgments about them, at least not at the time of the initial brainstorming. The following are samples of brainstorming topics:

- What would revolutionize how we educate our children about God?
- How could we change our Sunday school classrooms? Our sanctuary?
- How could our church begin to father fatherless children?
- How could we use our lawn as evangelistic space?
- How might intergenerational study work at our church?
- If time and money were no object, what could this class do for Jesus Christ?

After ideas are generated, the group might prioritize them. Those that receive the highest ratings could actually be seriously explored.

Rita and Kenneth Dunn suggest the following values of brainstorming.

Brainstorming is:

- *Stimulating.* It offers a unique, freewheeling, exciting, and rapid-fire method that builds enthusiasm in nearly all participants.
- *Positive.* Quiet and shy students usually become active participants because they are not put down; their contributions are masked by the group process. Conversely, those who usually dominate endless

[*Cont.*]

discussions are structured into offering succinct suggestions.

- *Focused.* Diversions and distractions are eliminated. Stories and speeches irrelevant to the question or otherwise not pertinent are eliminated.
- *Spontaneous and creative.* Students serve as a sounding board that generates new ideas. Creativity is realized during the momentum of the process.
- *Efficient and productive.* Dozens of suggestions, facts, ideas, or creative solutions are generated in a matter of minutes. Additional steps or plans of an activity can be brainstormed, as well as more specific answers for general responses (subset brainstorming).
- *Involving and image-building.* Self-image is enhanced for students who see their ideas listed. Group pride and cohesiveness increase, too, as members begin to feel a part of the unit that created the lists.
- *Outgoing and problem-solving.* The results are recorded and may be modified and used in new situations.[4]

VISUAL

Stick-Figure Bible Praise

(Children and young teens)

Pick a section of Scripture that children would understand, a section that provides opportunity for visual imagery. Divide the verses into sections and have students draw the different parts of the verse. For example, children might enjoy this way of celebrating a completed unit on who God is.

Each would read Revelation 4:11 three times, and then draw a stick-figure picture of the different parts of the verse.

> *You are worthy, our Lord and God,* [first drawing]
> *to receive glory and honor and power,* [second drawing]
> *for you created all things,* [third drawing]
> *and by your will they were created and have their being* [fourth drawing].

Perhaps the best drawings could be combined, duplicated on a transparency, and used as the basis for a Scripture reading in a worship service.

Free Visuals

(Older elementary through adult)

Tear pictures from magazines or newspapers on the general topic the group is studying. Ask students to share original stories growing from the pictures about what is going to happen.

Faces

(Older elementary through adult)

Ask participants to draw a face on a paper plate as a reminder of an assignment or commitment. For example:

- In a teen or adult class, have the students draw the face of a relative with whom they are having difficulty. Tell them to keep it in front of them this week during their devotions.
- For a teacher training meeting, ask the teachers to draw a face that represents a student for whom they are praying. Suggest that they keep the plate in front of them while they prepare the next unit's lessons.
- For young teens, have them make a face mobile of the kids in their school who have trouble accepting themselves.

Another use of faces employs "How do you feel?" sheets. People who are not used to talking about their emotions can "hide" behind the sheets. Having it in front of them makes talking much easier.

When using this sheet, ask participants to make their "face" decisions alone and then share what they chose with the class or several friends. For example, in an adult class, if the subject were creativity you might ask . . .

- What face represents how you feel about your own creativity? This church's creativity?
- When you think of your own child-raising and the creative energy you are putting into it, what face do you pick?
- When you think of the most creative person you know, which face seems most appropriate?
- Based on our study of creativity so far, what face would you like to be representative of you six months from now?

Carry the assignment further by asking students to put those feelings from the sheet into some other form—a drawing, a written description, a song, or a mime. Set your students free to use their function preferences.

The symbol sheet on the next page can be used in the same way as the faces.[5]

- Which symbol represents our church?
- Which symbol do you think nonattenders in our community would pick for our church?
- Which symbol represents our "competition" in this community?

- Which symbol describes our singles ministry?
- Which symbol should we accept as a six-month goal for our church?

[Cont.]

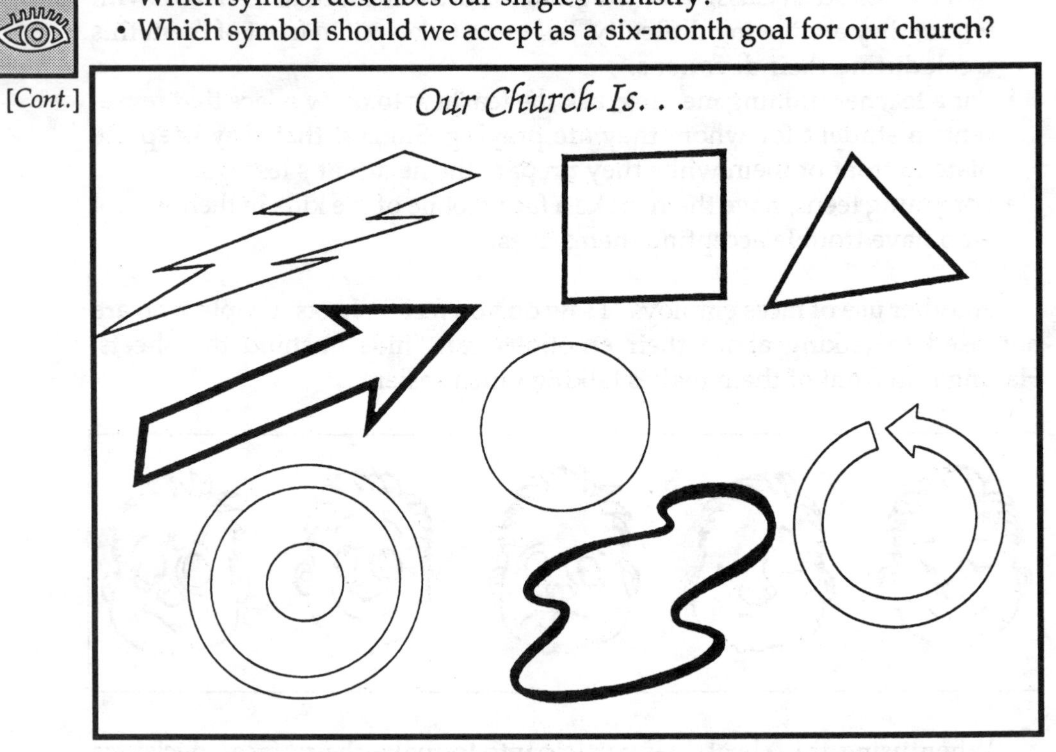

The most obvious use of the illustration at the top of the next page is in Bible study for youngsters. As they hear Matthew 18:2-7 being read, for example, they draw the expressions on the listener's faces:

> "I tell you the truth, unless you change and become like little children, you will never enter the kingdom of heaven. Therefore, whoever humbles himself like this child is the greatest in the kingdom of heaven. And whoever welcomes a little child like this in my name welcomes me."

However, Dynamic Learners in an adult class, studying the same passage, might enjoy drawing the answer to this question, "If these adults were our class members and we were showing our true expressions based on our actions, what would those expressions look like?" This activity would help them decide what their personal response to the passage should be.

The same picture already referred to can be used with any number of Scripture passages.

Godly Graffiti

(Youth and adults)

Tape butcher paper on the four walls. Divide groups into four teams. Each team is to design a graffiti board that contains illustrations of the primary principles studied in Scripture and the contemporary implications

of those principles. Groups may want to use large pieces of chalk for fuller coverage of the sheets.

When groups have completed their boards, each should share what it has done.

An alternative might be to leave the graffiti sheets up throughout a unit. Ask teens and adults to add their comments each week at the beginning and end of the study. On the final day of the study, use the graffiti sheets to review the study and discuss what's next.

Puppets

(Children and young teens)

Teaching experiences that involve puppets can, if they are correctly age-graded, capture the three learning modalities: Tactile/kinesthetic in the making and movement; Visual in the designing and the viewing; Auditory in the presentation and hearing.

Make inexpensive puppets from fast-food hamburger boxes, scraps of fabric, colored construction paper, glue, tape, and pins.

Directions for making the puppets: Cover the front of your box with skin-colored construction paper. Then paste on eyes and mouth. The top part of the mouth should be pasted to the top part of the box. The bottom part of the lips should be pasted to the bottom of the box. This way when you hold the

[Cont.]

back of the box, you can move the front open and shut and it will look like the box puppet is talking.

If you put on a Bible-time play, cover the top and the sides of the box with a piece of fabric so it will look like the headdress people wore in Bible times. If you are doing a modern play, use hats and scarves. Paste the headdress only on the sides and the top part of the box. Leave room at the box top for you to fit your hand between the fabric and the box.

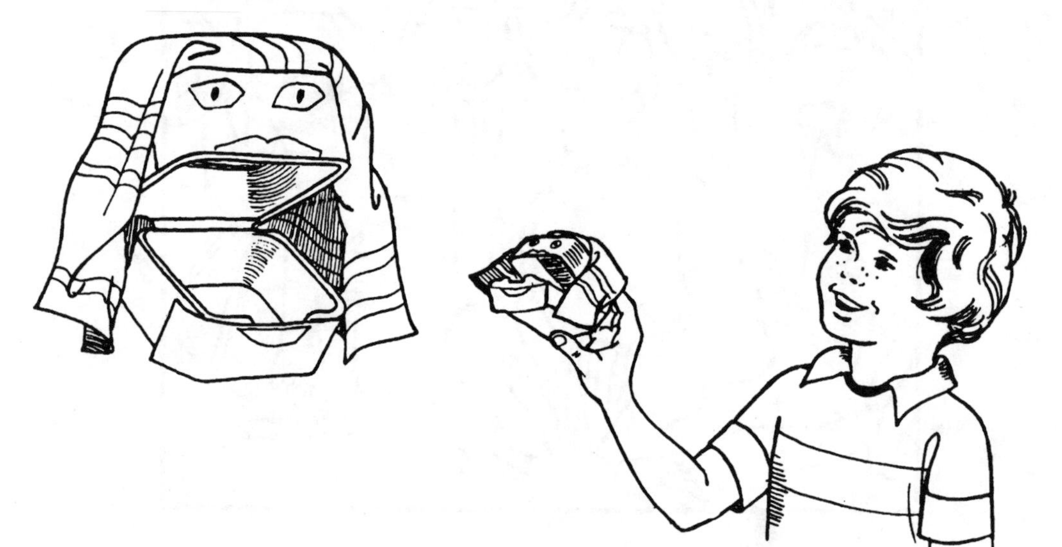

Dynamic Learners excel in teaching others what they have learned. Encourage their creativity with the script, sound effects, staging, and even marketing the puppet show.

Picture This

(Elementary through adult)

A little boy announced that he liked radio better than television because the pictures were better. Sometimes the pictures in our heads are much more compelling than those we see on paper. So use this mind's skill in the teaching process!

Ask students to picture themselves in the situations about which you are reading or talking. Guide their picturing with questions: What do these people look like? How do they feel? What smells do they smell? What can they touch? For example, consider a lesson on living our faith. You want to suggest various work projects to adults. As the students visualize themselves in these situations, the Lord might actually nudge them into involvement.

Nursing home: You are in a nursing home caring for an Alzheimer's patient. She is only in her seventies, but she acts much older. She smells slightly of urine and heavy perfume. She smiles vacantly at you and you decide to take her on a walk. She gets frightened when you take her arm. She cries out.

Crisis shelter: You are at a safe house for abused mothers and their children. A girl not much older than your high school daughter comes in with her two children. She's smoking. When you tell her smoking is not allowed in the shelter she swears at you. The youngest child is crying and when you offer to hold him the mother looks both grateful and angry.

Adults would then discuss these situations, using what their minds saw, to explain what they smelled, felt, heard.

Another example of "picturing" might make a Bible story come alive, opening the emotions of students whose ears have been hardened to a story through overfamiliarity. This use of picturing would work best in the Imaginative and Analytic quadrants of the Learning Style Cycle.

Consider this example by John Fischer from his book, *On a Hill Too Far Away*:

> The wounds on his hands bled slowly. Pressure from the weight of his body held back the flow. If there had been no other sounds that afternoon, it probably would have sounded like the slow, steady drip off the eaves of a mountain cabin on a damp, foggy night.
>
> But there were many sounds. Taunts from the soldiers, weeping and wailing from the women near the feet of Jesus, even careless laughter from children playing haphazardly around the perimeter of crucifixion hill, oblivious to the significance of this particular execution. Small dark puddles would gather briefly under the arms of the cross, only to be covered by the shuffle of a guard's feet. And then it would start in again: drip . . . drip . . . drip—little landings seen but not heard.
>
> Mary saw them. She stared at the puddles through bloodshot eyes while his life flashed before her, and it seemed to her that the earth swallowed his blood as if dirt had been created for this. As if it were drinking its fill and would thirst no more.
>
> Then she slowly turned her eyes up to his face, and her breath failed. He already had her in the grasp of his eyes. It was the first time he had looked at her from the cross, and his eyes were full of the deepest despair and the deepest love she had ever known. It seemed as if she were falling—falling into a bottomless abyss. She looked until she could look no more and turned her eyes away so she could catch her breath again. Once more her gaze went to the small puddle in the dirt, and it seemed now that she, and only she, could hear the drops landing, loud enough to shut out all other sounds.[6]

Color Blocks

(Youth and adult)

Ask students to express answers to questions in color and explain why they picked the color they did. This helps equalize people who are familiar with the "correct" answers and those who are new to a Christian group.

[*Cont.*]

- What color is this church's attitude toward people of different nationalities?
- What color is Christ's message that we studied today?
- What color are the people in this church when it comes to living out our Christian standards? What color are our teenagers?

TACTILE/KINESTHETIC

Clay in Class
(Children)
Clay Map

Children start with a flat surface, clay, toothpicks, and construction paper. The surface becomes a "map" of the world, province, city, or community. Students then mold clay items and attach them to their map surface.

For example: If the topic were people around the world who need our prayers, the child might draw a map of the world. Using clay she would create figures that represent people from each country she prays for. Every time she remembers to pray specifically for that country, she sticks a toothpick with a construction paper flag on it into the clay.

Another example might be: A student creates his own community.[7] On the flat surface, he draws roads and streets of the town and colors them. He might decide to use pebbles or cat litter to pave the roads. Buildings and the names of the people who live in each house could be added. Every day that he acts toward his neighbors in a way that would please Jesus, he could add a toothpick flag.

Both of these examples would grow as the child's participation in them grows.

A Teacher Training Idea

Empty the junk drawer of spools, pine cones, safety pins, Band-Aids, tops, etc. Spread these things on the floor. Give each teacher a small amount of clay to fashion into a pedestal. Then he or she should pick an item that will become a symbol of a goal for the class during the next quarter, and attach it to the pedestal. The teacher should keep this item in a place where it will be seen often as a reminder to work toward that goal. For instance, a teacher might pick the pine cone as a reminder that her primary class may not show great growth in one year, but the truths she is teaching could someday be used by God in mighty ways.

Clay Picture

Clay must be soft. The child spreads it very lightly on a piece of cardboard, making a craft project that reminds him or her of the day's assignment.

A simple outline picture works best: a girl praying, praying hands, open Bible. Children use their fingers as a brush. Encourage them to come up with their own patterns, designs, and finger strokes.

Alternative Bible Verse Memorization

(Children and youth)

[*Cont.*] Many students do not excel at Bible memory. We must affirm these children when they do, in fact, know what the Bible says. They have written its words on their heart, even though the exact wording may get a little scrambled. Once we have found ways to test the heart knowledge of these children, we must celebrate these alternative ways of learning with as much enthusiasm as we applaud traditional memorization.

Here are several ideas that include success possibilities for students of different modalities. Imaginative, Common Sense, and Dynamic Learners may all prefer this type of verse learning to the traditional word-for-word recitation.

Living Memorization

Give students a list of verses that are to be lived. They find ways to live those verses, and get a Christian adult to sign a sheet explaining how the student did it.

Visual Memorization

Students design and implement an artistic project that illustrates the verse. As part of the illustration, students may want to include the actual words of the verse. A student could design a cross-stitch of the verse. Or, a student may do a pen and ink sketch. Another may do a collage that visually interprets not only what the verse says, but also what it means to him or her.[8]

Teach the Verse

Students should find a way to teach what the verse means to another group of learners. For example, they might write a play to show what the verse means, do a video, or even an interpretive dance.

Video Creativity

(Youth)

Sunday school teachers have yet to explore what can be done when students put their creative energy into using tools that are now available. Students are held back more by their less technically literate teachers than they are for lack of equipment and ideas. More than half (55 percent) of all Americans are "technophobic" to some extent. Thirty-three percent of those are teens.[9] Since video is less threatening than computers and often easier to adapt to a classroom, start with it.

One idea might be to make a movie that will be an outreach tool. Friends and parents will come to see something their kids have created.

My first personal exposure to video came when I was working in the religious education department at Tachikawa Air Force Base in Tokyo during the Vietnam war. The chaplains decided that this tool—a new hand-held video camera—might be just the thing to put their program on the map. I was put in charge of the junior high department and the camera. The young teens decided they wanted to write and star in a movie of the life of Joseph, the unit they had just finished. The final result was terrific, at least in the eyes of the kids. They invited their parents to the chapel on a Friday night to see it. It was the Christmas season and I didn't expect anyone to show up. But I was wrong. The room was full of proud parents.

Another option would be to assign video interviews that can be used in class. Interview people who live within three blocks of this church and ask them what they think of our church. Ask people on the street what the most important part of Christmas is to them. Students could video people answering the question, "What is sin?" or ask other teens to define "family."

If they aren't going to shoot a movie, you could assign teens to find one- and two-minute segments in rented videos to illustrate points of upcoming lessons.

Even without videos, you can get kids to think in movie patterns. For instance, have triads list all the Old Testament events they can think of in three minutes. Groups will probably think they are trying to get a longer list than the others. When the time is up, assign them the task of using their list to tell the redemption story. Not only does this exercise get the creative juices flowing, but it also involves young people in critical thinking.[10]

Theological Miming

(Older elementary through adults)

Students will develop fifteen-second mimes that illustrate some aspect of a concept. Words like these stretch students' thought in mime preparation and discussion following each mime: love, faith, church, family, prayer, redemption. (A mime activity also makes an unusual video homework assignment.) Bob Samples offers the following example of effective mime:

> I once asked a class of sixth graders in the Bedford-Stuyvesant borough of New York to "move in such a way as to demonstrate what *freedom* means." After some hesitation, a tall student stood and walked heavily forward to the front of the room. I heard the audible reaction of the other students and saw the look of dismay on the teacher's face. The student stopped, stood straight, and announced that he was about to demonstrate Freedom! He began to take a long stride across the room. Halfway through the stride he came to a shattering stop. A look of panic crossed his face, and, for all purposes, his right foot was riveted to the floor. His body lurched forward, then backward, but his right foot stayed locked to the floor. He jerked and lunged, but the foot wouldn't budge. He tried to pry the foot loose with a nearby chair—and commandeered a broomstick, which also failed to move the foot.
>
> We are all transfixed by the performance. Then his entire body relaxed. He smiled widely at us all, bent over, and deftly slipped his right foot out

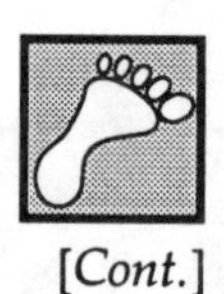

[*Cont.*]

of its shoe and walked away with a lilt—leaving the "anchored" shoe behind. The class broke into applause, the teacher relaxed, and the student took several bows and returned to his seat. I asked if he could tell us what his movements told us about what freedom means. He said, "Sometimes you have to give up something that matters to you so that you can have it [freedom]."

. . . His teacher later confided in me that this student was *the* problem student of the school and that he virtually held the class hostage for his whims. The teacher also said this was the first assignment he had voluntarily engaged in since school had started. For this student, a path had been opened that promised sophisticated communication.[11]

Strobe Theater
(Youth)

Students develop a pantomime and act it out under a strobe light. For example, a class could follow the life of a contemporary prodigal with their actions while an expressive reader presents the Bible story of The Prodigal Son from a paraphrase.

Notes

1. Dynamic Learners develop methods and new procedures that have the rest of us saying, "Great idea! What a revolutionary way to approach that problem." Munir Fasheh's story demonstrates the creative methodogy of a woman who must have been a Dynamic Learner. It was "a common scene on the West Bank and the Gaza Strip. A number of soldiers were harshly beating a young man in his early twenties in the central district. Several women rushed toward the scene shouting and trying to pull the soldiers away from the young man. Suddenly, a woman carrying a baby ran up and started shouting at the young man, 'I told you not to leave the house today, that the situation is too dangerous. But you didn't listen; you never listen to me." Then she turned to the soldiers and said, 'Beat him; he deserves this. He never listens. I am sick of my life with him.' Then back to the man she cried, 'I am sick of you and your baby; take him, and leave me alone.' She then pushed the baby into his arms and ran away. The soldiers were confused. Finally, they left the man and went on. A few minutes later, the woman reappeared, took back her baby, told the young man to go to his home and wished him safety and a quick recovery." It was only then that Fasheh realized that the man and the woman were total strangers to each other. Her solution exemplifies the creative solutions that Dynamic Learners generate.—Munir Fasheh, "Community Education," *Harvard Education Review*, Vol. 60, No. 1, February 1990, p. 30.

2. Merrill Harmin, *Inspiring Active Learning—A Handbook for Teachers* (Alexandria, Vir.: Association for Supervision and Curriculum Development, 1994), p. 25.

3. Carl Heine, "Worship Celebration Suggestions," *The Idea Book* (Elgin, Ill.: David C. Cook Publishing Co., 1988), pp. 6, 7.

4. Rita Dunn and Kenneth Dunn, *Teaching Students through Their Individual Learning Styles: A Practical Approach* (Reston, Vir.: Reston Publishing Co., Inc., 1978), pp. 71, 72.

5. "Something very different happens in the mind of a person when he or she is forced to process a tried-and-true, rationally biased, well-understood cognitive concept in a new way. First, different parts of the brain-mind system get involved. . . . Second, . . . the brain-mind system tends to establish a metaphoric interrelatedness of concepts rather than rationally separating concepts and skills into more discrete, concrete forms," wrote Bob Samples in "Using Learning Modalities to Celebrate Intelligence," *Educational Leadership*, October 1992, p. 62.

6. John Fischer, *On a Hill Too Far Away* ©1994 by John Fischer. Published by Servant Publications, Box 8617, Ann Arbor, MI 48107, pp. 31, 32. Used with permission.

7. Marlene LeFever, *50 Days for Jesus to Visit My Neighborhood* (Wheaton, Ill.: Chapel of the Air, Inc., 1988).

8. Charles Fowler, Director of National Cultural Resources, Inc., and the author of *Can We Rescue the Arts for America's Children?* pointed out that the best schools seem to also have the best arts program. "The arts are not pretty bulletin boards and bunnies," he said. "The arts penetrate what science cannot explain" (ASCD Conference, "Emerging Images of Learning," March 20, 1994). Can his observation be translated into our Christian education settings? Are the classes where students are learning the most also be the classes that honor the artistic intelligences as much as they honor the intellectual intelligences?

9. Reported in *Research ALERT*, October 1, 1993, p. 4, from reports from Dell Computer.

10. When we encourage critical thinking we are raising students who can analyze their faith and discern truth. Richard Paul, talking about secular teaching, also presents a caution to Christian educators: "The pace of change in the world is accelerating, yet educational institutions have not kept up. Indeed, schools have historically been the most static of social institutions, uncritically passing down from generation to generation outmoded didactic, lecture-and-drill-based models of instruction. Predictable results follow. Students, on the whole, do not learn how to work by, or think for, themselves." (From Richard Paul, *Critical Thinking—What Every Person Needs to Survive in a Rapidly Changing World* [Santa Rosa, Calif.: The Foundation for Critical Thinking, 1992], p. 55.)

11. Bob Samples, "Using Learning Modalities to Celebrate Intelligence," *Educational Leadership*, October 1992, p. 65. Reprinted with permission of the Association for Supervision and Curriculum Development. Copyright ©1992 by ASCD. All rights reserved.

14

Do-It-Yourself Lesson Plan

Christian education by its nature is a "preparadigmatic" discipline, in the sense that it lacks one dominant framework that guides all thought and practice. Naming the preparadigmatic nature of Christian education celebrates the place of freedom and creativity in responding to the challenges of teaching and learning in the Christian faith.
—Robert W. Pazmino

The Learning Style Cycle presented in this book gives valuable clues, a creative rationale, for structuring Christian education classes into a four-step sequence that utilizes the learning strengths of all students. The more we know the more difficult—but effective—our teaching can become.

It's important for every teacher to keep up with new discoveries about how people learn. Biblical truth is unchanging, from age to age the same. But as our knowledge about how God made us deepens, the ways in which we teach that truth will change. Change is always difficult. The human mind treats a new idea the way the body treats a strange protein; it rejects it. Smile, but break the tendency to live that quip.

To prepare yourself for change, complete the following three assignments.

Assignment 1

Do a comparison check on a number of different curricula to find ones that are making the most effective use of the Learning Style Cycle—starting by using the learning skills of the Imaginative Learners, moving to the Analytic Learning, next to the Common Sense Learner and finally preparing students to make a difference by using the learning skills of the Dynamic Learner.

Follow Up

Set your teacher's guide and your attendance book side by side. Go through a quarter's lessons looking at the methods that are used. Beside each, write the names of the students you think will benefit from it. Ideally, your curriculum should involve all students—no matter what their modality preference: Auditory, Visual, or Tactile/Kinesthetic.

Assignment 2

Try your hand at a lesson development. Fill in the following model using the learning cycle. Choose "The Love of God" as your theme.

Age Level: _____

Scripture Basis: ____________________

1. Imaginative Learners: How will you get students to answer the question, "Why is this subject important to me?" Give students an opportunity to talk with each other. Make use of what they already know. Add no new information. You want them to finish the section feeling, "Yes, I bring something of myself to this subject. I have something to contribute. I need this and I'm ready to learn more."

Imaginative Learners will shine.
Overview of what students will do in this section:

Modalities used:

Auditory

Visual

Tactile/Kinesthetic

2. *Analytic Learners:* Take the students into Scripture. This is the heart of the lesson. For some students the content itself will be new. For most, you will be bringing additional meaning or depth to previously known facts. This part of the cycle helps students answer the question, "What content do I need to know?"

Analytic Learners will shine.
Overview of what students will do in this section:

Modalities used:

Auditory

Visual

Tactile / Kinesthetic

3. *Common Sense Learners:* Students practice what they learned and see if what the Bible taught really does apply to them today.

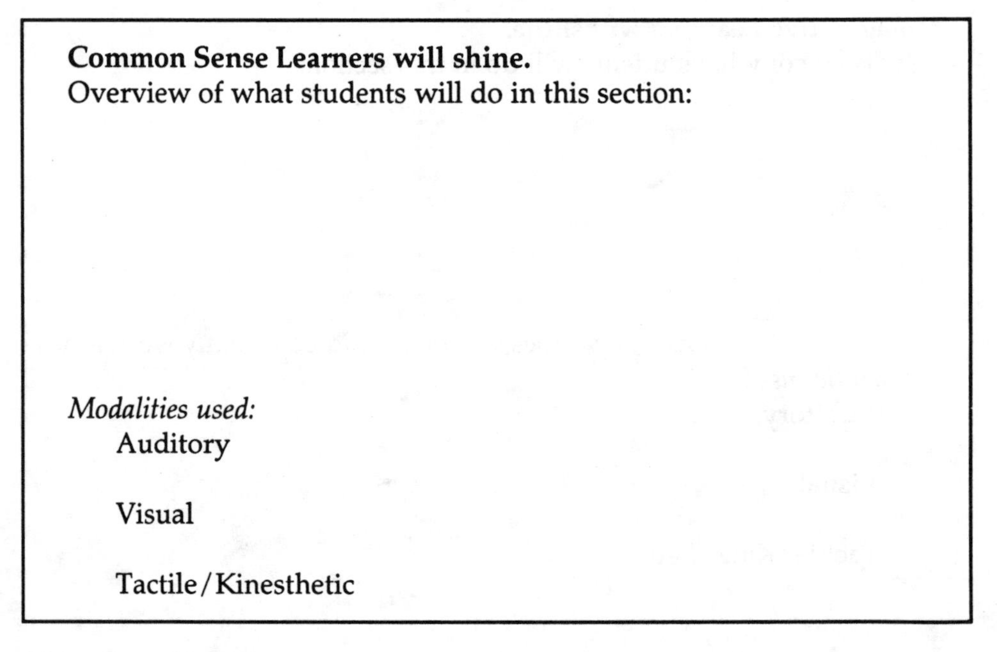

Common Sense Learners will shine.
Overview of what students will do in this section:

Modalities used:

Auditory

Visual

Tactile / Kinesthetic

4. *Dynamic Learners:* Students need to do something original or personal with the content, as they answer the question, "What can this become?" Know where you want the lesson to go, but allow plenty of room for students to add their own ideas.

Dynamic Learners will shine.
Overview of what students will do in this section:

Modalities used:

Auditory

Visual

Tactile/Kinesthetic

Assignment
Teach the lesson you have developed. Ask yourself:

- Which style of learner enjoyed my lesson most? Why?
- Which style of learner may not have learned up to his or her full potential in this lesson? Why?
- How did my own preferred style influence my first two answers?
- Were the four learning style questions answered? If not, what were the weaknesses?

    1. Imaginative: Why study this lesson? Why is it important to me?
    2. Analytic: What do I need to know?
    3. Common Sense: How does what I've studied actually work today?
    4. Dynamic: How can I put it into practice this week? What can it become in my life?

- Did I make use of the three modalities? What percent of my lesson was auditory? Visual? Tactile/kinesthetic? Fill out the chart on the following page.

Modality	My % Goal*	My Lesson %
Auditory	20	
Visual	40	
Tactile/kinesthetic	40	

*** This percentage goal is appropriate for students from about age ten on up. If you taught slightly younger children, you would want less auditory. When teaching children ages six and seven all methods should include the tactile/kinesthetic.**

- What things did I learn about myself through this exercise? What things did I learn about my students?

Part V

Learning Styles: Not Just for Teachers

Don't be polite. Bite in.
Pick it up with your fingers
and lick the juice that may run down your chin.
It is ready and ripe now, whenever you are . . .
—Poet Eve Merriam

Eve Merriam's description of how to approach a poem[1] could apply to learning styles, too. We can bite into the ideas that are ripe for a number of applications. In this section, we'll look at three.

Chapter 15 deals with recruiting volunteers. What superintendent or director of Christian education wouldn't put this task high on a priority list? When people are approached to do jobs that fit their learning style strength, they are more likely to volunteer and enjoy the assignment.

In Chapter 16 pastors and worship leaders will see how incorporating learning styles can enlarge what people get from and give to the Sunday morning service.

Marriage and learning styles: most people marry someone in an opposite learning style quadrant and they spend the rest of their lives trying to get the other person to think right—the way he or she does! God could use Chapter 17 to help enrich your marriage! In addition, He could use it to rebuild relationships with your children, who, because they are so very different from you, may feel unloved and unimportant to the family.

Chapter 17 is also important to teachers. People you teach come to you for prayer and advice. If what you know about learning styles might help someone who is struggling with a difficult family relationship, share these ideas—and if that person is an Analytic Learner, lend him or her this book!

Note

1. "Lick the Juice That May Run Down Your Chin" by Lorna Van Gilst, *Christian Educators Journal*, February/March 1989, p. 4.

15

Learning Styles and Recruiting Volunteers

A person's vocation is where their deep joy meets the world's deep need.
—Frederick Buechner

When I have asked superintendents and directors of Christian education, "What's the most difficult part of your job?" no one even thinks about an answer. It's instant: "Recruiting! And the second most difficult is . . . recruiting!"

Recruiting volunteers by using learning styles won't solve all the problems, but it could be one tool God uses to help.

The learning style approach is to ask people to do jobs in programs—Sunday school, clubs, vacation Bible school—that fit their preferred learning styles.

How Leaders Determine Volunteers' Styles

First, ask them! People can tell you how they prefer to learn and, by inference, the types of services that would most interest them. However, instead of putting people to work in their strength area, leaders often plug anyone they can find into the empty holes. Sometimes that works. (Never underestimate the genius of the Holy Spirit's participation in our bungling efforts.) But frequently, that approach makes poor use of people-skills. Mismatched volunteers "unvolunteer" themselves as soon as they possibly can.

The "Quickie Survey" (page 170) may give leaders some clues about the service preferences of potential volunteers. It won't tell everything, but it can serve as a conversation starter. A high number for statement . . .

"A" may indicate an Imaginative Learner.
"B" may indicate an Analytic Learner.
"C" may indicate a Common Sense Learner.
"D" may indicate a Dynamic Learner.

Quickie Survey

Name: ______________________________

Phone Numbers: Day ______________ Evening ______________

We have a lot of service opportunities in our Christian education program. Not all of them involve teaching. Please fill out this survey by writing 4 in front of the statement that is most like you, 3 next to the statement that is quite a bit like you, 2 beside the statement that isn't much like you, and 1 beside the statement that is least like you.

When something you might enjoy is available, we'll call you. Together we'll pray about the opportunity. (Returning this survey does NOT mean you have volunteered!)

___ (A) I like working with people and building friendships. I enjoy talking and listening to others.
___ (B) I enjoy searching for the right answers that solve problems and helping others understand those answers. Studying and reading are enjoyable to me.
___ (C) I enjoy getting involved in specific projects that have a beginning and an end. I like active participation.
___ (D) I enjoy doing creative things that differ from the norm. I thrive on change and doing things I've never done before.

Volunteer Ideas

Be creative in the service ideas you present. Consider some from the list below. Once a person has been successful as an usher, for example, he or she might be open to volunteering in other areas. Or the volunteer may find a service slot that he or she doesn't want to give up.[1]

Imaginative Volunteers

The following are activities that Imaginative volunteers would enjoy.

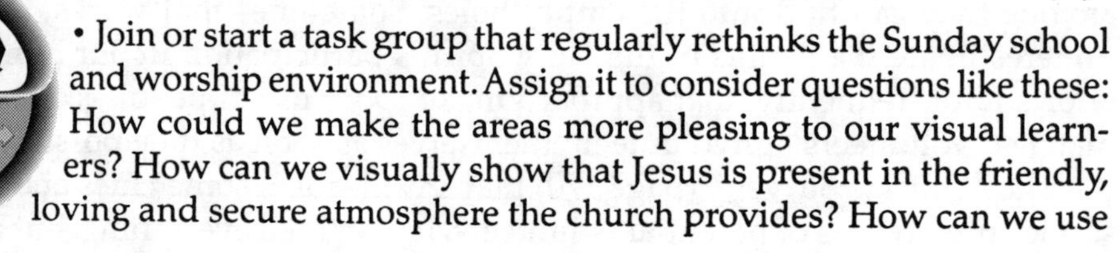

• Join or start a task group that regularly rethinks the Sunday school and worship environment. Assign it to consider questions like these: How could we make the areas more pleasing to our visual learners? How can we visually show that Jesus is present in the friendly, loving and secure atmosphere the church provides? How can we use our spaces to communicate something about the nature of the church and perhaps even our theology?

- Work on a quarterly, computer-generated newsletter for parents that will emphasize the parties, outings, and life response activities our church program offers. Include several ideas at each age level for parents to use at home to further the teaching that took place in class.
- Plan an every-six-months "coffee and talk" time for parents and teachers. The objective would be to have both groups get to know, trust, and share with each other.
- Be a children's greeter each week, welcoming youngsters into worship and Sunday school.

> "I don't teach," Daniel Brady of Casper, Wyoming, said. "My Sunday school job is to meet every one of the kids in our elementary class as they arrive. Then I officially escort them to the classroom. The boys love it. I make a big production out of the walk. I don't have the gift of teaching, but I can talk and laugh with kids and let them know that they are very special to me, this church, and to God.[2]

- Periodically (possibly each quarter) brainstorm ways to get more neighborhood children involved. Consider different learning style preferences and evaluate the existing programs. What type of child is being overlooked?
- Be in charge of treat time for clubs, children's church, or vacation Bible school. Tie the treats to the lesson in some way so that the food reinforces what is actually being taught.
- Be a nonteaching parent on the Christian education committee. Your job is to chronicle the results or lack of results of the program in which your child is enrolled. Be the reality check.
- Develop a Christian education logo that emphasizes the mission statement of our church.
- Sponsor clinics for teens. For example, one could be on how to show Jesus' love to little children when teens volunteer to work in the church nursery.
- Periodically (possibly every six months) brainstorm ways to use the mail to affirm people—teachers, students, those who are sick, etc. One teacher used postcards to breathe Christian reality into her class.

> Many of the young teens in my class could retell every Bible story correctly and recite Bible verses by the dozens. From their over-saturated perspective, the Bible held nothing new for them. It was boring.
>
> Postcards became my tool for breathing Christian reality into that class. "Mr. Myers from Philadelphia has cancer," I explained. "Let's send him postcards to let him know we're thinking about him. Even though you've never met him, I know he'll enjoy hearing from you."
>
> Each week for the last eight weeks of his life, Mr. Myers received forty-five postcards. Before he died, he dictated a letter through his wife to the

class: "Your postcards are wonderful. For years I've known about Jesus, but I've never been willing to accept Him. Your cards are a demonstration of His love to me, and I want you to know that they played a part in my becoming a Christian this week."

Bible class was never the same! Suddenly Christianity was not facts and names and memorized words. Christianity was a power that changes lives.[3]

- Be an in-class hugger and teacher helper with no responsibilities for the children other than building friendships with them. Teacher Holly Bahich from Crestwood, Illinois, said,

> I'm a "huggy" person and encourage my students to hug. "Jesus likes hugs, too," I told them. "By obeying Him and doing things that make Him happy, we are sending our hugs to Him."
>
> Hugs caught on! Now we regularly exchange happy, sad, lonely, excited, and even scared hugs.
>
> One little girl came up to me after Sunday school and just stood there looking up at me. I asked her if she wanted her hug and she [nodded] her head like a happy little puppy. Hugs are great—for me, for kids who often desperately need them, and for our Jesus who, I suspect, is 100 percent in favor of them.

Analytic Volunteers

The following are activities that Analytic volunteers would enjoy.

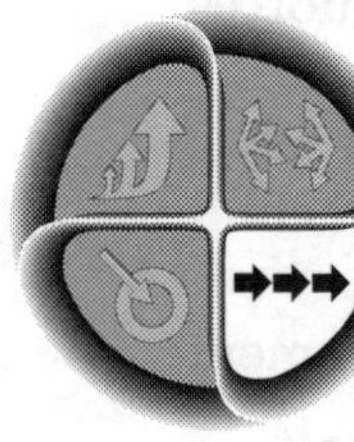

- Join a task force to study our Sunday school curriculum. Sometimes the most creative insights come from people who are on the edge of something, rather than being head-over-heels involved. So a nonteacher who enjoys evaluating process and results will be a great asset.
- Many church libraries, especially the Christian education section, could use new materials. Every six months, investigate what books are available and which would be helpful to teachers. Plan ways to acquire them.
- Regularly develop "marketing" ideas to get children, teens, adults, and teachers using the books in our church library.
- Annually develop a summer reading list for children and their parents. Since all parents are interested in teaching their children good values, even if they are not Christians, why not send the list to parents in your community, along with a cover letter on your church letterhead?
- Serve as a Brain Buddy to a gifted student. Spend time with this student and participate with him or her in enriching activities. One example comes from Lively, Ontario.

> "Stacy's too smart," Helen Smith said, "you'll lose her." The new plan seemed to make sense. There weren't enough kids for two classes, so the

kindergartners and first graders would study together. "No!" Helen said. "It won't work."

Helen had been teaching for thirty years, and she volunteered again. "Even if Stacy is the only child in my first grade class, she will learn about Jesus in a way that's just right for a child her age and her intelligence.

- Provide weekly ideas, perhaps published in the church bulletin, on how parents and their children can memorize Scripture. This story came from Mary Ellen Miller, Cochrane, Alberta.

Assistant teacher fourteen-year-old Steve Miller took Adrian as his special project. He worked hard to teach a Bible verse to the Downs Syndrome child. Then came the Sunday when Steve's attention paid off. "He cares for you," Adrian recited. Everyone celebrated. It was the first time Adrian had ever put four words together to form a sentence that made sense.

- Head up a quiz team committee. This team will work with a number of churches to set up quiz teams in which church teens (and perhaps adults) compete by answering Bible questions.
- Plan an annual evening for adults where people representing the four learning styles share how faith can be lived in this culture. For example, if you used a panel format, it might include a guidance counselor (Imaginative), doctor (Analytic), lawyer (Common Sense), and homemaker (Dynamic).
- Take on a one-year Christian stewardship project. Give a teen group $100 which they are to invest and grow for a Christian project over the next year. Educate the students in ways to make money and guide them throughout the entire project. As affirmation, publish updates in the church bulletin each quarter.
- Collect illustrations that teachers can use in their classes. The more up to date the illustration, the better. Transfer the stories onto computer so teachers can have instant access to them.
- Set up an all-church telephone prayer chain for students involved in Sunday school. It happened this way in Newhall, California.

Baby Frey was near death. Without encouragement from the adult teacher or pastor, all forty members were contacted and 95 percent of them showed up at the church at the height of Los Angeles rush hour to pray for that child's life. God answered prayer.—Mike Broyles.

- Schedule lecture series on community topics, and encourage church members to bring guests.
- Serve as back-up to a teacher, providing geographic and historical information on each week's lesson.
- Volunteer to teach. The following is an example from S. Lorraine Reed, Tulsa, Oklahoma.

My dad used to say, "I want one of my six kids to do something with her life."

So off I went to law school. But when I graduated I knew practicing law wasn't the direction God had chosen for me. So I'm back in school studying Christian education. This time I'm sure! My Heavenly Father wants me to do something important with my life, too.

- Tutor a child who needs special help.

Common Sense Volunteers

The following are activities that Common Sense volunteers would enjoy.

- As part of the summer program, share something from your own experience that would help students grow in faith. For example, one elderly man, who would never dream of teaching, had worked for years on his family genealogy. He helped the junior class build their spiritual genealogies. His project included their taping testimonies of relatives who were Christians and recording stories of how they came to Jesus. The project got some parents involved who had previously seen Sunday school as a babysitting service.
- Administer a bulletin board that spotlights worksheets and projects that students of all ages—including adults—have done.
- Set up an annual workday program where parents and other church members share with teens and older elementary students what they do for a living, their preparation for their jobs, their responsibilities and their challenges. Strong Christians might also share how they live their faith on the job. Michael Keller from Regina, Saskatchewan, benefited in this way.

My folks were divorced. The Sunday school teacher who made a difference in my life was a hockey player who spent time with me outside class. God knew I needed a special man in my life and He provided him.

- Plan an annual meeting with parents and teachers to talk about learning styles. Encourage them to identify their preference and the preference of their children. Encourage discussion between parents with different styles. For example, groups of mixed-style-preference parents might talk about how they deal with discipline, how they handle homework problems, how they facilitate Christian education in the home.
- Plan an annual teacher training meeting where teachers will go through their leader's guides and identify what child would prefer each activity. Evaluate the curriculum in terms of style. What student types are most affirmed? What students may feel left out or under-appreciated?
- Oversee a cross-generational mission project.
- Set up a round-robin magazine exchange for parents. Many parents would

like to have more information on doing a better job, but helpful magazines are too expensive. The church should subscribe to several and route slips could assure that the magazines move from person to person. Each year at subscription time, evaluate which magazines, secular and Christian, are most helpful to your people.

- Organize a list of people who would be willing to do occasional demonstrations in class. Tie the demonstration to what will be studied that day. Leslie Miller from Vancouver, British Columbia, benefitted from this idea.

> I loved my sixth grade Sunday school teacher. She was a hairdresser and every week she'd give us almost-adolescent girls beauty tips that somehow always led us into the Bible. The Sunday I found out this "with it" lady was a grandmother, I almost died!

- Ask parents to videotape television programs that deal with specific issues their children are covering in class. Make these available to teachers.
- Train teachers in how to use the technology the church has, and introduce them to technology that you think would be helpful in the future. Take them step-by-step through the processes that make these tools helpful, rather than scary. Consider making yourself available the first few times a teacher uses a new piece of equipment. This example comes from Warrenville, Illinois.

> I chose my career because I was influenced by two Sunday school teachers. My junior high teacher was totally blind. He taught me how to do audio recordings. Together we wrote and recorded Christian "radio programs" for class. In high school I had a young teacher who got me interested in video. My work was used in class, club, and the main worship service. Today I'm vice president of a video company, and frequently use my skills to produce videos to teach Sunday school teachers. How's that for God's full circle!—Darren Gould.

- Tape the adult Sunday school lesson to send to sick class members. Conclude with a personal message or enlist another person to add the "hello and we miss you."
- Take on tasks for the sick or elderly, and organize older children, teens, and adults to help you.
- Help teachers with interest and learning centers, collecting materials that will enable children and teens to work independently on projects. Develop unique centers. For example, young teens could make their own ink to write favorite Bible verses on homemade parchment paper. Or, teens could learn how to change oil in a car, a great service project or a missions money-making project.
- Organize sports teams and find creative ways to insure that more than exercise is happening. It worked in Eden Prairie, Minnesota, for pastor Leith Anderson.

At our church, all softball leagues must be made up of 20 percent non-Christians. We average 40 percent. Softball is our outreach, not just an exercise program.

It's fun to watch the Christians squirm when their best hitter is thinking about becoming a Christian—and if he does before the end of the season, their percentage of non-Christians will be too low and they're afraid they'll have to forfeit the championship.

Dynamic Volunteers

The following are activities that Dynamic volunteers would enjoy.

- Brainstorm ideas for holiday programs, and how to appropriately involve children in the worship services. Consider only things this church has never done before. For example, how would a Christmas program be structured around the architecture of the church building?
- Oversee a church graffiti board inside—or maybe even outside—the church.
- Dream up creative ways to raise money for specific Christian education projects. The ideas will range far beyond the traditional car wash or bake sale.
- Be the adult adviser to children or teens and produce a unique church newsletter.
- Partner with a group of parents who have children in the Sunday school to go through the curriculum or club programs and suggest ways others in the congregation could add to what is taught. Leave the assignment somewhat open-ended, but build around the question: "What could we do if we had the time, money, and energy to make what happens in this setting more effective?"
- Pick a "weird" kid and befriend him or her.
- Plan an annual weekend retreat between parents and teens. Find new ways for them to share who they are and what their goals and aspirations are for themselves and each other.
- Every six months, dynamic and imaginative learners should brainstorm unique ways to affirm people who are away from the congregation or people who are deserving of an extra thank-you. Encourage this group to have fun with their ideas. Could they send a balloon-o-gram? Or, for a sick child, how about taking photographs of the kids in the class making funny faces and captioning the faces?
- Plan a Christian education yearbook that can be photocopied for each student.

Notes

1. Ramona Warren Tennison, director of Children's Ministries at First Baptist Church, Elgin, Illinois, has less trouble getting volunteers than many leaders. Her approach is to ask people, "Which of these three jobs would you most like to do?" When given a choice almost everyone she approaches is able to pick one that he or she finds attractive. With a choice they can also fit one that matches best with how they like to learn.

2. Unless otherwise noted, the examples of volunteers in this chapter previously appeared in *Teacher Touch* and were collected and written by Marlene LeFever and published quarterly by David C. Cook Church Ministries. *Teacher Touch* is designed to affirm Sunday school teachers and other Christian education volunteers in their important and challenging work and to give them opportunities to encourage others with the stories of their ministries.

3. Marlene LeFever, "Care Mail," *The Christian Reader*, January/February 1993.

16

Learning Styles and Worship: A Sense of Koinonia

Each of us has what I call a leading instinct of the soul.
—Gordon MacDonald

One elderly woman shared, "I come to this church because we stop after the sermon to hug each other and say, 'The peace of God be with you.' That's the only time all week I'm touched by another person. Often I feel as if God is in that touch."

"That's my least favorite time," another countered. "I'm uncomfortable when people I don't know very well come up and hug me."

These people have different learning styles. They don't leave those styles at the Sunday school classroom door. They bring them into worship. Their style affects how they worship and often what church they choose to join.

Pastors can increase the number of people who feel comfortable in their churches when they pay attention to learning styles and make certain that there is a place in each service where people who prefer any one of the four styles will feel comfortable. Not only pastors but worship leaders and those who plan worship in any setting—camp, retreats, children's church—can benefit by considering the style preferences.

Meeting God in Worship

The point in the worship service where different people meet God may be totally different—a reflection of their preferred learning style.

Imaginative Learners, feeling-directed people, may feel God's presence during communion, the celebration of the Eucharist. Like the woman above, they may need the touch of another person when people greet each other.

Imaginatives may feel God's presence during the coffee hour when they, along with others of their faith, share and pray together. They covet the special feelings that let them know that they belong to an active community of faith.

Analytic Learners, thinking or intellect-directed people, may feel God's presence through content—the sermon. When the preacher is able to share some new insight with them, touching their minds with new thoughts about God, they know they have worshipped.

Common Sense Learners, practical people, worship through sensation, hands-on experience, and social action. They may not feel God's presence in the corporate worship service as much as they do when they are building new cribs for the nursery, washing the communion pieces, or mowing the church lawn for Jesus' sake.

Common Sense Learners have a practical, sensible faith. It makes more sense, they conclude, to be Christian than not to be, especially when they consider what types of people they would be without Him. Faith is validated as they analyze how they have matured and become more like Christ.

Dynamic Learners, intuition-directed people, will often worship at unexpected moments through what they describe as mystical experiences. This could be during a liturgical dance or a beautiful number sung by the choir. Their intuition confirms for them that God does exist. While Imaginative Learners may feel an emptiness within that draws them to Christ—capsulated by Pascal's statement that there is a God-shaped vacuum in the heart of every person that can only be filled by God Himself—the Dynamic Learners have a sense of fullness that hints that there is a "bigness" or soul within that lives forever, something that can be accounted for by nothing but God. Both perspectives lead seekers to Christ.

> Each has a unique part to play in the church's total ministry. Some find meaning in analyzing church doctrine; others, in fixing up the church building; some, in discovering new ways for the church to relate to the community; and others, in performing a service for the needy. All are expressing their response to Christ in ways particularly meaningful to their dispositions. All build up the body of Christ in their own way. When everyone can participate, almost imperceptibly a sense of koinonia arises.[1]

"Knowing our leading spiritual instinct," writes Gordon MacDonald, "will help us identify the situations in which we can most naturally enter God's presence. Being aware that others have different instincts can prevent us from judging them as inferior and help us appreciate the diversity in the Christ-following family. We cannot prescribe any single way as best for all."[2]

Yet, how often we try—even with our own spouses and children. A person's preference can lead to a disdain for those who hold the opposite preference. Suzanne M. deBenedittis notes that our predominant style takes "energy away from its polar opposite."

> Thus one's very strength is also one's weakness, since too much energy spent in one direction makes for an unbalanced life and a distorted view of reality. For example, when mystical types are told to "come down from the clouds," what is meant is their need to be more practical. They need to "get their feet on the ground" and be in touch with sensible reality. If they do not, they are dismissed as impractical, unbalanced, or "out of it." So too the pragmatic are chided for not being able to "see the forest for the trees" when they tend to become overly concerned with the details and lose the greater vision of life.[3]

A wise worship service planner will try to incorporate elements that touch each of the four learning styles. Churches that put total emphasis on the Analytic sermon as the central element may find the congregation filled with Analytic Learners all happily taking notes. But those who do not fit that pattern will not be comfortable with the church. The church will lose their important variety of gifts.

When Spouses Have Different Worship Styles—A Personal Illustration

(As I mentioned earlier my husband is an Imaginative Learner. I am the opposite—a Common Sense Learner.)

"How great thou art!" Singing that wonderful song made me want to laugh out loud. I looked over at my husband, and tears were running down his face.

"What's wrong?" I whispered.

"How can you sing that song and not cry?" he said.

Jack and I express our love for God in different ways. We serve God differently. This spiritual difference is a struggle-point in our marriage, but it also makes us stronger. It's helped us realize how creative our Savior is! He can take two such different people, and make both of us feel at home in His love, even though we may not feel at home in the same church, especially when worship is structured around the preferences of only one or two styles.

Jack wants a warm church, a church filled with people who hug and get together for breakfast during the week. I want a teaching church, one that puts at least as high a priority on knowing what we believe and making Christianity work as it does on interpersonal relationships. Jack sees the great vision of what Christ brings to us—the big picture. I get involved in programs, asking the practical questions.

We attend church together on Sunday. I *love* our church and our pastor. What a great preacher! I always have Post-It notes in my purse so I can write down the new ideas in his sermon. I often transcribe these on Monday and file them where I can use them.

Jack *likes* our church, but his hug quota is not being met. So to meet his needs he has joined the growing ranks of people who attend two churches. On Wednesday nights, he goes to a church where people who arrive late stop to kiss a few friends on their way to finding a seat. Love for God is expressed more emotionally at this church. Jack raises his hands as the group sings praise songs. He gets together with friends afterward to pray at the front of the church.

A wise worship planner will use elements that touch each style.

George Barna predicts in his book, *America 2000: What the Trends Mean for Christianity*, that more and more people will be multiple church attenders. They will go where their needs are met, and, as in our case, if the marriage partners have different needs and one church does not meet both sets of needs and gifts, the wise couple will find ways for both partners to grow.

The sermon is usually the part of the service where Jack and I most obviously differ. A conversation on the seven-mile drive home from church often goes something like this:

Jack: I didn't get anything out of that sermon.
Marlene: You're kidding! I bought the tape.
Jack: But it was on Hur! I never even heard of Hur.
Marlene: That's the point. Lots of Christians who serve God are almost anonymous, but like Hur, they are important to God's plan.
Jack: Another thing! When church is over, I wish you wouldn't be in such a big hurry to leave.
Marlene: I feel silly just standing around looking for people to talk to.
Jack: But that's the most important part. This morning Bob shared some real struggles. I wish you could see how important coffee time is!

Jack and I can learn a lot about God from each other when we're willing to let the other one teach. For example, I won't let him live Christianity on the feeling level alone. Content is necessary; knowing what we believe keeps us from heresy or getting involved in cult-ish or unexamined practices. On the other hand, he knows that emotions and intuition are important. Jack won't let me pile Christian fact upon Christian service upon Christian fact without understanding what it means to love and accept people for Jesus' sake.

Jack and I struggle with how to affirm each other's different needs for worship. It's all too easy to feel that my way is best and he should just conform. The following action steps have been helpful to us. They don't eliminate our struggles, but they keep us from hurting or denying the Holy Spirit's unique work in each other.

Ideas to Consider

Pastors and worship leaders may want to share these ideas with couples in the church. These practical ideas are designed to help couples who are struggling with finding ways to be at home in the same church when they have very different styles.

1. *Talk about your differences.* Laugh over them. Let your spouse know you respect his or her way of thinking, responding, worshiping.

In worship, you're meeting your Heavenly Love. Share with your earthly partner how love is exchanged between you and Jesus. Help each other understand how different and special each Christian is.

2. *Consider different churches* if one partner is not satisfied or growing. It's possible that a church has such a strong emphasis on one type of worship that people who worship differently will never feel comfortable. For the left-out partner, Sunday worship becomes a tribulation to be endured.

Parents with children have an additional consideration. Many decide that their children's needs for learning and worshiping are more important than their own. If a church's Christian education program appeals to the children, adults may put their preferences for corporate worship on hold. My parents did this for me. I needed a strong youth group that was involved in lots of projects, so my parents picked a church that had that feature. The Sunday I left home for college, they went to a new church that was more satisfying to them. To their credit, they never let me know about this gift until I no longer needed it.

3. *Support your church.* First, and easiest, support with money. Jack and I tithe at our Sunday church, and he gives special gifts to his Wednesday night church. But often our worship style will determine how we support in service. He helps set up men's sharing groups. I have a postcard ministry to shut-ins. He plans hospitality events in our church and home. I enjoy teaching elective classes and teacher training. But in each of our activities, the other affirms. My ability to teach is not more highly honored than his ability to make others feel the love of Christ.

After twenty years of marriage, we've found a better way.

4. *Encourage your spouse's spiritual disciplines.* Jack and I can't study the Bible together. We've tried and it doesn't work. We learn and respond in totally different ways. After bouts of Bible study, we'd end up feeling decidedly uncoupled.

After twenty years of marriage, we've found a better way. We support each other's individual growth in spiritual disciplines and private worship. For example, almost every spring Jack goes on a prayer retreat for a week. My response to this trip used to be (and sometimes still is), "Hey, if you've got the money for a retreat, you could use it to take me on vacation. Instead, you leave me alone, and . . ."

Every year it's hard to see him go, but I know that his retreat conversation with God makes a year-long difference to him. His spiritual mountaintop is not mine, but that doesn't make it wrong. Just different. As a Christian couple we become stronger together when as

Christ's children, we nurture our differences.

God can be worshipped in spirit and in truth, and that worship can involve talk, songs, upraised hands, laughter, tears, hugs, cooking, and even a long, well-crafted sermon!

Worship Talk

The following five sentences are discussion starters. They can be used in a number of ways. A pastor could print them in a bulletin insert to gain valuable information about the congregation. Worship committees might discuss them and use the results to make sure someone from each learning style quadrant is included on the committee to represent all those in the congregation who have strengths in that style. Couples and parents with teens may also find it helpful to build a discussion around them.

1. I feel closest to God when I'm . . .
   - ❑ singing hymns.
   - ❑ listening to the sermon.
   - ❑ participating in communion.
   - ❑ doing Christian service.
   - ❑ Other ___________________________

2. Which of the following worship activities is easiest for me? Which do I enjoy most?
   - ❑ Prayer in small group.
   - ❑ Prayer by myself.
   - ❑ Bible study in a small group.
   - ❑ Daily devotions.
   - ❑ Sharing my faith with a friend.

3. The thing I like best about our church is:
   - ❑ My friends.
   - ❑ Sunday morning service.
   - ❑ Sunday school, youth group, or small group.
   - ❑ The pastor.

4. Which of the following gifts would I most enjoy giving to Jesus?
   - ❑ Four hours of praise.
   - ❑ Four hours of in-depth Bible study of praise passages.
   - ❑ Four hours of really messy clean-up around the church.
   - ❑ Four hours of sharing Jesus with a suicidal friend.

5. If we changed churches, I would want our new church to put the most value on:
   - ❑ Christian education.

❑ Small groups.
❑ Spiritual gifts.
❑ Hospitality.
❑ Preaching.

Ideas: Reach All Worshipers

Pastors, worship committee members, and others in the congregation involved in structuring the worship service will find the following idea-starters helpful. They are designed to encourage churches to incorporate people with very different learning styles into the church's praise and worship of God.

Imaginative

- Make certain there is a time to touch in every service. Not everyone will welcome this touching. Annie Dillard tells about a New York congregation that fired its minister because he insisted on their "passing the peace" which in liturgical churches involves shaking hands with people sitting around you in the worship service. The church fired the man because they were unable to adjust to touching others.
- Invest in banners. Change them several times a year.
- Encourage a bulletin board committee to keep the foyer or narthex inviting and unpredictable.
- Publish activities that are open to everyone, with directions on how to get to homes where they will be held.
- Plan two or three greeters, in addition to ushers, to welcome everyone—not just new people.
- Provide time and space for a coffee hour after every service, structuring it briefly by suggesting people talk to each other about a specific topic. For example, talk with one or two people about a time when God's presence was evident to you this week.

Analytic

- Include quotes in sermons from books that would stimulate growth. Then make those books available.
- Provide written outlines of sermons. A mother shared:

> My teenage daughter has a three-by-five card taped to her bathroom mirror: "I Am God's Servant. What Will He Have Me Do Today?" Our pastor tossed out that question before concluding his sermon. He wouldn't let us leave his sermon in the pulpit. In the form of a specific question for us to wrestle with, he sent it with us to our homes and work places.
>
> Bulletin inserts with sermon fill-in-the-blank outlines transform my junior high son from a mere spectator into an active listener. (Pencils are stationed beside hymnals in the pew racks.) The outlines also can be referred to during the week or compiled in a notebook for future reference.[4]

- Plan sermons that have a beginning, middle, and an end. If you can't put the message of the sermon into a single sentence, you probably aren't clear enough about what you want to say.
- Provide background information in a bulletin insert about the form of worship or church theology.
- Plan songs that fit with the worship aim, and if helpful give background information on the songs.
- Encourage people to read the pastor's text for next Sunday as part of this week's Bible study. People will be ready to hear the sermon in a deeper way.
- Set up a "study book" lending library for people who want to read serious theological books.

Try something from another worship tradition.

Common Sense

- Never end a sermon without providing ways people can get involved with its challenge.
- Provide quiet time, even in the middle of a sermon, during which people think about how what is being said applies to them.
- Provide opportunities for people to move during the service—kneeling, raising hands, standing, bowing heads. In *Celebration of Discipline,* Richard Foster wrote, "God calls for worship that involves our whole being. The body, mind, spirit, and emotions should all be laid on the altar of worship. Often we have forgotten that worship should include the body as well as the mind and spirit."
- Find a way to identify visitors without embarrassing them. One church has all regular attenders stand up so those still seated can see who knows about the church and who can answer questions.
- Find ways to affirm those who serve the church through physical labor.

Dynamic

- Encourage people to come to church ten minutes early and spend time praying that God's presence will be felt throughout the service.
- Aim for excellence in music. Occasionally include some radically different type of Christian music.
- Don't always do things in exactly the same way every Sunday. Vary the pattern and capture the Dynamic's attention. Any change is helpful.

Dynamics will enjoy what is different; however, many in the congregation will find it suspect. Avoid some of the pitfalls by staying away from theatrics or the unusual just for the sake of innovation, suggests Rev. David R. Mains, Director of Chapel of the Air. Don't push the congregation too far too fast. Pastors beg for trouble when they insist on pushing beyond the acceptance level of most members. Always begin where they are and build involvement and acceptance as congregational tolerance changes. Use small, pleasant surprises. Don't try to be shocking.[5]

"God sat next to me at today's worship."

For some churches who have not encouraged Dynamic Learners, they may find coming up with something new very difficult. As the quip goes, they've been doing exactly the same thing for years, long before the Dead Sea became sick. Pastors in this predicament might consider the ploy used by a businessman to encourage change. Every few years he "dies." He sends out a memo and formally announces his death. This is his way of forcing the company to rethinking everything. Employees—and parishioners—resist change, but this wise leader moves them away from the old way of doing things by saying, "That was the way things were done by the last, late president. He's dead. Now, how shall we proceed?"

- Add the element of surprise to worship. "God sat next to me at today's worship," a young woman told me after a creative worship service. "I never felt Him so near."
- Provide means for anonymous feedback on the worship, possibly a suggestion box.
- Consider different ways to present Scripture. For example, choral reading, a person "signing" along with the spoken words, men and women on left and right sides taking turns.
- Try something from another worship tradition. For example, after the hymn of praise encourage people to give God a praise offering—clapping in joy that He allows us to worship Him.
- Try a short dramatic reading or a mime.[6]

Assignment

Seekers are attracted to churches that meet their needs or that speak directly to their interests. If they are lonely and the church offers friends, they may come and meet the Greatest Friend. If they have always felt that Christianity is for people who need others to do their thinking for them, they may be attracted to the scholar-preacher or Christian education classes that deal with tough issues. Not all our approaches to announce to our market areas that we are open for business will reach all people. So we must plan a variety of approaches, becoming all things to all people so that all have an opportunity to hear the Gospel.

A few years ago, David C. Cook Church Ministries, a publisher of curriculum and other products for the church, did a mailing to youth leaders based on their learning style preference. The letter explained a little about the four basic learning styles and encouraged each leader to choose the response to the mailing that felt most right to him or her.

The Imaginative Learners were told to call an 800 number that would allow them to talk to a Christian education consultant about the benefits of these products to their program. They could also, the letter suggested, have a representative visit their church.

The Analytic Learners were given an address to write for an annotated bibliography on learning styles and how these findings could be applied to their ministry. They would also get samples of the product and a study sheet to guide them through it.

The Common Sense Learners could send for samples that they could use with their teens to check if this new material was really everything the company's advertising said it was.

The Dynamic Learners were encouraged to tell the company how they would like to be exposed to the youth materials. It would follow their lead. Use this mailing as an idea-starter. How could you structure a mailing from your church that would attract a variety of people to your place of worship?

Learning Styles Help You Reach Your Church Community

Some Christians know more about the trees that grow in their church neighborhoods than they know about the people who live behind those trees. The following ideas just might get you past the foliage and into people's homes. No one idea is right for everyone, of course. You might want to start with the ideas in the quadrants where you suspect your church is most lacking. Remember that the best idea is always that idea you come up with. Here are several in each quadrant to get you started.

Imaginatives in Our Church Neighborhood

- Plan a neighborhood picnic—no service, just free food. Encourage people to come and get to know you. You may want to give a walking tour through the church. Sometimes people are afraid to come to our churches because everything about them is unfamiliar. This example comes from Debbie Hill, Anchorage, Alaska.

> My pastor husband teaches a class for people who are just getting interested in the church. Part of the class is a church tour. "Why does your church have a Jacuzzi?" a young woman asked.
>
> "That's for baptism."
>
> "Oh," said the woman. Then came her next question. "What's baptism?" Christian education for today's adults!

- In a mailing, highlight the interpersonal relationship programs the church offers.
- In radio spots, have people share twenty-second testimonials on why they love your church.
- Plan a person-to-person phone or walking canvas of the neighborhood.

Analytics in Our Church Neighborhood

- Introduce your pastor in a mailing by giving credentials and background.
- Open your church library to people who would like to investigate Christianity.

- Plan church panels and debates on topics of Christian and neighborhood interest, and use the newspaper to advertise the event.

Common Sense People in Our Church Neighborhood

- Add how-to classes to the Christian education program and hold those classes in homes or neutral places. The following happened to Carson Pue in Vancouver, British Columbia.

> "So the pagan's selling the preacher!" Greg was a tough, foul-mouthed, award-winning real estate agent who got stuck selling my wife and me a house. He took a lot of ribbing from the other agents who figured he must be in pain spending hours with a dour, sour preacher. Instead we were having the time of our lives, laughing and building a friendship that continued after he sold us our house.
>
> I invited him to an adult Sunday school class I was teaching at a five-star hotel in our area. People who wouldn't come near a church building would show up at a hotel. My topic, "Why baby boomers find it difficult to believe," and the neutral location drew him in and kept him coming.
>
> About a year later, I asked him to introduce me to a new class I was starting. He did, and to my surprise he added that he'd become a Christian.
>
> That real estate agent had bought the idea of a heavenly home!

- Offer church news stories to the local newspaper. Include black and white action shots.

Dynamics in Our Church Neighborhood

- Bring in a drama or liturgical dance troop and invite the neighborhood.
- Offer free tickets to a Christian music concert where the music might not fit the world's stereotype of Christian music.
- Plan the most creative float for the town's parade.

Church Staff

Lyle E. Schaller suggests that harmony may not be the highest goal in building a church staff. He uses the metaphor of an orchestra: "Which is the higher priority, a superb performance or a happy and compatible collection of musicians?" A mature pastor may find "himself placing the superb performance higher on his priority list than the happy and mutually supportive team."[7]

A vibrant staff should have the strengths of each learning style. Consider a successful beehive. It takes all kinds. Some bees fly around and find new sources of pollen. Others in a well-ordered, controlled fashion bring the pollen back. Without all groups, there would be no honeycomb.

The more secure the senior pastor, the more likely that the staff will include people who are dissimilar from him or her. It is often easier to hire people who "think like I do" but who are just a little less experienced. These people make the boss feel good, and often the relationship they have is a comfortable one. Yet the church programs and services will have blind spots in them, if, for example, there is no Imaginative leader who is "out there" loving people into the sanctuary.

The same mix should be considered when church leaders look for people to fill committees. Leaders should find fully qualified people who are not all the same style. Those mixed groups will have a more difficult time working together than people who are all one style. But the results will be more rounded, and more people will feel at home in the church family.

Fill committees with qualified people of different styles.

Assignment: The Four Little Pigs—A Church Committee Tool

Read the following story of the Four Little Pigs as a parable of what often happens in the church. Act it out at your next board or church committee meeting and discuss whether it reflects what is happening at your church.

(The pig numbers reflect the four different styles: 1—Imaginative; 2—Analytic; 3—Common Sense; 4—Dynamic.)

The Four Little Pigs[8]

Once there were four little pigs who, as pigs have always done, wanted to wolf-proof their homes. They got together to build the best possible structure. This is the story of how the Four Little Pigs became the Three Little Pigs.

Pig 1: How is everyone today? How do you feel anyway? Is everybody okay? I just love this idea about the four of us building a house together.

Pig 2: Right. Speaking of the house, let's get to the point. We're behind schedule. Now where's that list? I believe we are in phase two of the initial planning stage. Yes, it's all right here . . .

Pig 3: Hogwash. Forget the list. Let's get on with it. Talk's cheap. We need to see some actual construction around here.

Pig 4: Now there's an idea! We could get started building! Or, maybe we should look around for some investment property. I saw a nice little piece of property down by the river. Water access on one whole side of the house. That would keep the old wolf thinking!

Pig 1: Speaking of the wolf. You know, I still say we could save a lot of hard feelings in the end if we would just sit down and meet with the wolf in person. I have this feeling that the wolf is probably not all that bad deep down inside. We just need to try to see things from his perspective. Being a wolf has a lot of hardship connected with it and I don't see why we don't . . .

Pig 2: Cut it. We're off the subject. The next item on the schedule is to discuss actual building materials. I have the list right here.

Pig 4: Did we remember to add all that extra stuff for the turrets? I really like turrets in a house. And what about bay windows? I think we should consider bay windows. Are they on the list?

Pig 3: Turrets are out. Entirely impractical. And bay windows would provide easy access for the wolf. Anyway, we've already decided what we need. In fact, I have actually picked up most of the stuff on the list. It was on sale. We got a good deal on it. I got brown tile instead of red. Easier to clean. I knew that as soon as I saw it.

Pig 2: Hold on. You mean you bought things that we didn't approve? You mean you changed the list?

Pig 3: Just staying on top of things.

Pig 2: Things are getting out of hand. I don't think I can continue with the house project in light of this recent insubordination.

Pig 4: I'm not sure I'm still in either. I don't completely buy leaving off the turrets. But maybe there's still hope if we consider a moat. What does everyone think about a moat?

Pig 1: I think we'd all feel a lot better if we'd just arrange to meet with the wolf. I just know he'd be sympathetic to our situation.

Pig 3: Forget it. I'm out. Too much talk. Not enough action. I've got the stuff I need. I'm building my own house.

Pig 4: So be it. I'm off to the realtor.

Pig 1: Well then, I guess I'll just have to go see the wolf myself. I'm sure he'll be understanding.

Discussion questions to get you started:

- What strengths does each pig bring?
- What is lost when each pig leaves the project?
- What kinds of little pigs do we have in church leadership? How is this a strength? Weakness?
- If we take this parable seriously, what changes might we make in church, board, committee, and volunteer leadership?

Notes

1. Peter Ainslie, "Personality Type and the Spiritual Life," *The Christian Ministry*, May/June 1989, p. 23.

2. Gordon MacDonald, "What's Your Worship Style?" *Discipleship Journal*, Issue 70, 1992, p. 32.

3. Suzanne M. deBenedittis, *Teaching Faith and Morals—Toward Personal and Parish Renewal* (Minneapolis, Minn.: Winston, 1981), p. 32.

4. Naomi Gaede Penner, "Sermon Variations That Made an Impression," *Leadership*, Spring 1990, p. 117.

5. Circle Church, an inner-city church that pioneered in experimental worship in the 1960s and 1970s, was excellent at finding the balance between what was new and

effective and what was new and shocking. Two examples from the ministry headed by David and Karen Mains:

(1) Once David was preaching about how we are the aroma of Christ—the smell of death to those perishing and the smell of life to those who are being saved. Clipped inside each bulletin was a perfume sampler that had been donated by a local department store. Everyone was asked to open their sampler at the same time. An incredibly beautiful smell arose from the congregation. David explained that Christians smell this sweet to God. (2) One Easter, the worship planners brought out carts of food from the Middle East—cheese, grapes, bread, and grape juice for wine. People formed into small groups, ate, and talked about the Risen Christ—what His resurrection meant to each of us. The celebration lasted for twenty minutes.

David Mains wrote about his own preaching: "I sometimes added a sensory appeal. Worship means attributing worth to God. It's possible to do that in ways other than hearing. Sight, touch, taste, and smell can also help worshippers experience the delightful presence of the Lord. Appealing to additional senses enhances the meaning of the worship experience." From "Sensory Worship Experiences," *Innovations*, Fall 1984, p. 9.

6. Analytics will have the most trouble with drama in the church. "I am more comfortable in the safe modes of academic endeavor, among the papers and the exams—it is a hard thing to be creatively dramatic. It beings tears to the eyes sometimes, and feelings of tightness and embarrassment at unaccustomed actions in sight of others. What are they going to think? Worse yet, what am I going to think of myself when I realize that all these unexplored possibilities are dormant in me? How hard it is to trust the flow that pulses in and through us." Quoted in "A Model for Aesthetic Education" in *Aesthetic Dimension of Religious Education*, edited by Gloria Durka and Joanmarie Smith (New York: Paulist Press, 1979), p. 146, and reprinted by Maria Harris in "Art and Religious Educaton," *Religious Education Journal*, Summer 1988.

7. Lyle E. Schaller, *The Senior Minister* (Nashville, Tenn.: Abingdon, 1988).

8. "The Four Little Pigs" by Mo Sanders, Staff Development Coodinator, Kenai Peninsula Borough School District. Used by permission of Excel, Inc.

17

Learning Styles: Loving Your Spouse and Children the Way God Made Them —Not the Way You Wish He Had Made Them

You married the woman because of all the things you find annoying about her, not in spite of them. If you'd have wanted someone more comprehensible, you'd have married yourself.
—Stanley Bing

One of the most important gifts we can bring to our Christian education assignments is our modelling of a working marriage and a working family. Knowing about learning styles can help us affirm the differences in our own families. Knowledge leads to celebrating differences, rather than squelching them.

Although this chapter talks specifically to married people, it could be very important to Christian volunteers who never married or never had children of their own. It provides clues that will help all teachers give wise council and advice to people who are looking for help with their marriages and children.

One father from Lancaster, Pennsylvania, was asked by his preschool son, "Daddy, how did you learn to be a man?" After thinking a minute the father replied, "My Sunday school teacher showed me."

God uses married women and single women, single men and married men to lay the foundation on which many children will later build their own Christian families.

Missy has surely played this role in the lives of many little children. This Springfield, Oregon, woman is eighty-seven and for the last seventy-nine years without a break, she has been teaching the four-year-old Sunday school class. She began when she was eight and was asked to baby-sit until the "real" teacher showed up. She's been there ever since. "It didn't take me very long to realize that you don't just baby-sit four-year-olds. You can teach them," she said. While she never married or had children of her own, only God knows what a difference her faithfulness has made in the lives of eight decades of little children.

Learning style preferences do effect marriages. Over 80 percent of us marry our opposite styles.

Imaginative and Common Sense Learners are opposites. So are Analytic and Dynamic. We are attracted to others in the dating process who think and respond to life in ways that intrigue us. He can fix things and make them work. She is a people person who makes parties fun. He is an abstract thinker who can come up with unique concepts she never dreamed of. She on the other hand is willing to do the craziest things, and is always tackling what no one else will dare.

Amy Grant said about her marriage:

> When Gary and I were having struggles, I remember looking at my mom and saying, "Don't you agree that this is the worst thing I've ever done?" And my mom just sat with me and said, "No, but these are hard times." I think the things you love about someone at first eventually drive you crazy. And the qualities you really come to appreciate in your mate are the ones that you only see after ten years of marriage.[1]

Connie Barrans, a special education teacher, and her husband Peter Barrans, a vice principal, from Scarborough, Ontario, wrote about their marriage.

> Couples marry out of the strong bond that unites them. They have many similarities and differences that complement their lives. Compatibility for each other is not just a passive role but an active participation in the relationship. Learning style has given our marriage new life. Instead of tolerating our differences, we now understand the diversities that make up our strengths and preferences. . . . Awareness of each other's style has increased our mutual dependence and sharing of strengths. Learning style has brought new meaning to the word compromise; instead of giving up, we give.[2]

OPPOSITES ATTRACT

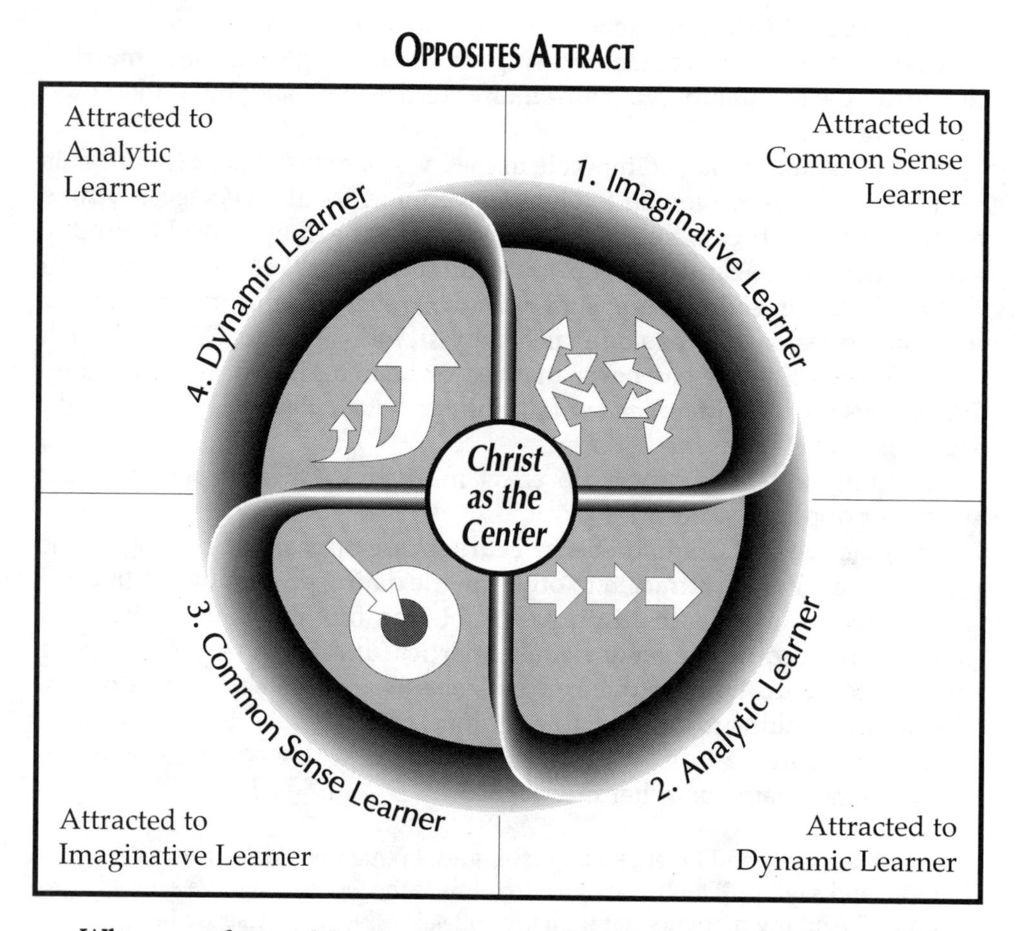

When couples with such different styles have children, those children may prefer styles that neither parent understands. In a family of four, all four styles may or may not be represented. In my family, for example, my father is Analytic, my mother Dynamic, and both my brother and I are Common Sense.

HUSBANDS AND WIVES—DISCOVERING YOUR STYLES

From the information in previous chapters, you can make an educated guess about the preferred style of your spouse and your children. Remember that no one falls completely into one quadrant, although many people have a strong, easily identifiable preference. But if you're not sure, try the following quiz.

You Say To-MAY-toe, I Say To-MAH-toe

The following questions are meant to be fun. Discuss them together (or make them available to couples in your church). They may help you place yourself and your spouse into your strength areas.

1. My idea of a great date is to:
   A. Throw a party. (Imaginative)
   B. Go to an art film. (Analytic)
   C. Play baseball. (Common Sense)
   D. Take a balloon ride. (Dynamic)
2. My reaction to finding out we're going to have our first baby might be to:
   A. Call all my friends and tell them the good news. (Imaginative)
   B. Check out every book on parenting from the library. (Analytic)
   C. Build a cradle. (Common Sense)
   D. Sign the baby and myself up for a telephone talk show visit on her twelfth birthday. (Dynamic)
3. My basic attitude toward money is:
   A. Make people happy with it. (Imaginative)
   B. Make it work for us. (Analytic)
   C. Sensibly save. (Common Sense)
   D. Money is for spending. (Dynamic)
4. My vacation ideas include:
   A. Going places with my friends or to visit friends. (Imaginative)
   B. Visiting places we've never been and learning about them. (Analytic)
   C. Going somewhere to participate in the sports action. (Common Sense)
   D. Heading east. We've never gone east before. (Dynamic)[3]
5. When I look for a place to sit in church, I:
   A. Sit where I do because it's with people I enjoy. (Imaginative)
   B. Choose my favorite pew. (Analytic)
   C. Sit where I can get out as soon as the service ends. (Common Sense)
   D. Sit in a different place each week, trying to find where the sermon is the shortest. (Dynamic)
6. When I fight with my spouse, I say:
   A. "You hurt me. You made me feel worthless and stupid." (Imaginative)
   B. "You're not being logical. If you would just listen to me, you could get it right." (Analytic)
   C. "You're not making sense." (Common Sense)
   D. "Okay, let's just look at this from another perspective." (Dynamic)
7. In organizing our family budget, I would:
   A. Make coffee. This would be a great time of togetherness as we plan for the future. (Imaginative)
   B. Plan exactly what we need for the kids' college and retirement and

work back from there. (Analytic)

C. Buy a budget book and record everything we've spent over the last year so we can develop a workable budget. (Common Sense)

D. Budget? What's a budget? (Dynamic)

8. In picking a church to attend, the most important thing to consider is:

A. The friendliness of the congregation. (Imaginative)

B. The correctness of the theology. (Analytic)

C. The Christian service in which I can get involved. (Common Sense)

D. The uniqueness of the ministry. (Dynamic)

Based on the choices I've made so far, I suspect:
My preferred style is: ______________
My spouse's preferred style is: ______________

Learning Styles and That Man God Gave Me: A Personal Illustration

Let me demonstrate how learning styles work in a marriage by sharing how my husband Jack and I realized that we had different learning styles. We see life differently and respond differently to what we see. When we began to understand how each of our minds worked, we realized that unless we could appreciate and affirm each other's difference, our marriage wouldn't work.

Several years ago, the magazine *Today's Christian Woman*,[4] asked a number of people who had been involved in the magazine over its first ten years to write short articles about what had been the most significant thing that had happened to him or her during that decade. Together Jack and I decided that discovering the differences in learning styles was our answer. It may not seem major at first, but it helped us learn to communicate more effectively, and that is a big deal. It made us better Sunday school teachers. It helped us affirm each other's very different talents and gifts.

I remember the day Jack threw his pencil across the table, banged the Bible shut, and announced that studying together was bad for our marriage. I agreed. We just didn't think the same way. I'd be doing the word studies and working on a life response problem and he'd be staring out the window, smiling.

"Hey, we're supposed to be studying the Bible." I'd give a wifely tap on his workbook where he ought to be recording his conclusions.

"I am," he'd say, his eyes focused somewhere out there. "Do you think these paragraphs could be painted using all new symbols? I think color is easier to understand than words."

Jack first attracted me because he didn't think or react to situations the way I did. From my perspective, he was intriguingly weird. It was one of the reasons I married him. Yet I spent the first years of our marriage trying to get him to be more like me—to do things the "right way"—my way!

My changing-Jack agenda began on our honeymoon. This unique human being started talking about his high school years and how he had hated English. "All those word constructions," he said with a laugh. "I'd rather talk English than write it. Adjectives are only fun when you can get someone to react when you use them."

How could he feel that way? English was my favorite subject because it made so much sense; I used it every day. Deciding to teach him to think right about English, I spent the better part of two days trying to give him the thrill of diagraming a sentence in the Mexican sands. He put up with my fervor as long as he could also work on his tan and take frequent swimming breaks. Instead of enjoying his mind, I tried to change it.

The attraction became the frustration.

The very things that attracted me to him became the things that most frustrated me.

I loved his artistic nature. "What do you mean you want to paint our house purple?" I'd sputter. "What about the resale value?"

I loved his creative flair. "You spent big bucks on real crab for your friend's party? That's awful." I'd wave the checkbook and assume my hungriest poverty-stricken look. "What's wrong with imitation crab? No one but you would know the difference."

I loved his genuine concern for people. "How can you spend all night listening to Ray?" I'd felt neglected. "It's a waste of time. He doesn't need a listening ear, he needs a cork."

The frustrations over differences worked both ways.

He loved my organizational skills. "You didn't have to orchestrate every minute at dinner. It's okay to have an empty space." He'd smile to lessen his resentment. "You sounded like a canary in overdrive."

He loved it when people thought I was smart. "Why do you have to study so much? You'll go blind."

He loved my excitement about things to be done at church. "I've got a revolutionary idea," he'd finally yelp. "Why don't you let the church form a committee that doesn't include you?"

God placed us together. We never doubted that. But to make the togetherness work, we had to accept our differences. Jack doesn't think wrongly. He thinks differently.

Our two biggest achievements this last decade were learning to affirm the way each other thinks and to grow by modeling each other's strengths.

Paul Pearsall, author of *The Ten Laws of Lasting Love* (Simon & Schuster) which is based on his twenty-five years of counseling couples, said, "Men and women have fundamental differences, and couples need to celebrate that. For instance, men *do*, women *feel*. A woman tells a man she's sad, and he tells her he'll wash her car for her. She has to realize that washing her car is his way of expressing love."[5] Learning styles show us that sometimes the roles are reversed—men *feel* and women *do*—but Pearsall's basic idea is right. We marry people who are quite dissimilar from ourselves and our love has a better chance of prospering if we see these differences as part of God's plan, when we celebrate God's smartness in matching us in these ways.

Team teaching Sunday school illustrated to my husband and me how much more effective in God's service we were as a team than we ever would have been as individual teachers. I love teaching, so I would prepare the lesson and spend hours collecting the materials. Much time and planning went into every lesson. Jack, meanwhile, would pray for the kids. He would sit in class and simply exude niceness while I interacted with the teens. When they had a question about their faith, they came to me. When they had personal hurts and their worlds fell apart, they would go to Jack. He would love them and hug away some of the pain.

I resented that. I did all the "real" work and he was the part of the team that the class loved. I'd find myself secretly competing to prove to myself that I could be as nice as Jack.

It took a long time before I saw God's genius in teaming Jack and me.

It took a long time before I saw God's genius in teaming Jack and me. Those kids needed the practical Christian teaching I had to give them. They needed to understand the faith they were struggling to live. But they also needed the prayers and hugs that came so naturally to Jack.

It's not that I can't sit still long enough to pray for the kids or form my arms into a decent circle and squeeze, but those things don't come naturally. I have to announce to my mind, "This child needs to feel loved. Perhaps through my caring she will see beyond me to my Lord who loves her unconditionally. So stop being so self-conscious and hug her."

It's not that Jack can't hit the books and construct a logical explanation for baptism, but it doesn't come naturally. In that area, he sweats and I glow.[6]

Following Jack's example, I've grown as a people lover. Jack exudes people-love. A homeless person can be walking down the block and on the opposite side of the street and pick out Jack as an easy mark. The person will ignore everyone else and head straight for him. "Quarter for a cup of coffee?" Jack always gives it. From my perspective he should never give money to someone like that. "He'll just drink it," I announce with my middle-class logic. "You're contributing to the problem."

"What he does with the money is his concern," Jack explains every time. "How I respond to him is what God holds me accountable for."

Jack's love knows no bounds. Behind the train tracks, a small shanty town has evolved. Cardboard and abandoned cars, metal sheets and unpainted boards press against each other to form shelters. Jack parks his car near there on his frequent trips to that part of the city. He got into the habit of waving to a man who sat outside one hovel balancing himself on a three-legged chair. Sometimes they would talk—weather, food, city politics—the same kind of stuff you'd talk about with your friends. One day he gave the man a five-dollar bill and thanked him for always being there to smile and wave. I ranted and raved. "The guy always makes me feel good," Jack explained. "I wanted him to know I appreciated him."

I will probably never show people love in the automatic way Jack does. For one thing, it wouldn't be as safe for a woman to do some of the things Jack does. But for another, he's not me. I want his strong points to rub off on me while I still keep working on my own. Because I have watched and admired Jack, I can work with people more easily than I used to. I can work at helping people feel comfortable around me. I can model Jack and be a better conversationalist and small group member. Jack shows me how Jesus would act in situations where I wouldn't be as aware of His presence.

One afternoon, I went to pick up the car in a parking lot, and a man on the street asked me for a quarter. Jack must be rubbing off, I thought. There were other people around, but this man specifically picked me. I felt as if I had passed a test.

"Here are three dollars to get yourself some bacon and eggs, too," I said. The man looked at me in amazement, grinned and sputtered, "Hey, lady, where are you from?"

Some of my good learning patterns have rubbed off on Jack, too. He's getting a little more organized. He's developed a love for some books without pictures, and he can now share his faith aloud in front of a group.

For us, our different learning styles have been a life-changing discovery. God made both of us right. Those two minds can work together in different ways to do more for Christ than either of us could do alone.

Children's Styles[7]

Discovering how each child in your family learns and responds will help you build a healthier, more productive family. Or, if you're a teacher or church leader, share this information with families who are part of your ministry.

Affirm Your Family's Strengths

Sometimes parents find it difficult to accept their children's differences and strengths. What mechanically inclined father understands his bookworm son? What quiet, sophisticated mother totally relates to an attention-seeking, free-wheeling daughter? But acceptance is imperative to successful child and family development.

Joshua was one of four boys in his family, and a member of my Sunday school class. All the boys followed in their father's footsteps as football players. One Sunday, however, Joshua shared that he wanted to drop football so he could be in the school operetta. How, he asked the class, should he approach this with his father? The class prayed and the next week Josh's report proved how very wise that father was. "I will support you in whatever you decide. I have a son, not a football player," he said. That man showed up for all three performances and the dress rehearsal. The boy continued to pursue the arts and is now a Christian filmmaker. Who knows what Joshua's future would have held if he had been "forced" into becoming someone he didn't want to be.

Replace the Negative with Positive

The school system usually affirms the Analytic student. Those who do not fit the Analytic pattern may be given negative labels that they accept as true. How long, for example, does it take for a child to know that the Wren Reading Group isn't as prestigious as the Robin Reading Group?

But concerned parents can make the difference. One mother shared that she rewarded her daughter with a dollar for every "A" on her report card. Her son was smart, but not school smart. He got a dollar for every course he passed. "My daughter used to complain about how unfair this arrangement was. It doesn't mean that I love him more. Both children are equally intelligent, but school was made for people who learn the way she does. School teachers didn't teach the way my son's mind works best."

Christian education systems exist to serve children.

When you determine what learning style is strongest in your child, work with the school to capture that strength. If your daughter would get much better grades if she could talk through her tests, find out if that is possible. If your son needs hands-on work in order to understand, encourage his teachers to structure homework assignments that allow him to use his strength.

School systems and Christian education systems exist to serve our children. As a parent, you need to make sure your children's strengths don't get missed, because if they do, children may limit themselves for the rest of their lives.

Provide Same-Style Role Models

"When I think of a real role model, I think of my church club leader," said Phillip. "He knew how to set up tents and shoot cans on fence posts. My own father was afraid of bugs. His idea of roughing it was to stop at a motel without a reservation."

Wise parents encourage friendships between their children and Christian adults with whom they can relate. This is especially true during adolescence. Children will pick mentors—and it is important that they have adults who can help them develop in ways that may be foreign to their parents.

Family Devotions with Style[8]

Spiritual growth experiences can be planned around the learning styles of your students.

For the Imaginative Learner

Plan growth activities that involve the whole family talking together.

- Dig through family picture albums and tell stories about people who were Christians.
- Act out the story from the Bible.
- Work together to draw one symbolic picture of how each family member feels about living for Christ on the job (children's jobs would be school).
- Memorize Scripture together—an activity that will not come easily to these children. Sit family members two by two facing each other. As they say the verse, make up a hand rhythm to do in time to the words. For example: clap, clap, snap, snap, hands together twice, repeat.

For the Analytic Learner

These children will want you to do most of the talking, but make certain you are telling them something new, something they can think about. Eric, a first grader, likes to listen to his mother tell the Bible story in order—first things first. If she forgets something and adds it to the story later, he doesn't like the story as well. Knowing the content helps him grow spiritually.

Here are some activities that children like Eric would enjoy.

- When you tell or read a story about Jesus, encourage children to write a list of words that help explain what Jesus is like. They can only pick words that can be shown to be true through the story you are telling.
- Play Bible tic-tac-toe. Ask children questions and when they answer correctly they get to place their X or O.
- Ask children to read the Bible verse to themselves and then make a list of ways they have seen people live, or not live, this verse.
- Practice reading the Scripture together and talking about what the passage means. Students in fourth grade and beyond may enjoy a map or key word study.

For the Common Sense Learner

These children enjoy using their hands to build things that share what they are learning about God. Amanda falls into this group. "I don't like Bible club," she told her mother. When her mother questioned her, she realized that Amanda was saying that the club program didn't include anything that was exciting to her. She felt different and left out because none of the activities allowed her and her special learning abilities to shine. Her mother made a daily effort to prove to Amanda that God made her mind different—not wrong.

Some activities that would appeal to a child like Amanda are . . .

- Teach while you work together on a service project—perhaps washing the church windows or cooking a turkey for a large family who don't have an oven.
- Go on nature walks around your house, especially in the winter season. Pick up things that illustrate God's creation. Spend an hour building a collage of what the children found.
- Encourage a child to develop a computer game that will help others learn the truths about Jesus' life.
- Work with the child to draw a maze worksheet. At the middle, put a Bible verse that the family is learning. At each of the dead ends, draw signs that tell some of the things that keep us from obeying the verse.

For the Dynamic Learner

These children will want to start with the parent's idea and grow that idea into something uniquely their own.

- Write and put on a play that tells others about God's love. Videotape it. Invite another family over for pizza and to see the video.
- Make a list of ways people in the neighborhood might know this family is Christian even though the neighbors haven't talked about "religion."
- Have each family member share how he or she feels about Jesus by using only motions—no words.
- Provide some unique materials such as clay, Popsicle sticks, and plastic flowers. Have children come up with ways to use these items in service projects or even as ways to help them memorize Scripture verses.

Family Camping

Camp can be a life-changing experience. The whole body gets involved in learning new things in a new setting, and when that happens, the camper will have those peak experiences that combine head knowledge and heart knowledge.[9] Peak experiences can change the direction of a camper's life forever. These can have a long-term, life-changing effect on children.[10] What a perfect place to encourage children's spiritual growth.

"My father used to make us sit around the campfire and listen to him read a chapter or two from the Bible," an older teen said. "I hated camp devotions. The bugs would bite and he would read on and on. If I ever have kids and take them on a camping trip, you'd better believe I'll leave Sunday school at home."

Good idea. Leave Sunday school at home. Bad idea, if it means this some-day-father won't make use of his environment to help teach his youngsters.

Camping is a great place to try creative things that would be impossible in a living room. Parents can structure spiritual growth occasions that target their child's strongest learning style.

The best ideas are those that parents come up with for themselves, but to get parents thinking, here are some suggestions.[11]

Camping with an Imaginative Child

Imaginative children love colorful learning atmospheres, so the out-of-doors is perfect for them.

- God Made Me and Said, "Hey, Be My Friend!"
- Text: John 3:16-21.

Give everyone in the family several minutes to collect things in nature that are colorful—yellow, red, brown, white, black, green, etc. Then read the Bible text and stop to ask questions that can only be answered with colors that they have picked. Encourage each person to share why.

The best ideas are those that parents come up with for themselves.

Here are some color ideas.

1. Pick a color that represents someone who believes everything in these verses. Share why you picked the color you did.
2. What color would you pick for a person who just couldn't believe the good news of these verses? What things might this person doubt? What answers do you have for these doubts?
3. Pick your favorite verse from these six verses. What color is the verse?

This is a familiar passage, but the color study will be different for everyone in the family. The colors will help everyone look at content in new ways.

Camping with an Analytic Child

Even in the wilderness, this child will be happiest with a mind-expanding, content-based study. Try a simple inductive Bible study.

- God Made Me and Said, "Hey, Very Good!"
- Text: Genesis 1:27, 28

Clear a patch of dry ground or sand and write these verses with a stick. Then have the child use a "pencil" stick to do this study.

1. Circle everything in these verses that God made.
2. Underline everything God did to show how much He loves people.
3. Double underline the words that are most important to you today.
4. Detective question: What are five or more things you can guess about God from these verses, even though the verses don't actually tell you?

Camping with a Common Sense Child

This activity is a type of inductive study. Because it has a slightly different twist to it, most Common Sense children will enjoy it. It appeals to their need for proof that Christianity makes sense—that there is something important to be learned from the Bible. Analytic children should also do well with it.

• God Made My Mind Right!
• Text: Genesis 7:17-19; 8:1, 18, 19

Give these directions to your family: Find a bug—one that doesn't fly. Spend five minutes using your mind to study the bug. It's wonderful how much you can learn just by looking. Draw pictures of your bug. Do diagrams to show its parts. Use your mind! Study your wonderful bug. Check out how many legs it has. Does it have eyes? Can it hear? What colors are on it? How does it move? Can it bite? Is it scared of you?

At the end of five minutes, give yourself a grade on how much you discovered about your bug.

Now study the Bible verses for the same amount of time. Use your mind to learn just by looking. Draw pictures of what you learn. Consider drawing diagrams of how different words connect to each other.

Someone asks you, "Why did God give people minds to make choices instead of making them robots who are always good?" Clear off a spot in the ground. Use a stick to draw a picture of your answer.

Camping with a Dynamic Child

If you have a Dynamic child, you have a kid who gets excited about an idea and runs with it. Unfortunately, the opposite is also true. If she or he doesn't get excited, the idea will be labeled boring. This child is often a natural leader who leads by strength of personality. If she or he is bored the child may pass that attitude on to the rest of the family and your camping devotions may be ruined.

Dynamic children don't like to be told exactly what to do. Instead, they like to be given an idea-starter and take off from there. Sometimes their ideas don't work. This rarely bothers them, because they can immediately change gears and be off working on another idea. They need you, the parent, to be the catalyst for their action. A wise parent will capitalize on the Dynamic child's willingness to experiment.

Camping offers a great opportunity for Dynamic children's growth. Just about any creative idea will be greeted enthusiastically. Suppose, for example, you were studying how wise Solomon was to follow God's rules. His ability and wisdom are exemplified in the building of the Temple. We know that he had palm tree and chain designs in his main hall. A parent might suggest that the child pretend that Solomon has asked him to come up with an outdoor design for one of his little halls in the Temple. The child has to find leaves and anything from nature to make the design. The design has to be at least a foot long. It can be held together with sticks, glue, pins, or staples.

Dynamics would know exactly what to do in an open-ended assignment like this. They might incorporate flowers and berries and nuts into a chain that they use to decorate large leaves.

Dynamic children can work by themselves, often mentally competing with the rest of the family to do the "best."

Camping offers a great opportunity for Dynamic children's growth.

- God Made My Body—My Legs, My Arms, My Strength
- Text: I Samuel 17:41-50

This study will appeal to the Dynamic child because of its uniqueness and potential for creativity.

Everyone in the family should find five stones that are flat enough to draw on. One of the stones should be small. Use crayons for drawing. Give your family the following directions:

1. On your first stone, draw a picture of how David must have felt when the giant was making fun of puny him.
2. On your second stone, write or draw a thank-you to Jesus for making your body and for making you strong enough to do things for Him. You may be His David for this year!
3. Decorate your third stone with colors that show how you feel about the special body God gave you.
4. On your fourth stone, write the name of a family member. Then sometime tomorrow, give that stone to that person and say, "God made you special. He loves you and I do, too."
5. Your last stone is a very small one. Put this one in your pocket where you can feel it occasionally. When you do, remember that God made your body, and He made it wonderful.

Church Activities That Click

The closer children come to adolescence, the closer parents need to look at their church's youth program. Does it offer anything that enhances your child's strength areas? Or is everything geared to the Imaginative or Analytic learner when your child is a strong Dynamic? If there is no place in the church program where your child can shine, he or she may see little reason to participate. "I want to shoot a teen video for our Christmas program," said fifteen-year-old Sandi. "But my youth leader wants us to sing a few songs like we always do. Church is boring. It's as if God and I don't speak the same language."

Imaginative Learners need opportunities to serve others—to work in the nursery, visit elderly people, act as church greeters. Analytics need to explore their faith with someone whose mind they respect, to study what Christians believe and why. Common Sense Learners need hands-on projects built around the church, mission trips, opportunities to raise money for furthering the Gospel. Dynamic Learners want creative opportunities. If the idea is new and different, they'll be excited about participating.

We do not serve a God who created us with a cookie cutter—each person pressed into the same shape from the same lump of dough. Perhaps we're

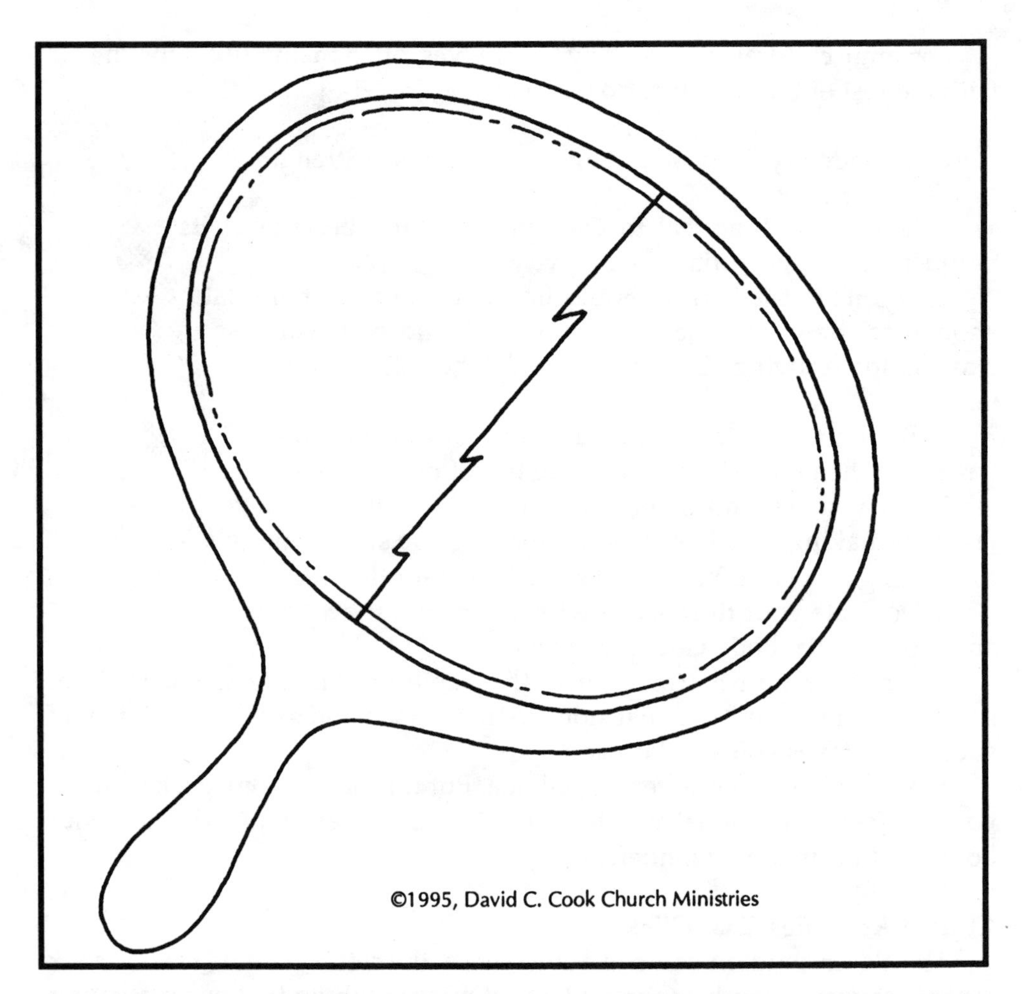

more like the Pennsylvania Dutch funnel cake. The cook pours the mix from a paper funnel and as it hits the hot grease, the batter breaks up into different shapes and patterns. No two funnel cakes are ever alike. Yet, every cake is delicious.

Assignment: Draw Your Mind[12]

Photocopy the mirror on the top of this page so that each person in your family has a copy. (Eight-year-old children and older should enjoy this activity.) On the one side, draw a picture using symbols and doodles and even a few words, if you must, to illustrate how others view your mind. On the other side, show how your mind really works. When you have spent about three minutes drawing each side, share your work with other family members. You may be surprised what you learn about each other.

On the next page are a couple illustrations to get you started.

Jack Richardson, Minneapolis, Minnesota, felt he was definitely strongly Analytic. He explained his drawing: "People see my mind as little boxes all lined up in neat little rows. They are right, but not completely right. I can

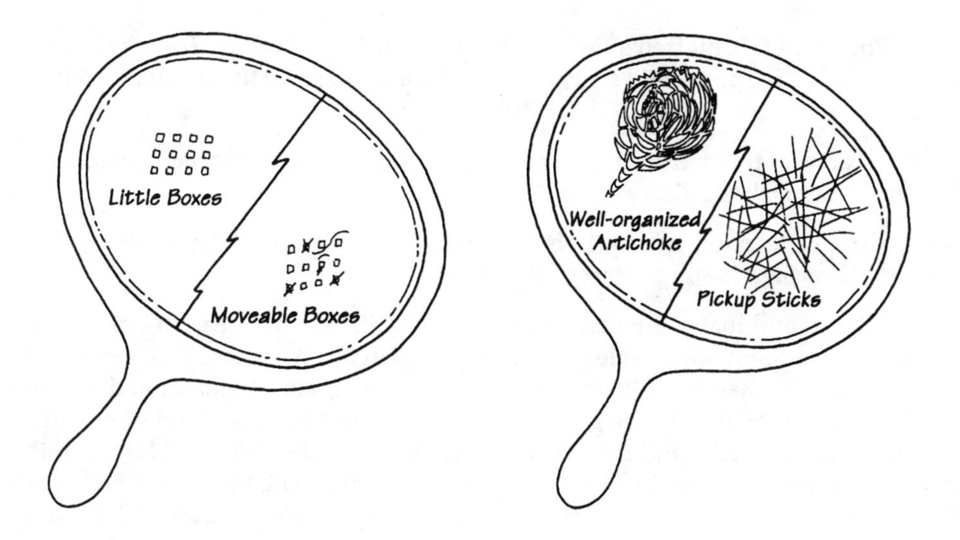

move those boxes around when I need to."

Anna Waterhouse, Arcadia, California, is a Dynamic Learner. She said people look at her mind as if it were a game of pickup sticks. "They are wrong," she said. "My mind is more like a very well-organized artichoke."

Notes

1. Dale Hanson Bourke, "Down on the Farm with Amy Grant," *Today's Christian Woman*, September/October 1990.

2. Peter Barrans and Connie Barrans, "Learning Styles and Compatibility," *Learning Styles Network Newsletter*, Winter 1993, p. 3.

3. Interestingly, there may be more Dynamic responses out there than we realized. According to the "1993 Outlook for Travel and Tourism," fewer than half of the United States travel customers have a particular destination in mind when they visit a travel agency. Only 36 percent have a general idea where they would like to go, and 19 percent have absolutely no idea!

4. Portions of material on pages 196—199 were previously published in an article by the author: "Opposites Distract," *Today's Christian Woman*, July/August 1988.

5. Cheryl Lavin, "Fast Track," *Chicago Tribune Magazine*, June 27, 1993, p. 12.

6. I interviewed another team-teacher couple for the newsletter *Teacher Touch* (David C. Cook Church Ministries). These two followed the same pattern Jack and I did with our teens when they taught preschoolers. She prepared the lesson, set up the room, taught the lesson. His job as the Imaginative Learner of the two was to count the number of children who did not have active fathers in their homes and divide by the number of minutes in the class hour. And that's how long each child got to sit on his lap.

7. Portions of "Children's Style" were previously printed in *Today's Christian Woman*, "What's Your Child's Style?" by Marlene LeFever (September/October 1991).

8. Portions of this section appeared as "Be a Faith-Shaping Teacher" by Marlene LeFever in *Evangelizing Today's Child*, November/December 1987.

9. Karla Henderson and M. Deborah Bialeschke, "Camping and the Split Brain Theory," *Camping Magazine*, March 1986, p. 19.

10. "We found that camp was a fun, active, positive living/learning experience which brought about observable changes in group-living skills, and that these objectively measured changes in behavior were supported, corroborated, and supplemented by additional evidence gained from case studies, interview, questionnaires, critical incident reports, and the evaluation team's own observation. Moreover, the qualitative data confirmed that the changes were not transient, but seen as lifelong in their impact."—James C. Stone, "How Camping Helps Children Grow," *The Education Digest*, May 1987, p. 48.

11. These ideas are edited from *God's Special Creation—Me* by Marlene LeFever, a Shaw Bible Discovery Guide for Campers (Carol Stream, Ill.: Harold Shaw Publishers, 1989). Used with permission.

12. Permission is granted to photocopy the mirror on the top of page 206 for use in family and Christian education settings.

Part VI

A Step Farther

We can all operate in all four learning style quadrants,
but given the opportunity, like ET, we phone home.
—Bernice McCarthy

We create best in our own image. That's fine for kids who are like us
and awful for those who are different.
—Rita Dunn

The mail arrives and with it newsletters about the newest research in learning styles. Month by month the knowledge base and the implications of that base grows, giving teachers more and better tools to do their jobs.

Bernice McCarthy

In Chapter 18, Bernice McCarthy, the educator whose terms we have used in this book to describe the four quadrants, shares her unique contribution to the learning style research. She divides each of the four quadrants into two parts—a right brain/mode function and a left brain/mode function—turning the learning cycle into eight steps, rather than four.

Christian educators, Christian education students, Christian school teachers, and parents who home school will want to look closely at her work.

Rita Dunn and Kenneth Dunn

Rita Dunn and Kenneth Dunn have explored additional avenues of learning. Chapter 19 will overview twenty-one elements of learning, covering—among other issues—the role lighting, room design, eating, and time of day play in the learning process. (Chapter 9, "Do You Learn Best by Hearing, Seeing, or Moving?" used information from the Dunn model of learning styles.)

These two models overlap in several areas. Both consider right and left brain/mode functions of learning. Both consider auditory, visual, and tactile/kinesthetic modalities.

In several cases, the models use the same words to explain different aspects of learning styles and this may be confusing. When Bernice McCarthy talks about the Analytic Learner, she is referring to the student who is most at home in Quadrant Two of the learning cycle. When Rita Dunn talks about the Analytic Learner, she is referring to the student who is most comfortable with left brain activities.

Use the next two chapters as an invitation to study more widely in the growing and exciting world of learning styles.

18

Bernice McCarthy and the 4MAT System

The goal of education should be to help our students develop the flexible use of their whole brain.
—Bernice McCarthy

The brain is divided into two hemispheres—the right brain and the left brain. The two halves of the brain, joined by the corpus callosum, work together. People use both sides of their brains, of course, but many people have a preference—a dominance.[1] Some do better with right brain activities, while others do better with left brain activities.

Left Brain Functions

- Right-hand control
- Speech
- Written language
- Number skills
- Reasoning
- Scientific skills

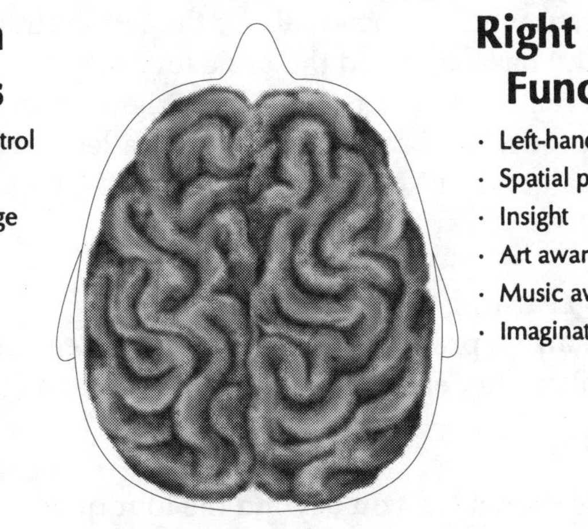

Right Brain Functions

- Left-hand control
- Spatial perception
- Insight
- Art awareness
- Music awareness
- Imagination

While both halves work together, they do process information differently. For example, speech is a function of the left brain. Spatial capability, how we move within a space, is a function of the right. The left brain processes information sequentially—first things first, second things second. The right brain perceives, absorbs, and processes information even while it is in the process of changing.[2]

Educators have been big on the verbal, left hemisphere development and have neglected the right. For example, teaching often affirms people who solve problems by looking at their parts, but misses people who learn by looking at the whole and intuiting solutions.

Both brain hemispheres should be equally important.

Hemisphere Functions

Left Brain (Most teachers affirm these functions)	**Right Brain** (Most teachers are uncomfortable here)
Does verbal processing (speech, writing)	Does visual-spatial processing (drawing)
Likes sequence	Likes random patterns
Structured	Fluid and spontaneous
Analyzes	Synthesizes
Controls feelings	Free with feelings

Science, as it is usually taught, would be a left-brain course—focused outward. Its equivalent in Christian education might be the study of theology. Art, on the other hand would be a right-brained focus—focused inward. In Christian education this might translate into a person's sensitivity to following the lead of the Holy Spirit.

We have been good with the left brain activities, but not as effective with the right. Einstein provides a caution to educators when he said, "The intuitive mind is a sacred gift; the rational mind is a faithful servant."

To incorporate what is known about the left brain and the right brain, Bernice McCarthy has expanded the basic four-step Learning Style Cycle to an eight-step cycle. Using her terminology, right brain functions are called right mode functions. Left brain functions are called left mode functions. See how the familiar quadrant chart on the following page becomes an eight-step pattern.

The Eight-Step Learning Style Cycle

Bernice McCarthy, president of Excel, Inc. and learning style researcher/ practitioner explains her eight-step teaching cycle in a conversation with the author.[3]

LeFever: Bernice, what led you beyond the four quadrants to incorporating

THE 4MAT® SYSTEM

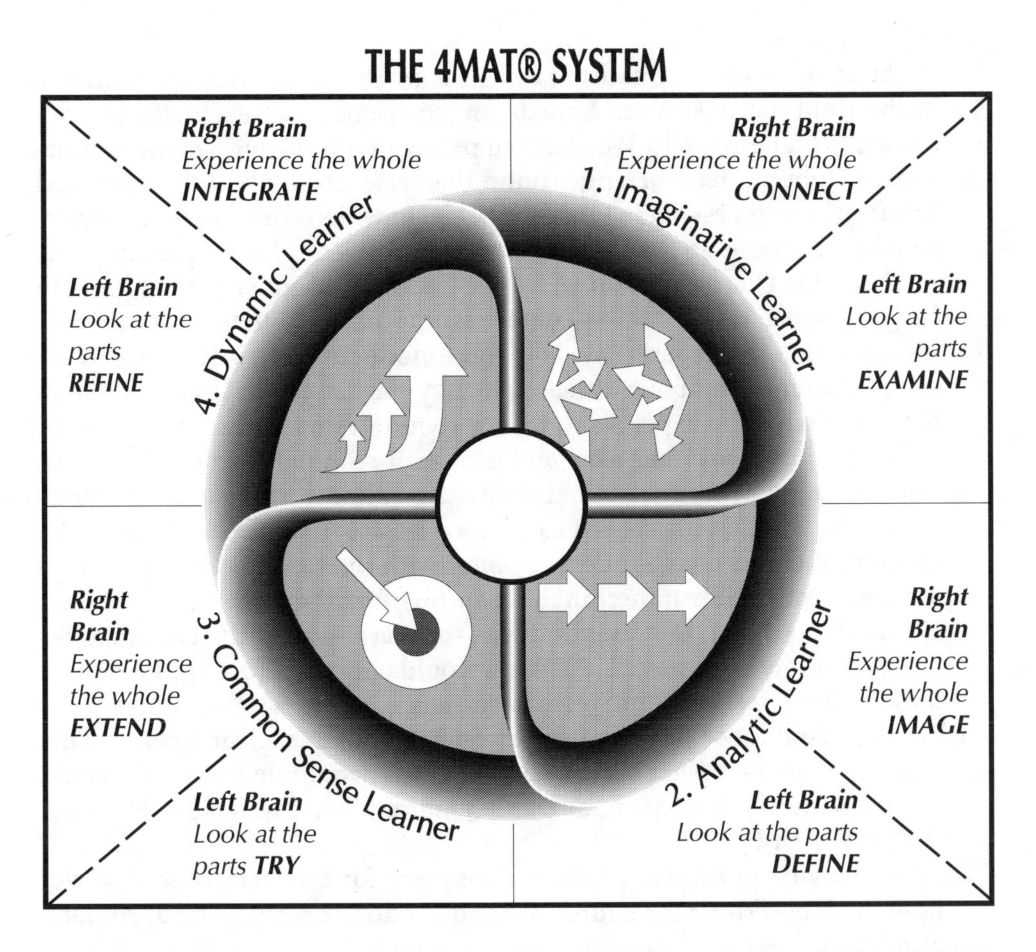

hemisphericity—right- and left-mode thinking—into your Learning Style Cycle?

McCarthy: I found people who approached learning with a penchant for the right mode and people who approached learning from the left in each of the quadrants. It became obvious that each of the four quadrants would be richer if teachers used both right-mode and left-mode functions.

LeFever: Your model suddenly becomes more difficult.

McCarthy: Perhaps, but also more effective, I think. I could have left it at a four-step model. I chose not to, and now, with the current research on hemisphericity, it appears it was a good decision.

The value of right- and left-mode processing helps us move in teaching from whole to part and back to whole again. Teachers are accustomed to teaching from part to whole, but there is equal value in teaching from whole to part. Another way of stating this is that teachers need to alternate between synthesis to analysis.

Follow this pattern and I think you'll see how much sense it makes. Each of the four quadrants contains two steps—a right-mode step and a left-mode step. (See the figure above.)

Start, of course, in Quadrant One (Imaginative Learners)—specifically, in the right-mode section. I create an experience that each student can *connect* with personally. We start the process with the whole, the synthesis, the right mode. Working around the cycle clockwise, I then proceed to left-mode processing in Quadrant One, in which we *examine* these personal connections so that all of us in the group learn from everyone else.

Now for Quadrant Two (Analytic Learners). I must get students to *image* in some way how the content is important to them before I take them to what the experts say. This right-mode imaging is the big picture of the content I'm about to teach. If they participate in imaging, when they hear what the experts say, they respond, "Ah, I already know that." *This is the most important place on the cycle.* It stimulates students to continue learning. It connects what they already know to the new learning.

LeFever: Stop and let me see if I can plan a lesson so far. In a lesson on the concept of church, say, students *connect* with the topic by doing twenty-second mimes to illustrate church. Then, together, they might *examine* their observations. Next, they might draw—or *image*—what the church looks like in their own experience. All these would happen before I guided them into the Bible, perhaps into a study in Acts.

McCarthy: And those pictures would constantly loop back and connect the students with their personal experiences as they continue around the circle.

Then, during the left-mode part, Quadrant Two, students study what the experts say.

LeFever: Finally an easy step! This is the place for Bible study to discover how the Bible *defines* the church. Christian educators are good at content.

McCarthy: Secular educators, too.

Then comes left-mode processing in Quadrant Three (Common Sense): students *try* or test their understanding of the content.

LeFever: Many teachers think only these latest two steps—Bible study and trying out how those facts work today—are teaching, and the rest is filler.

McCarthy: They're doing what I call pendulum teaching. Teaching that swings only between content and testing of that content is not adequate teaching. The material never makes a life difference to the students.

That difference begins in the next step, the right-mode part of Quadrant Three. Students leave the realm of the familiar and begin to create from what they have learned. They add something of themselves. They *extend* what they know beyond where the teacher took it.

LeFever: In our lesson on church, then, students might compile as many characteristics of the church as they can find in Scripture and prioritize them in the order that their own church seems to think is the most important. This helps them experience how important this Bible study is for them today.

McCarthy: Now it's time for the students to be creative—my favorite part! In Quadrant Four's left-mode section (Dynamic Learners), students *re-*

fine the usefulness of what they have learned. Finally, they use right-mode processing to *integrate* what they have learned into their own lives: they personally do something with the information and find a way to share it with others.

LeFever: So in our lesson on church, students would look for a way to respond to what they have learned—perhaps writing an acrostic prayer thanking God for church. Then they would find a way to use that acrostic during the week—perhaps as a prayer-starter that would remind them to pray for ten people from their church every day.

Dabble a bit in science fiction, Bernice. If Christian educators followed your teaching plan, how would our world be different?

McCarthy: Fun question for someone like me who lives in Quadrant Four! One thing we know for certain is that when teachers do the first three steps, memory is enhanced. We also know that when they take right-mode steps, students make intellectual leaps. Students who were not successful in school suddenly begin doing very, very well when right-mode activities are added.

Conversely, look at the students who already do well in school. What are they missing? What is not being developed in their lives?

LeFever: Some left-mode students I've taught do very well in content, but have poorly developed interpersonal skills. Often they are not expanding their creativity.

McCarthy: Right you are! My science fiction conclusion: If we implemented learning styles, we'd have a smarter, more whole world full of people who feel good about their minds.

LeFever: My favorite line coming up: Let's start teaching children the way God made them instead of the way we wish He had made them.

How the Eight-Step Pattern Works in Curriculum

Quadrant One: Imaginative Learners

1. Right Mode—Enter the learning experience. *Connect* with the topic. This section is based entirely on past experience and what students suspect or intuit about the subject.

2. Left Mode—*Examine* and discuss what has been done in the right-mode experience.

Quadrant Two: Analytic Learners

3. Right Mode—See or *image* the experience. Students will begin to think about the concepts that are part of the lesson.

4. Left Mode—Expand content by learning new material. Look at the parts and define what needs to be known.

Quadrant Three: Common Sense Learners

5. Left Mode—Practice defined givens. *Try* them. Test them to see if

they work and how they work.

6. Right Mode—Students *extend* what has been learned by adding something of themselves.

Quadrant Four: Dynamic Learners

7. Left Mode—Students develop originality and *refine* the effectiveness of their personal additions to the content.

8. Right Mode—To totally *integrate* what they have learned into their lives, they must use it, moving out of the classroom and into their own personal applications.

Now, let's put the sequence to work to see how a unit teaching plan might be developed. Below on the left side is an example of how an elementary teacher might teach a unit on grasshoppers.[4] On the right side is an example of how the book of I John might be taught at a Christian high school. Pay particular attention to the right-mode activities.

> Typically, Bible study techniques are left brain oriented. Whereas in order for the text to leap off the page, to assume a life of its own, and to challenge the reader to grow, the right brain needs to be engaged. The text cannot really be grasped if imaginative right brain activity is ruled out.[5]

All students would participate in all activities, but each would shine in the part of the lesson that is his or her greatest strength.

GRASSHOPPERS	I JOHN
IMAGINATIVE LEARNERS	
1. Right Mode—Connect	
Students observe grasshoppers inductively.	Students read I John as a choral reading while listening to the first movement of Beethoven's Fifth. The teacher is creating an experience to help teach the content.
2. Left Mode—Examine	
Students discuss what they had seen and record that information on a big sheet of paper.	Students discuss this experience and look for possible similarities between the themes of the music and text. They list the biblical themes.

Grasshoppers	I John

ANALYTIC LEARNERS

3. Right Mode—Image	
Students bring in their own collection of grasshoppers and collect data on them.	Students discuss the themes they have identified in I John and personally prioritize them.

4. Left Mode—Define	
Teacher teach the stages of grasshopper growth.	Teacher lectures on the symphonic development of I John.

COMMON SENSE LEARNERS

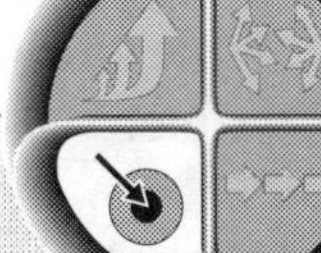

5. Left Mode—Try	
Students would work in workbooks and do text activities to show mastery of information about grasshoppers.	Students use a week's worth of news stories to develop color charts showing contemporary themes identified in I John.

6. Right Mode—Extend	
Students identify different types of grasshoppers in their collections and plan projects.	Students look for implications for themselves in I John's primary themes and personalize the chart.

DYNAMIC LEARNERS

7. Left Mode—Refine	
Students write plans for their grasshopper projects and contract with the teachers on creative ideas.	Students plan to use symphonic structure to teach the adult class what they have learned.

8. Right Mode—Integrate	
Students do their projects and share them with others.	Teens teach the adults.

Move through this pattern one more time by looking at the Parable of the Sower. All students will participate in all eight steps, but each will be most at home in two of the eight that fall into a primary learning preference.

Lesson: Parable of the Sower

Imaginative Learners: Why do I need to know this?

Teacher's Role: Motivator, getting the students excited about what is to come and being a witness to what they do.

1. Right Mode (Connect)—Students work in small groups to pantomime what it means to be a missionary. During this process students enter into the missionary experience rather than examining it from the outside.

2. Left Mode (Examine)—Students discuss the pantomime, examining its validity. The primary method is discussion, and in this left-mode step the students switch their focus from an inward, right-mode one to an outward one.

Analytic Learners: What do I need to know?

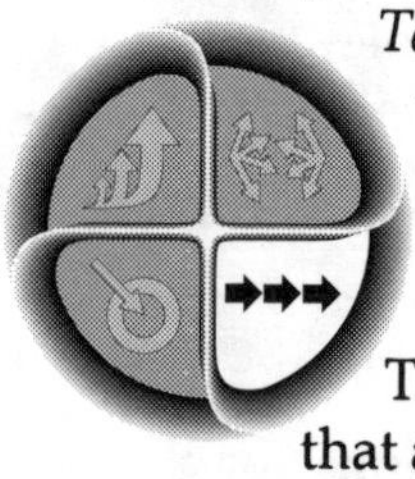

Teacher's Role: Traditional role of teacher, telling the students what they need to know in order to gain greater insight into the subject, or guiding the class to sources that will help in this learning process.

3. Right Mode (Image)—Students read the Parable of the Sower. Together the students and teacher discuss the various characteristics that allow this story to be labeled a missions parable. They compare this parable to the points made by the mission mimes the groups developed earlier.

Methods here should be informational, but the information should be based on the experience that the group has had. The information presented will include the class reactions to that experience.

4. Left Mode (Define)—Teacher lectures on the concept of biblical missions. Students may take notes as they follow along on an outline.

Common Sense Learners: How does this work today?

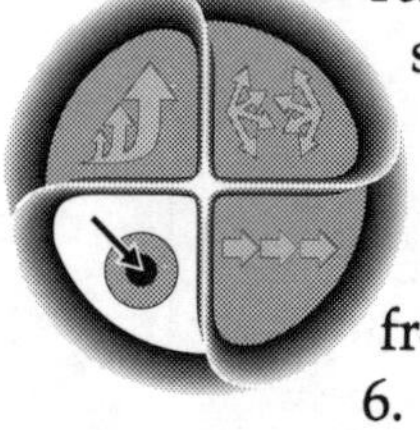

Teacher's Role: Coach. The teacher sets up tests that allow students to see if missions principles found in the story of the sower are valid today.

5. Left Mode (Try)—Students develop a computer-generated flowchart on how a contemporary sower sows. Content should come from a quarter's worth of their church's missionary letters.

6. Right Mode (Extend)—In self-chosen groups, students try out

what they have concluded by structuring interview questions and interviewing a missionary or someone who has had extensive sower experience.

Dynamic Learners: What can this become?
Teacher's Role: Evaluator or guide. The teacher probes, enlarges ideas, encourages, and challenges. The teacher allows the students to experience self-discovery as they take what they have been taught a step further by adding their own creativity to it. I like this definition of teaching that is lived out in this Dynamic step: "Teaching is participating in the student's own continuing creation of life."[6] In this step, a teacher must allow students to teach what they have learned to themselves and to others.

7. Left Mode (Refine)—Students write a prayer handbook for their church on how to best support their "sowers."

8. Right Mode (Integrate)—Students introduce the congregation to the handbook and demonstrate how to use it.

Recap

In the first quadrant, the teacher gives students a reason for what they have been studying. In the second, the teacher teaches it to them. In the third, the teacher allows students to try what they have learned for themselves and in the fourth, the teacher encourages students to expand what they have learned beyond what they have been taught.

The Pattern[7]

1. CONNECT: Creating an experience (right mode).
2. EXAMINE: Reflecting/analyzing the experience (left mode).
3. IMAGE: Integrating reflective analysis into concepts (right mode).
4. DEFINE: Developing concepts/skills (left mode—what usually happens in school).
5. TRY: Practicing defined givens (left mode—what usually happens in school).
6. EXTEND: Practicing and adding something of oneself (right mode).
7. REFINE: Analyzing application for usefulness (left mode).
8. INTEGRATE: Doing it (right mode).

EXCEL'S RESOURCES: TEACHING WITH 4MAT®[8] (SECULAR)

All materials listed on the following page are available from Excel, Inc., 23385 Old Barrington Road, Barrington, IL 60010. Phone: 800-822-4MAT. Write for the 4MAT Product Guide with a complete listing of products and seminars available through Excel.

Introductory Format Products:

The 4MAT System: Teaching to Learning Styles with Right/Left Mode Techniques, 1981, 1987 by Bernice McCarthy. This essential resource introduces the reader to the 4MAT system. The book contains fifteen unit plans showing 4MAT's applications in K—12 classrooms. *The 4MAT Workbook* is also available.

4MAT in Action, 3rd Edition, 1995 (two volumes: K—6 and 7—12). Contains 115 unit plans from secular content areas, including science, math, music, and literature. Includes step-by-step demonstration of lesson planning for Christian school or home school teachers.

4MATION—Lesson Plan Management Software for the Macintosh and Windows. With *4MATION,* teachers can create 4MAT lessons, cutting planning time to a minimum. Contains 260 lesson and unit plans.

Learning Differences: Designing Instruction with the 4MAT System. A two-part video program with an overview of 4MAT and demonstrations of 4MAT working in the classroom.

Parent Presenter's Kit is designed for making presentations to parents.

A Morning with Bernice McCarthy Audiocassette. This forty-five-minute tape is an excellent tool for introducing and reinforcing the 4MAT system.

Assessment Tools:

Learning Type Measure (LTM). This assessment tool helps identify an individual's learning preference and provides a method for applying this knowledge to develop strategies for improved teaching, communication, or management. A presenter's manual and kit are also available.

Hemispheric Mode Indicator (HMI) helps you identify your preference for either right (synthesizing), left (analytic), or whole-mode processing. A technical manual for the *HMI* is also available.

Teaching Style Inventory (TSI) is a self-assessment tool that helps the teacher identify their teaching style.

Leadership Behavior Inventory (LBI) helps you evaluate your leadership style.

Notes

1. What we know about how the right and left brain work is open to continued study. See "Right Brain, Left Brain: Fact and Fiction" by Jerre Levy, biopsychologist at the University of Chicago, *Psychology Today,* May 1985, p. 38. Levy's conclusion is that each hemisphere has special abilities, but people use both all the time.

2. "These distinctive functions of the two hemispheres are verified not only by brain research and experimentation but also in case histories. Gardner (1993), in pointing out that musical 'language' and spoken language involve two distinct brain functions, recounts two stories: how one composer suffered a left-hemisphere stroke,

which impaired verbal language but did not impair musical composition abilities, and how another composer suffered right-hemisphere damage with no ill effect in the ability to speak and teach music but in losing interest in composing and enjoying music. My personal experiences in working with a brain-damaged adolescent, who could not speak in complete sentences but who could sing all the words to songs, forever dispelled for me any doubts about brain-function lateralization and convinced me as an educator of the importance of at least these two kinds of knowing" (Paul Bumbar, "To Know God . . . But How?" *Religious Education*, Vol. 86, No. 1, Winter 1991, p. 124).

3. Marlene LeFever, "Waste No Minds," excerpts reprinted from *Youthworker Journal*, Summer 1991, pp. 94–100. ©1991 by Youth Specialties, Inc., 1224 Greenfield Dr., El Cajon, CA 92021. Used by permission.

4. Grasshopper illustration was used by Bernice McCarthy at an Association for Supervision and Curriculum Development seminar, Vancouver, British Columbia, 1986.

5. Richard V. Peace, "Imagination and Bible Study in Groups," *Christian Education Journal*, Vol. XIII, No. 3, p. 64.

6. Anabel Proffitt, "Liberating Education," *Religious Education*, Vol. 88, No. 1, Winter 1993, p. 12.

7. Bernice McCarthy, *The 4MAT System—Teaching to Learning Style with Right/Left Mode Techniques* (Barrington, Ill.: Excel, Inc., 1987), p. 122.

8. 4MAT and 4MATION are federally registered trademarks of Excel, Inc.

19

Rita and Kenneth Dunn and the Twenty-One Elements of Learning

We have redesigned our nineteen-by-thirty-foot space, bringing in individual desk lamps, room dividers, milk crates, beanbag chairs, a couch, and tables. Students who work best in bright light are encouraged to sit near a desk lamp. Students who prefer a warm area are encouraged to sit by the wood stove or wear a sweater. Those who need sound are given headsets and audiocassette tapes that play wordless music. Students who need quiet wear ear plugs or earphones with no music.
—Idaho teachers Vic Koshuta and Paula Koshuta

People almost always respond positively to the idea of learning styles. "Yes," I'm told after leading a seminar on the subject, "that makes sense." The easy part is affirming that learning styles makes sense. The difficulty comes when teachers have to rethink their curriculum structure and the methods they use within that structure. Without responsive changes, teachers become a little like the drunk fellow on the plane. He was very loud and abusive. Seated directly behind him was a well-known, respected evangelist. In an effort to quiet the man the flight attendant said, "Sir, do you know who is sitting right behind you?" The man turned and, sure enough, he recognized the preacher. He announced, "I'm so glad to meet you. I went to your crusade and it changed my life!"

Lighting, bean bag chairs, noise, quiet, time of day: People who care about the teaching and learning process are looking at things that might effect learning, things that weren't seriously considered even just a few years ago.[1]

If we are to reach all students, teaching to learning styles will require changes in how the curriculum is structured. The four-quadrant Learning Style Cycle gives us a teaching pattern to follow.

Other researchers supply additional clues to solve the puzzle of learning. Pulling all of this information together and restructuring what happens in the learning process is a bit like rebuilding a 747 while it's in the air.[2]

But we have to try! Claudia Arp, coauthor of PEP (Parents Encouraging Parents), said, "God gave that kid everything that kid needs to be everything God wants him or her to be."[3] Our job as teachers is to encourage that developing child, making certain that everything we do develops skills and abilities, rather than stifles them.

No matter if each child doesn't fit the traditional pattern. God can use her. God can use him. God uses differences for His glory. As we teachers model that affirmation, our students who model us will also accept those who don't fit into our "smart," "A-level" categories.

Twenty-One Elements

Educators Dr. Rita Dunn and Dr. Kenneth Dunn[4] have identified twenty-one elements that effect how students learn. Each is identified in the following visual outline.[5] When the elements that are important to a student are present in the learning situation, the student will succeed. When too many are missing, the student may fail.

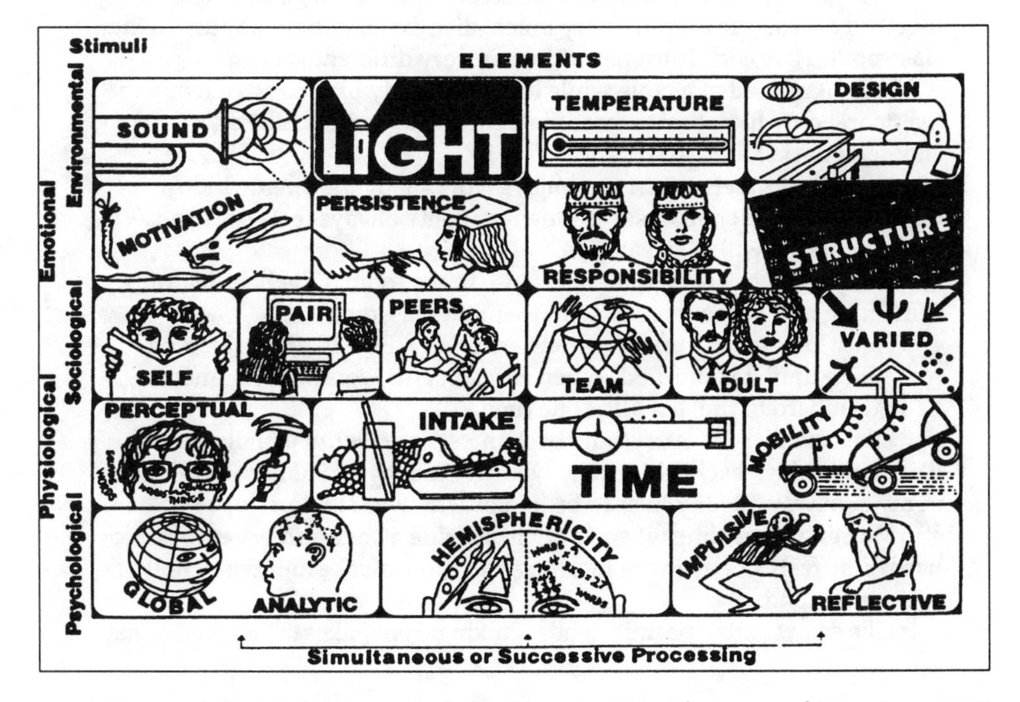

In testing more than 175,000 children in grades three through seven,[6] researchers found that children could give valuable clues as to which of the twenty-one elements were important to them. They also had little trouble identifying their teachers' preferences.[7]

Those students who need the elements that the traditional schools provide will thrive. Students who learn best in ways that run counter to the school (or Sunday school) will not.[8]

Dunn's work is particularly helpful to parents. In a family with three children, it is not unlikely that one of the three will learn differently from the school pattern. Rather than being celebrated as "learning different," that child may be mislabeled, "learning disabled."[9] A parent's understanding of the elements of learning that effect each child will help him or her help the child. Knowing may also help the parent help a child's teacher do a more effective job.[10]

Two Smart Elephants

As you read the story of two elephants, Ellie and Fonty, excerpted from the booklet "Elephant Style,"[11] think of the children who concern you. Who is an Ellie? A Fonty? In a traditional classroom, one of these elephants would be considered a good student and the other could have scholastic problems. Yet both are equally smart elephants. They just learn in very different ways.

> Ellie and Fonty are the best of friends. They do everything together. They even look like each other except Ellie wears a T-shirt with stripes and Fonty wears a T-shirt with polka dots. They play together. They eat the same foods, usually peanut butter ice cream. They even go to school together. So you see they are very much alike except when they are in the classroom. They each learn new things in very different ways.
>
> Ellie likes to sit at a table while learning. Fonty likes to stretch out on the floor. Fonty likes to sit where the light is very bright. Ellie always chooses a darker area to work in.
>
> Ellie always feels warm and enjoys working by the open window, especially when a cool breeze is blowing. Fonty always feels cold and enjoys working with a sweater on.
>
> Fonty can work even if there is noise in the room. Ellie likes learning something new when there is no noise in the classroom.
>
> Fonty likes to do something new every day. Ellie likes working on something until it is finished. When Fonty begins working on something, he finds it hard to finish it all at one time.
>
> Ellie usually puts everything back in its place. Fonty usually doesn't like to put things back where they belong. Ellie says, "I like to do my work in my own way." Fonty likes to be told exactly what to do.
>
> Morning is the time when Fonty feels wide awake and eager to work hard. Ellie feels sleepy in the morning and more awake and ready to work in the afternoon.
>
> Ellie enjoys eating peanuts while working. Fonty likes to eat only at snack

time. Ellie can't sit still while working and likes to get up and walk to different areas in the classroom. Fonty can sit still forever until something is done.

Some students cannot learn unless a particular element is present or absent.

According to Rita Dunn, a few students cannot learn unless a particular element is present or absent. For example, noise. Some students need a lot of noise in order to learn. Others need some noise. A few need to learn in absolute quiet. Others prefer a rather quiet environment. Still others are not affected one way or the other by noise. That group will be captured by their interest in the subject, how they feel about the teacher, and the relevance they place in what is being presented.

When students are taught in ways that complement their styles, leaders will see significantly increased achievement, improved student attitudes, and fewer behavior problems.

Environmental Elements[12]

The first four elements of learning are environmental: sound, light, temperature, and design. Each of these can be addressed in a Christian education setting—but not without some creative thought and a learning style champion who believes teaching to style can make a difference.

Sound

A parent calls to her child, "Turn off that music so you can study!" That mother may be cutting down on the effectiveness of her child's study if he studies best when there is noise in the background.

The need for sound remains fairly consistent for children during the elementary years, and increases as adolescence begins. It then returns to its previously normal state after adolescence.

Many underachievers work best with sound. Why? One possibility is that sound forces them to focus on what they need to do. Without noise, they hear non-sounds, like people hearing sounds in the quiet night that keep them from sleeping. The "quiet" is a loud distorter that keeps them from learning. "We have done what is wrong, and we have done it with conviction," quips Rita Dunn.[13]

People with a need for constant noise may be annoying in the classroom or even in a worship service, because if the noise they need for learning isn't present, they may make their own noise. They might hum to themselves or mutter. In the work place, the sound-makers may constantly whistle.

To reach these students, some of our activities must involve noise.

In the four-quadrant Learning Style Cycle, we can suspect that many students who test high as Imaginatives, Common Sense, and Dynamic would need some degree of noise, while most Analytic students would find noise a detriment to learning.

About one percent of all students need absolute silence.[14]

Light

Light affects more people than sound.

Many young children have difficulty with bright light, especially fluorescent light. Some white light contains ultraviolet rays which are irritating and may even cause low-grade headaches. Yet for many Christian education classrooms, fluorescent light is still being used because it is less expensive. What a shame. Our young children operate on the feeling level. ("My stomach hurts," the three-year-old said. "Don't you feel it?") They feel the love of Jesus, the love of their Sunday school teachers, and the love of the church for them. Those feelings may affect their attitudes toward church and their decisions concerning the Gospel for years to come. When we create an atmosphere in which many of our children are not comfortable, we may have saved a few dollars, but at what cost?

We thought for years that preschoolers need the lightest classrooms. Not so. They need happy and bright classrooms. But every three to five years, statistically, people need more light. Our classrooms for seniors should be the brightest.[15]

There is a saying, "If you think education is expensive, try ignorance!" This comment is not so funny in the light of the functional illiteracy that seems to be increasing both among those students who drop out of school and even those who finish high school.[16] Lighting may play a part here.

Most poor readers read better in low light, perhaps for much the same reason many people need sound to block out distractions. The low light will cause the words to stand out on the white page. In the Sunday school classroom, it can be a very Christian thing to screw out a light bulb and allow students to sit where they are most comfortable.[17] Don't worry about eye strain in low light. Readers only need enough illumination to see print comfortably.

Temperature

"A sweater is what my mother makes me put on when she's cold." A child should be able to work in whatever temperature is best for him or her. Cold affects more students negatively than does heat.

When a child has one bad year, when too many of the elements are against him or her, when his teacher's preferences are opposite from his or hers and that teacher makes no allowances for differences, the child can be negatively affected forever.

Christian educator Wesley Willis said, "There are good teachers and there are not-so-good teachers. But the ones who really make me nervous are the ones who assume their learning experiences to be the normative. One professor explained his teaching theory in this way: 'Whatever I liked as a student is what I do in class, and I never will use methods I don't like.' When I asked him about those students who learn differently from the way he learned, he looked incredulous."[18]

Design

Some students work best at desks, but a surprising number learn best when they are allowed to spread out on rugs or couches. The need for informal design increases with adolescence. Yes, a strong case can be made for adding beanbag chairs to the Christian education budget.

Take a poll among your church's Sunday school teachers. How many get ready for their lessons by finding a comfortable, soft chair, or propping themselves up in bed, or stretching out on the sofa? The casual setting makes studying easier, more enjoyable. Why do we assume that our students are different from us?

Look at room design in terms of what needs to be accomplished by the people in that setting rather than in terms of what learning spaces have traditionally looked like. This will require a whole new attitude—one like grandpa has when he feeds Kjersten.

Look at room design in terms of what needs to be accomplished.

> The other day I was feeding Kjersten, the world's most perfect grandchild. She had climbed up on a small bar we have between the kitchen and dining room.
>
> She would stand up, lie down, put her head between her knees, lie on her back and stand on her head. Wherever her mouth was, I would put the food. But if she had been my child, I would have had her sit up straight and clean up her plate, and not squirm—and both of us would have had a miserable time.[19]

One researcher discovered that when students who needed informal design had their needs met, they tested 20 percent higher than when they were in a formal setting.[20] There is only one chance in a thousand that the room design wasn't responsible for the improvement.

Those students who respond to the more formal desk and chair setting are able to adapt to an informal situation much more easily than those who need an informal setting are able to adapt to formal. Darrian, who likes a desk, can just put his back up to the wall and make a desk from his lap. Josh has much more difficulty making a beanbag chair out of a traditional desk.

> In Lancaster, Texas, a teacher told the class a story about an elephant who couldn't sit still. He hopped up and down, squirmed, and constantly dropped things. He was so busy with everything except listening that his grades weren't very good. It wasn't because he didn't want to learn. He just couldn't keep his mind on things, no matter how hard he tried. The teacher asked the class, "What do you think the little elephant's teacher could do to help him?" This discussion led to the student's parents bringing in a small couch for their son's use in place of the desk. The other youngsters didn't care; they weren't jealous. After all, they had suggested it as a solution for their friend's problem. He could not sit at a desk and pay attention at the same time.[21]

Assignment

An Environmental Experiment
SOUND, LIGHT, TEMPERATURE, DESIGN

In the block below, draw what your own or a typical Sunday school room at your church looks like.

An Environmental Experiment
SOUND, LIGHT, TEMPERATURE, DESIGN

In the block below, design a setting for the age level you teach. Take into consideration as many of the four environmental elements as possible. Start out grand—don't put limits on the time it would take to reconstruct or the amount of money it could cost. Just work on the ideal.

Consider asking several other people from your church to come up with their plans. Compare notes. Pick those things that are feasible and take steps to implement them. When others in the church become aware of the importance of environmental elements to learning, they may be willing to work with you to make the wish list a priority.

Emotional Elements

The next four elements of learning are emotional: Motivation, Persistence, Responsibility, and Structure. All except Persistence may change with time.

Motivation

When the class subject is of immediate interest—the Christian and sex, for example—young teens are motivated to pay attention. However, when the subject seems a little drier (the importance the Trinity plays in my understanding of my faith), the unmotivated student may drop out. The motivated student will continue to learn.

Unmotivated students need short assignments.

Motivated students need to be told when they are to learn, what they are to use as resources, and how they can tell when they have reached the learning objective.

Unmotivated students need short assignments, few objectives, frequent feedback, supervision, and genuine praise. If confirmation class contains these elements, for example, they may actually enjoy the training!

Motivation is linked to achievement. The higher the achievement, the more motivated the student becomes.

Persistence

Persistent students will stick with a subject until it is done, even if they do not see immediate use for the information. They can't stand to see something remain undone, and they feel unsettled if they stop a project in the middle.

Students who are low in persistence live for the present, dislike being organized, and push the rules, often very creatively. High school drop-outs often test low in persistence, although quite often, not low in intelligence.

One way to work with students who are obviously intelligent and yet seem totally disinterested is to give options or choices of things to do in class. Instead of announcing which verses will be memorized in the coming quarter, give students their choice of eight out of twelve. Break learning into small pieces so unmotivated students can succeed at small tasks.

Does paying attention to this and the other twenty elements make a difference? Research in secular settings says it does. Brightwood Elementary School, Greensboro, North Carolina, was an impoverished, minority district where children were reading at the 30th percentile in the California Achievement Test (CAT). The teachers began to teach to the elements of learning and the school moved up to the 83rd percentile, one of the highest in the state.[22]

What would similar research show if it were done on a Sunday school class, a youth group, or a weekly club program?

Responsibility

Responsible students will do what they are told. Nonresponsible students need to know why they are doing something and what makes it important to both the teacher and themselves before they do it.

Responsible kids conform. They do what they are told.

Nonresponsible students achieve best when the teacher gives them choices that show they have completed the assignment and learned the material. The more non-directive the teacher is, the better. The teacher dare not talk down to nonconformists, but respect the way they think.

Structure

Externally structured students, students who march to the authority of a teacher, need to be told by the teacher exactly what is expected (when the paper is due, how long it will be, what resources should be used). Internally structured students, students who act as their own stimulus, want to do things their own way.

Externally structured students are the ones who always have their term papers done a week early. Internally structured students may be finishing minutes before the paper is due.

Both groups get the work done, but they follow different "mind schedules." Externally structured students can explain why they were early: "I was afraid all the books would be checked out of the library." "I wanted to make certain that the teacher read my paper." "I was afraid I would get a headache on the day it was due and not be able to finish." "I worry until it's done." Internally structured people have an impressive list of self reasons why it's best to wait until the last minute. "I need time to get my thoughts organized." "I work better under pressure." "I had too much other stuff to do." "It wasn't something I felt was important." Mozart probably had a strong internally structured preference. He never committed anything to paper until all the musical score was completed in his head.

Sociological Elements

The six sociological preferences identify what kind of group setting works best for the student.

Learning by Self

Most gifted learners prefer this. We need to limit how often we use gifted students as "student teachers" to help others in the class.

Learning with Pair

Pairs can be self-chosen or teacher-chosen.

Learning with Peers

"Students learn an enormous amount from each other."

The whole class might work together on a project. The teacher is not an active part of the process. Some students are incapable of learning from an adult, no matter how good that teacher is. Maybe the teacher makes them feel uncomfortable, shy, or even scared. When they work with peers, they feel free to learn.

Teachers who get feedback from their students about class structures that allow them to be successful discover some surprising things:[23]

Students learn an enormous amount from each other.

When students make their thoughts clear to others, they gain greater clarity for themselves.

Students decide what it is they want to understand.

Students know what they know and what they believe.

Students have the powerful experience of having their ideas taken seriously, rather than simply screened by the teacher until he or she gets the "right" answer.

Learning on a Team

A team may include a teacher or children who are younger and older. In a team the students are working toward a common goal.

Cooperative Learning[24] is a team learning tool that needs to be given some consideration in Christian education. "None of us is as smart as all of us" is an assumption this teaching pattern makes. Cooperative Learning is a set of teaching methods in which students work in small, mixed-ability learning teams. The students in each group are responsible not only for learning the material being taught, but also for helping every other member of the team learn. In a youth group setting, for example, Cooperative Learning would demonstrate how students learn biblical content while practicing what it means to love their neighbors as themselves.

In twenty-six controlled studies, researchers found that in twenty-one Cooperative Learning situations, students had higher achievement, two had mixed results, and three yielded no significant differences. The more complex the learning task, the better the grades.

Cooperative Learning is structured around five tenets.

1. Positive Interdependence. Students sink or swim together. They talk more. Students in groups of three are talking one-third of the time. Each person can be a tutor or have the advantages of being tutored by someone who speaks his or her language.

Students stay together for an extended period of time. The purpose of the group is to give peer support and to increase the probability that members attend school or Sunday school and apply themselves to learning and practicing what they have learned. In effect, Cooperative Learning is creating family groupings. In churches that are struggling with how to provide family for children who have never been part of a functioning family, Christian educators could creatively adapt aspects of Cooperative Learning.

2. *Face-to-Face Interaction.* Groups are formed by the teacher. Students in those groups promote each other's learning by helping, sharing, and encouraging. Cooperative Learning assumes that whoever explains, learns.

3. *Joint Rewards.* Groups are working for an incentive that can't be reached by individuals. It has to be reached by the whole team. "I don't succeed unless you do," is the mindset. While not every student will have the same goal, every student must meet the goal set for him or her. The award is important. However, it doesn't have to be something of monetary value. It could be a paper certificate, pizza with the pastor, a tongue-in-cheek giant lollipop prize, or a mention in the church bulletin.

Every group can win, not just the group that achieves its goal first. For example, in a demonstration of Cooperative Learning at a Christian education conference, I used computer-generated certificates to encourage participants to memorize or paraphrase the following poem, "Foresight."

Foresight[25]
by Keith Patman

Before lambs bled in Egypt, One was given.
Before the worm tore Eden, pain was faced.
Somewhere, before earth's cornerstone was placed,
A hammer crashed in heaven—nails were driven.

4. *Individual Accountability.* Each member is also individually accountable. In the "Foresight" example, the "Awesome Group Award" went to every group in which *every* person memorized the poem. The "Super Group Award" went to every group in which *every* person paraphrased the poem. For the group to win, all members had to help each other.

For sample group awards see pages 234 and 235.

Most adults admitted that without the encouragement of their group, even though this was a workshop they had chosen to attend, they would not have considered memorizing a poem. In fact, many said they did not have the ability to do it. However, group pressure caused every small group except one to memorize, rather than paraphrase. Many people expressed surprise when the experiment proved that with the group's help, they could memorize.

5. *Celebrate Success.* Classes that have implemented Cooperative Learning have found that prejudice declines, even when some of the group members are handicapped or of different ethnic backgrounds. Race relations continue even after the teams are no longer together. Participants have a greater ability to view situations from others' perspectives. Ridicule practically disappears. Kids who are different continue to socialize during free time.

Awesome Group Award
Group Name: ____________
Group Member: ____________
You were great! What a group!
So Celebrate!
No one could have done it
without you.
Signed: ____________

Super Group Award

Group Name: ______________________

Group Member: ______________________

GOOD GOING.

Your group is very, very special.

Way to go!

Your group couldn't have

succeeded without you.

Signed: ______________________

Students have a higher regard for school and for the subject they are studying and for their teachers. And, finally, students develop more self-confidence.

For the majority of students who prefer to work in groups, the following summary applies.[26]

- There is evidence that most students perceive school as competitive.
- Students become more competitive the longer they are in school or the older they become.
- As Christians we believe that we are our brothers' and sisters' keepers and that we are called to love one another. Yet sadly, this message is not the primary one we model for our children in the Sunday school—or in the modeling we do in other church groups.[27]
- There is consistent research evidence that students will become more involved in instructional activities and tasks under cooperative rather than competitive conditions.
- Many students prefer cooperatively-structured rather than competitively-structured learning situations.
- Competition may be superior to cooperative learning when a task is a simple drill activity, such as a Bible drill, or when sheer quantity of work is desired on a mechanical or skill-oriented task that requires little if any help from another person. (Competition must not be on the primary agenda of the Sunday school.)
- In problem-solving activities, there is significant research support that indicates that cooperative goal structures result in higher achievement than do competitive goal structures or individualistic goal structures.[28]

Learning with an Adult[29]

A student who learns best with a teacher may socialize in a peer setting. He or she may have a great time but never learn anything.

Learning Using Varied Settings

In most Sunday school classes, this is the approach that will be taken.

Physical Elements

The next four elements of learning are physical: Perceptual, Intake, Time, and Mobility.

Perceptual

The perceptual element refers to the modalities through which the student prefers to learn—auditory, visual, or tactile/kinesthetic. This element was covered in Chapter 9, "Do You Learn Best by Hearing, Seeing, or Moving?"

Intake

"Take that gum out of your mouth," the schoolteacher says. Yet some of our students learn best if they are allowed to chew while they are learning. Think about what you do when you're working on a difficult task, such as preparing a sermon or a devotional for the women's prayer group or the lesson for the primary-junior Sunday school students. Many teachers munch popcorn or sip coffee. Why do we assume that if eating helps so many of us study better it wouldn't also help our students interact more effectively with their lessons?[30]

Why eating? Why does it help some students learn? We don't know for certain, but perhaps chewing is one of the body's adaptive strategies for increasing the arousal level of the neural system to help us focus on the task. In other words, the stimulation to the central nervous system by gum chewing may provide the system with a mild jolt, "acting like a nonprescription amphetamine to increase the flow of electrical current. The body has naturally fashioned a compensating mechanism for its low arousal level."[31]

Time

According to Dunn, the most important learning elements are light, design, and time of day.

Lyn Cryderman is an early morning person. His wife Esther is more awake late at night. For their marriage to work, they had to adjust to each other's time-of-day preference.[32]

> *Lyn:* Our biological clocks are set on different time zones. I like rising early and getting a fast start on the day, but I don't enjoy staying up late. Esther hates to get up in the morning, but she really starts to come alive as the evening progresses.
>
> *Esther:* When we were first married it would get to be 9:30 or 10:00 and Lyn would say, "I'm getting sleepy. Why don't we go to bed?" And I'd think, "What's wrong with this guy? I'm not even beginning to get tired."
>
> Or we'd be lying in bed talking. I'd be sharing my most intimate thoughts and I'd look over and Lyn would have fallen asleep. . . . After I complained about him conking out on me, he did something to help me see his perspective. He'd come into the bedroom after he'd been up in the morning to say, "It's a beautiful day outside. Why not get up and enjoy it?" . . . When I was half awake, he'd say, "What do you think about suffering in the world, Esther? Now would be a good time to talk about that, don't you think?"
>
> . . . What advice do the Crydermans have for other couples?
>
> According to Lyn, "Don't try so hard to change each other."
>
> Esther's advice: "The most important thing is to communicate lovingly and kindly. You need to say as gently as you can, 'Honey, I really do love you. I'd like to talk (or get up, eat breakfast, whatever) with you right now. But I'm just too tired. Can we wait until I'm awake?'"

Most important are light, design, and time of day.

Like the Crydermans, most students have a best time of day—for talking, studying, and taking tests. Catch them at that time, and they will achieve. Catch them during the biological downtime, and they are less successful.

Many students are not morning alert, but for most churches, this is the time serious Christian education takes place. For example, 28 percent of elementary students are early morning people. The rest come to life after 10 A.M., and most are at high energy levels between 10:00 A.M. and 2 P.M.[33] In a study by J. Virostko,[34] 286 elementary children were taught math in the morning and reading in the afternoon. When the subject was taught at the students' preferred time, they improved twenty-eight points on test scores. There is only one chance in a thousand that it was not the time of day that made the difference. The next year, the researcher taught the same children and another subject was put into the preferred slot. High grades were correlated with time of day and not with subject. This study won the Kappa Delta Pi International Award for the best educational research in 1983.

Research reported by Bernice McCarthy shows similar jumps.[35]

An educator from Lynnwood, Washington, designed an alternative for dropouts. School didn't start until 11 A.M. Students who had been missing fourteen days a semester missed fewer than three with the new schedule.[36]

Talented students in art, dance, drama, music, and sports often prefer afternoon and evening learning settings.[37]

Don't forget adults. Almost three out of four employed adults say they are more productive in the morning. One in five comes to life in the afternoon. Only 3 percent are most productive in the evening.[38]

According to Rita Dunn, time is the most significant variable. So if you can't make all the changes in your Christian education program that this research indicates ought to be made, start with time of day.

Assignment: Answer these questions with your church's ministry in mind:

- What times of day are the Christian education programs held?
- Would a student who learns best in early morning, late morning, early afternoon, early evening, or after 8 P.M. be at risk in your program?
- Most school-age students are not morning alert. What paradigm-breaking responses should a church leader make with regard to this information?
- School dropouts, underachievers, at-risk, and vocational education students (as a group) are not morning people. What paradigm-breaking responses should a church leader make with regard to that information?

Mobility

Fifty percent of junior high/middle school children can't sit for more than ten minutes. They have such strong biological urges that they need to move. Boys tend to require more mobility than girls. When they are encouraged to be passive in Sunday school, they may become discipline problems.

The less interested young children are in what they are learning, the more they need to move.

Psychological Elements

The final three elements of learning, as isolated by Dr. Rita Dunn and Dr. Kenneth Dunn, are psychological: Global / Analytic, Hemisphericity, Impulsive / Reflective.[39]

Global/Analytic

Some students learn best globally. They obtain meaning from broad concepts and then focus on details. They often learn best with music, low light, and an informal classroom. They are often labeled right-brain processors.

Other students learn successively, in small steps. These processors, labeled Analytics by Dunn, and corresponding to what McCarthy calls left-brain learners in all quadrants, prefer conventional, formal classrooms and structured teaching.

The school system—and often the Christian education system when it is patterned after the secular school system—favors Analytic students and neglects the global, right-brained ones.

Hemisphericity

This corresponds to McCarthy's right- and left-mode thinking, as explained in Chapter 18. Basically, left-brain thinkers are affirmed by traditional schools. Research on the right and left sides of the brain is far from conclusive. There is usually a dominance, but what we know about right and left brain is open to continued study.

Impulsive/Reflective

An impulsive student has difficulty thinking through an answer or process before talking about it or acting upon it. Students who want to please a teacher may try to act reflectively if they like the teacher and know that he or she values reflective patterns, but that behavior will be exhibited only when the teacher is watching. When the teacher is absent, the impulsive students revert to what is natural to them.

When students have an opportunity to shine in their own learning style, when the elements of learning that they need are present, they discover that it's fine to be different. Even more exciting, God can use their differences for His glory. They also learn that it's important to affirm those who don't fit the usual patterns. With this affirmation, they are learning the skill of encouraging.

Robert Fulghum demonstrates the importance of accepting all those who don't fit into our established categories in his essay, "Giants, Wizards, and Dwarfs."

Giants, Wizards, and Dwarfs[40]

Giants, Wizards, and Dwarfs was the game to play. Being left in charge of about 80 children seven to ten years old, while their parents were off doing parenty things, I mustered my troops in the church social hall and explained the game. It's a large-scale version of Rock, Paper, Scissors, and involves some intellectual decision making. But the real purpose of the game is to make a lot of noise and run around chasing people until nobody knows which side you are on or who won.

Organizing a roomful of wired-up gradeschoolers into two teams, explaining the rudiments of the game, achieving consensus on group identity—all this is no mean accomplishment, but we did it with a right good will and were ready to go.

The excitement of the chase had reached a critical mass. I yelled out: "You have to decide NOW which you are—a GIANT, a WIZARD, or a DWARF!"

While the groups huddled in frenzied, whispered consultation, a tug came at my pants leg. A small child stands there looking up, and asks in a small, concerned voice, "Where do the mermaids stand?"

Where do the Mermaids stand?

A long pause. Very very long pause. "Where do the Mermaids stand?" says I.

"Yes, you see, I am a Mermaid."

"There are no such things as Mermaids."

"Oh, yes, I am one."

She did not relate to being a Giant, a Wizard, or a Dwarf. She knew her category, Mermaid. And was not about to leave the game and go over and stand against the wall where a loser would stand. She intended to participate, wherever Mermaids fit into the scheme of things. Without giving up dignity or identity. She took it for granted that there was a place for Mermaids and that I would know just where.

Well, where DO the mermaids stand. All the "Mermaids"—all those who are different, who do not fit the norm and who do not accept the available boxes and pigeonholes?

Answer that question and you can build a school, a nation, or a world on it.

What was my answer at the moment? Every once in a while I say the right thing. "The Mermaid stands right here by the King of the Sea!" says I.

So we stood there hand in hand, reviewing the troops of Wizards and Giants and Dwarfs as they roiled by in wild disarray.

It is not true, by the way, that mermaids do not exist. I know at least one personally. I have held her hand.

Each person is special and must be valued. Teachers will have the risk-taker, the problem-solver, the data people, and the dreamers all in the same class. They must model for their students that all must contribute to Christ's cause.

Teacher Observation Checklist[41]

Fill out a checklist for every student.

Student's name: ______________________________

SOUND
- ❑ Works well when students and teacher are interacting.
- ❑ Enjoys studying with music in the background
- ❑ Complains when there is too much sound present
- ❑ Makes sounds or noises while working
- ❑ Reminds others to be quiet

DESIGN
- ❑ Has difficulty sitting in the traditional classroom
- ❑ Enjoys lying down while listening to stories
- ❑ Sits in chair correctly
- ❑ Stands to work on crafts or other projects

STRUCTURE
- ❑ Likes to complete a project independently after directions are given
- ❑ Likes to complete a project step by step
- ❑ Keeps work area neat
- ❑ Tends to misplace supplies

SOCIOLOGICAL
- ❑ Likes to work and play with classmates
- ❑ Likes to work or play with teacher near
- ❑ Likes to work or play alone
- ❑ Creates opportunities to visit with teacher

RESPONSIBILITY AND PERSISTENCE
- ❑ Quickly and neatly completes projects
- ❑ Quickly but not neatly completes projects
- ❑ Slowly and neatly completes projects
- ❑ Slowly but not neatly completes projects
- ❑ Sometimes does not complete projects
- ❑ Wants teacher to provide specific instructions
- ❑ Independently cleans up work area when craft or project is done
- ❑ Needs to be reminded to clean up area when craft or project is done
- ❑ Easily distracted while working on a project

MOBILITY
- ❑ Is frequently out of chair
- ❑ Often requests a drink of water or another excuse to move around the room
- ❑ Is extremely active during class activities

MOTIVATION
- ❑ Works best with much assurance from others
- ❑ Needs teacher feedback while working
- ❑ Works best when allowed to do a project creatively
- ❑ Does projects on own accord
- ❑ Volunteers information about past experiences

PERCEPTION
- ❑ Enjoys looking at books, filmstrips, and video
- ❑ Sits up front and is attentive during a Bible story
- ❑ Likes to listen to records or tapes while also participating in other activities
- ❑ Remembers well what others say
- ❑ Likes to visit
- ❑ Likes to draw or doodle
- ❑ Enjoys physically moving around during class

Assignment

Briefly review the twenty-one elements of learning and describe how attention to them would change your Christian education program in five or more ways.

1.

2.

3.

4.

5.

If you were a curriculum writer, what are five things from this chapter that you would want your writing to reflect?

1.

2.

3.

4.

5.

Notes

1. Portions of the following material were taken from Chapter 22, "Understanding Learning Styles," by Marlene LeFever (*Christian Education: Foundations for the Future,* edited by Robert E. Clark, Lin Johnson, and Allyn K. Sloat. ©1991, Moody Bible Institute of Chicago. Moody Press, Chicago, Ill. Used by permission).

2. Gordon A. Donaldson, Jr., Director of the Maine Academy for School Leaders and a professor at the University of Maine, used this analogy to explain how secular teachers feel about new ideas that force change. How much more true it is for Christian education volunteers who teach less than an hour a week!

3. Claudia Arp in a workshop, "Positive Parenting," Christian Booksellers Association, Denver, Colorado, June 28, 1994.

4. Dr. Rita Dunn is professor of the Division of Administrative and Instructional Leadership and Director of the Center for Study of Learning and Teaching Styles at

St. John's University, New York. Dr. Kenneth Dunn was superintendent of schools, Hewlett-Woodmere, New York, and Executive Director of the Education Council for School Research and Development. This talented couple combined research with classroom testing to give educators a large body of learning/teaching information.

5. This model is a developing one. When Dr. Rita Dunn and Dr. Kenneth Dunn first presented their research, they had identified only 18 elements. See their books, *Teaching Elementary Students through Their Individual Learning Styles* (Boston: Allyn & Bacon, 1992); *Teaching Secondary Students through Their Individual Learning Styles* (Boston: Allyn & Bacon, 1993). Chart used by permission of Dr. Rita Dunn.

6. Preference Inventories: "Learning Style Inventory" and "Productivity Environment Preference Survey," by Rita Dunn, Kenneth Dunn, and Gary E. Price (primary version available for kindergarten through second grade) ©1987. LSI is an inventory for the identification of how individuals in grades three through twelve prefer to learn. "Productivity Environmental Preference Survey" is an inventory to identify individual adult preferences of conditions in working and/or learning environments. ©1982.

7. Rita Dunn, "Can Students Identify Their Own Learning Styles?" *Educational Leadership*, February 1983, pp. 60-63.

8. The marketing departments of four universities experimented with teaching students to do their homework using processes that were appropriate to their learning styles. Simultaneously, but unknown to each other, all four came to the same conclusion. Marginal and underachieving students were unaware of their learning style strengths. When they were taught to use them, they showed statistically higher achievement. In one study, student retention was increased by 30 percent. (*Learning Styles Network Newsletter*, Spring 1990.) Also see "Effects of Learning-Style Intervention on College Students' Achievement, Anxiety, Anger, and Curiosity" by Lenehan, Dunn, Ingham, Signer and Murry, *Journal of College Student Development*, November 1994, Vol. 35. This study among nursing students showed those doing homework by making use of their strongest elements got higher science grades and grade point averages.

9. Truly learning disabled students do prefer some elements over others, and predictably, those elements differ from what the classroom usually offers. Studies on young adolescents found that they require (a) sound; (b) low light; (c) a warmer temperature; (d) an informal design; and (e) mobility while learning. They also were both (f) parent-and (g) teacher-motivated (from M. B. Madison's 1984 study of the learning style preferences of specific learning disability students [Doctoral dissertation, University of Southern Mississippi] and corroborated in K. P. Snider's 1985 study, "A Study of Learning Preferences among Educable Mentally Impaired, Emotionally Impaired, Learning Disabled, and General Education Students in Seventh, Eighth, and Ninth Grades As Measured by the Learning Styles Inventory" [Doctoral dissertation, Michigan State University]. These studies were reported in *Learning Styles Network Newsletter*, Summer 1991: "How Do LD Adolescents' Styles Differ from Other Students?" p. 3).

10. East Texas State and St. John's University have developed a framework for helping parents understand and work with children through knowledge of learning

styles. East Texas University has established Parents and Learning Styles (PALS). Services include identification of children's learning strengths, a personalized learning-style plan, and workshops. Contact Dr. Joseph L. Vaughan, Texas Center for Learning Styles, East Texas State University, 2600 Motley Drive, Mesquite TX 75150. Phone: (214) 618-8734. St. John's University has a two-day parent component to its Learning Styles Leadership Seminar. Parents and their children learn about style, how they interact and support and inhibit each other, and how to use their styles to improve family relationships and academic achievement. For information contact Dr. Angela Klavas, Center for the Study of Learning and Teaching Styles, St. John's University, Utopia Pkwy., Jamaica, NY 11439. Phone: (718) 990-6335/6336.

11. Perrin, J. and Santora, S., (1982). *Elephant Style*. (Order from St. John's University Center for the Study of Learning and Teaching Styles, Jamaica, NY 11439. $10.00 includes postage.) Used with permission.

12. This multidimensional pattern of learning styles has won twenty-four major educational awards, two of them international.

13. This phrase, often repeated by Dunn in her workshops and seminars, should become a caution to all teachers not to assume what was done in the past was right and should, therefore, continue to be done in the future.

14. Many senior executives may fall into the group that needs quiet. According to "Quiet! A New Study Praises a Little-Understood Management Tool" (*Newsweek*, November 27, 1989, Special Advertising Section, page 18): "You won't find 'Quiet' listed in the curriculum of any business school. Yet, according to a study launched by the Northwestern Mutual Life Insurance Company, quiet time is one of the most important management tools used by top executives. . . . The study's key finding is that quiet plays a profound and active part in most top executives' methods and in their thinking as individuals. Executives will make an effort to schedule working time so that time for quiet is available. If quiet at the office is not available, some senior executives arrange quiet times away from the office, usually at home."

15. Most people are more optimistic in bright light. Churches may want to increase wattage in the low-light winter. Two percent or 150,000 western Canadians have Seasonal Affective Disorder (SAD) symptoms severe enough in November to benefit from treatment, according to psychiatrist Chris Gorman in Canadian Airline Magazine, *West*, November 1989.

16. David W. John, Robert T. Johnson, Edythe Johnson Holubeck, and Patricia Roy, *Circles of Learning* (Alexandria, Vir.: ASCD Publication, 1984), p. 4.

17. The principal of Lake Wylie Elementary School in Charlotte, North Carolina, did a study of the students in just one school. He found that 42 percent worked best in low light; 16 percent needed bright light; and 42 percent could work equally well in bright or low illumination (Pete Stone, "How We Turned Around a Problem School," *Principal*, November 1992, p. 33).

18. Editorial perspective by Wesley Willis, *Christian Education Journal*, Winter 1991, p. 7.

19. Chuck and Barb Snyder, *Incompatibility: Grounds for a Great Marriage* (Phoenix: Questar, 1988), p. 219.

20. Tom Shea, "An Investigation of the Relationship among Preferences for the Learning Style Element of Design, Selected Instruction Environments, and Readers' Achievement with Ninth Grade Students to Improve Administrative Determination Concerning Effective Educational Facilities" (Ph.D. Dissertation, St. John's University, 1983).

21. Ann Brigman, *Learning Styles Network Newsletter*, Spring 1990.

22. Unattributed, *Learning Styles Network Newsletter*, Spring 1990.

23. Eleanor Duckworth, "Teaching as Research," *Harvard Educational Review*, November 1986, p. 487.

24. Cooperative Learning was popularized by David and Roger Johnson, recipients of the 1987 National Psychology Award for Excellence in the Media. For more information see *Educational Leadership*, December 1989/January 1990 theme issue, "Cooperation Works." Some educators debate the validity of Cooperative Learning, especially those who work with gifted students.

25. This poem was published in *A Widening Light: Poems of the Incarnation*, Luci Shaw, editor. ©Harold Shaw Publishers, 1984. Reprinted with permission.

26. Basic summary points compiled by the National Education Association/ Summary of Research on Motivation ©1978. Presented by Marian Leibowitz, Educational Consultant, Lawrenceville, N.J., ASCD Cooperative Learning Seminar, July 20—August 2, 1990. Christian education comments added by this author.

27. I remember a contest at my church when I was about eight. A chalk artist was giving away a drawing to the person who could bring the most people to his series of meetings. I was determined to beat out my nearest competitor and actually celebrated when he got sick and could not continue bringing in his friends. I won the drawing, but the structure of that contest encouraged and rewarded my totally unchristian attitude.

28. See the following secular resources for additional information on effective learning for those students who learn best in groups: *Together We Learn* by Judy Clarke et al (Scarborough, Ontario: Prentice Hall, 1990); Spencer Kagan's *Cooperative Learning Resources for Teachers* (Riverside, Calif.: University of California, 1988), and Robert Slavin's resource *Using Student Team Teaching: An Overview and Practical Guide* (Baltimore, Md.: The Johns Hopkins University, 1986).

29. In studies on students with learning disabilities (Michael Kyriacou and Rita Dunn, "Synthesis of Research: Learning Styles of Students with Learning Disabilities," *National Forum of Special Education Journal*, Vol. 4, Nos. 1 & 2, 1994-95), researchers found that students with both learning disabilities and emotional handicaps needed tactual/visual and kinesthetic/visual resources designed to be used independently, and more mobility, intake, and structure than nonhandicapped students. They needed an authoritative adult nearby to provide immediate feedback when they had difficulty learning independently.

30. I once had an assistant who needed to chew in order to concentrate, but she was worried about gaining weight. So she bit into plastic pens. Every one of her hard plastic pens had teeth marks up and down their lengths and their tops were frayed into plastic "flowers." The pens still worked and since it helped her better enjoy her job, my response was, "Chew away!"

31. Stephen Garger, "Is There a Link between Learning Style and Neurophysiology?" *Educational Leadership*, October 1990, p. 64.

32. Lyn and Esther Cryderman, "Work It Out," *Marriage Partnership*, Spring 1991, pp. 10, 11. Used with permission.

33. "How Schools Are Using Brain Research and Getting Results," Association for Supervision and Curriculum Development, 1989 panel moderated by Leslie Hard. Tape number 2306. Statistic stated by panel member Dr. Rita Dunn.

34. J. Virostko, "An Analysis of the Relationships among Academic Achievement in Math and Reading, Assigned Instructional Schedules, and the Learning Styles Time Preferences of 3rd, 4th, 5th, and 6th Grade Students" (Ph. D. Dissertation, St. John's University, 1983).

35. "Building Application" from *The Clearinghouse Bulletin* produced by 4MAT©, Spring 1992.

36. Lucia Solorzana, "Is Your Child a 'Visual' or 'Walkman' Learner? Style Can Count," *U.S. News & World Report*, August 31, 1987, p. 62.

37. R. H. Andrews, "The Development of a Learning Styles Program in a Low Socioeconomic, Underachieving North Carolina Elementary School," *Journal of Reading, Writing and Learning Disabilities International* (New York: Hemisphere Publishing Corporation, Vol. 6, No. 3, July—September 1990, pp. 307-314 . Reported in *Learning Styles Network Newsletter*.

38. Reported in *Research Alert*, December 4, 1992, p. 6, from a national poll conducted by The Gallup Organization.

39. The curriculum quadrants in Bernice McCarthy's learning styles model and the Dunn and Dunn research overlap in several important areas. The overlap is especially obvious in global/analytic and hemisphericity categories.

40. From *All I Really Need to Know I Learned in Kindergarten* by Robert Fulghum. Copyright ©1986, 1988 by Robert Fulghum. Reprinted by permission of Villard Books, a division of Random House, Inc.

41. Adapted from a teacher checklist by Linda Loken Emery and used in Aberdeen, South Dakota, Public Schools. Reported by *The Learning Styles Clearing House*, November/December 1992, p. 112. This district's motto is, "If students don't learn the way we teach, let us teach the way they learn."

Conclusion

Thank You, God, for Teachers

The command Be ye perfect *is not idealistic gas. Nor is it a command to do the impossible. . . If we let Him—for we can prevent Him, if we choose—He will make . . . [us] a bright stainless mirror which reflects back to God perfectly . . . His own boundless power and delight and goodness.*
—C. S. Lewis

This book was dedicated to Sunday school teachers—Imaginative Teachers, Analytic Teachers, Common Sense Teachers, and Dynamic Teachers. Each strives to reach every student God has brought to the church, and with the Holy Spirit's help, they are succeeding.

Each teacher has a story, and from a spiritual perspective each story is a miracle, an affirmation that God is involved in our teaching.

The following stories are true.[1] Each story celebrates a volunteer teacher who is making a difference. Each is committed to the ongoing work in the church. I don't know what spots these teachers prefer in the Learning Style Cycle. Based on the slice of Sunday school life represented by their stories, I arbitrarily placed them in one of the four quadrants. Their personal learning style is not important; their determination to reach all students is.

I suspect every one of these teachers would agree with Dallas Seminary Christian educator, Howard Hendricks, when he said, "You can impress people from afar, but you can only impact lives up close."

Read the stories and celebrate that even though we don't know all the answers about the teaching/learning process, even though we often make mistakes, even though we may not always give the teaching assignment our best energy, God can use our gifts of time and service. We, Christian educators, make a difference!

IMAGINATIVE

Mr. Kerns Was Different

Mr. Kerns's eyes filled with tears as he moved away from the Sunday school lesson to tell us, his ninth grade class, about the decisions and emotions that had faced him since his wife gave birth to a Down's Syndrome child. He helped us understand how the largest disappointment in his life grew into the biggest blessing he had ever received. He wasn't just in our class to move word-for-word through a teacher's guide. He was there to share his life.—Columbia, South Carolina

Missing Piece

Something was missing in my life until I got involved in the three-year-old class. Those children made me feel good all over—right down to my shoes. I went from being the assistant to being the main teacher. Some of the parents were a little skeptical at first about a man teacher. The kids weren't. The only trouble is they can't sit in my lap as often because I'm teaching.

It's a shame they ever have to move to another class. I feel as if I'm losing my own children. Promotion is months away, and I miss them already.—Ephrata, Pennsylvania

Relaxing

My work week gets pretty hectic. Then comes my special time at church with my teens. We laugh and talk. I love relaxing with them. Suddenly I'm laid back and enjoying the Sunday job I do for Jesus.—Cedar Hill, Texas

ANALYTIC

Why I Teach

I teach because I am the father of Aaron and Rachel. People in our church have made substantial investments in the teaching of my children, and now it's my turn.—Toronto, Ontario

Young Tim

Fifteen-year-old Tim was on the fringes of our small church, the only teen in a busy, older congregation. "We'll lose him if someone doesn't take the time to make him feel important," I thought, and with that thought came the knowledge that God had assigned the job to me. Hot chocolate and conversation kept us studying the Bible together and today he's a church leader.—Watford Herts, England

Carpenter—Not!

Christian education is more than what happens in the classroom. As a public school teacher, Bruce knew that Mark had been hospitalized for depression. He missed so much school that he fell behind and that added to the pressure he felt.

"I used to feel bad about not being good with building projects the church had," Bruce admitted. "But God showed me that instead of standing around banging my thumb every time I tried to hit a nail, I should concentrate on what I can do. I'm a teacher and I volunteered to tutor Mark free for Jesus' sake." Mark made the honor roll last semester.—Franklin, Pennsylvania

Sensible Choice

In our small church, we have an active young adult class because a baby boomer came back to teach. He had dropped out of church for ten years. Then he started calling me with his questions, and I would pray every time the phone rang because the questions were so hard. When he became convinced of the Christian answer, he was impossible to stop. He started teaching and a number of new people have joined our church through his class. Today people from his class are our most active church participants and hold most of the major offices in the church.—Rockford, Illinois

Good Teacher

I thought Sunday school was a great way to help kids learn to be moral and make right choices. If they were good enough, I thought, they would get to know God. Then our church got a new pastor who decided to visit my class. After hearing my lesson, the pastor said, "You have all the skills and the kids like you. But I suspect you don't really know Jesus Christ. Let me explain how to get to know Him." I listened, and accepted God's saving grace. Now when I teach, I really teach!—Trout Creek, Ontario

COMMON SENSE

Kick Ball

"Would you take my place for a minute?" a fourth grader asked me. I jumped right in. I may be 64 and the senior pastor, but I love Vacation Bible School and a good game of kick ball. It was a great game, too, right up to the minute the ball and my knee connected and I tore some ligaments. I hobble a bit now, but I'm getting better. I'd do it all over again. I don't think there is such a thing as a pastor getting too involved in Christian education. These kids are our future.—Fort Wayne, Indiana

Tools for Ministry

When I started ministering at this church, Eric's name kept coming up—how he didn't like youth group and wasn't too keen on God either. I targeted him in my prayers, and the Lord used a job I once had at a bike shop to bring us together. I heard Eric had a new mountain bike that didn't work, so I stopped by his house to see if we could fix it. Later when his mom told him I was the youth leader he said, "Wow! Finally someone cool at church." I'm not cool, but I do enjoy loving teens unconditionally.—Midland, Michigan

The Wiggles

It was my Sunday off from teaching. I was enjoying the worship service when the usher plopped nine-year-old Justin next to me. Part of me wanted to yell, "Unfair." I knew my quiet time with God had just ended. Justin can't listen and be still. He's all noise and rattles and whispers and squirms. I know how difficult being still is for him, but during prayer, I couldn't take it anymore. I reached over and held him in a tight bear hug. For a short time, he relaxed and enjoyed the touching. The church has got to find a way to hold on to kids like Justin. We can't lose them by expecting them to learn about God in stillness and quiet, ways that are impossible for them.—Reading, Pennsylvania

DYNAMIC

New Way

When I came to this church, Koreans were teaching the old way—teacher talks and students listen. We had forty-five minutes of student quiet. I brought in methods and ideas about how kids learn, and we've had a 90 percent turnaround. Sunday school is alive and creative.—Houston, Texas

It's Him

I've got a former headbanger in my youth group. He comes complete with three-color hair and an enthusiasm for Christ that won't quit. No, I don't mind his hair. That multi-colored head is him. And, he reaches kids the one-color-hair kids can't!—Seattle, Washington

Teacher Training

Instead of our regularly scheduled leaders' meeting, we rode around with the police for one night. We got a dose of reality. ". . . and the cop was yelling, 'Kick the knife away,' and I was grabbing a blanket to cover the naked woman and . . ." Only when we know how our kids live outside our church can we bring them our real Jesus in a way they will hear and accept.—Houston, Texas

Piglet

When my teacher's guide provided a life application story about a pig, I got the idea of bringing a live piglet to class. Piggy was very well behaved! The children will never forget the lesson they learned the Sunday piggy came to Sunday school.—Hamburg, Pennsylvania

Senior Sweat

I may teach elderly people, but there's no way we're going to sit around and get dusty. I knew I was successful when I heard an eighty-year-old student grumbling, "I don't think a body should have to work this hard on Sunday."—Carrollton, Missouri

Married Team

Team teaching with my wife Donna has been great for our marriage. We come at teaching in opposite ways. She's highly organized and I'm a little looser. For our senior high class to work, we have to talk to each other—lots. Talk and handle conflicts and talk and play. We've never talked so much. Team teaching means no communication problems!—Eskridge, Kansas

---

Note

1. These stories previously appeared in *Teacher Touch* and were collected and written by Marlene LeFever and published quarterly by David C. Cook Church Ministries. *Teacher Touch* is designed to affirm Sunday school teachers and other Christian education volunteers in their important and challenging work and to give them opportunities to encourage others with the stories of their ministries.

Select Bibliography

Armstrong, Thomas. *In Their Own Way: Discovering and Encouraging Your Child's Personal Learning Style*. Los Angeles: Jeremy P. Tarcher, Inc., 1987.

————. *Multiple Intelligences in the Classroom*. Alexandria, Vir.: ASCD, 1994.

Cherry, Clare. *Creative Art for the Developing Child: Teacher's Handbook for Early Childhood Education*. Carthage, Ill.: Simon & Schuster Supplementary Education Group, 1990.

————. *Creative Play for the Developing Child: Early Lifehood Education through Play*. Carthage, Ill.; Simon & Schuster Supplementary Education Group, 1976.

Cherry, Clare; Goodwin, Douglas; and Staples, Jesse. *Is the Left Brain Always Right?—A Guide to Whole Child Development*. Carthage, Ill.: Simon & Schuster Supplementary Education Group, 1989.

Clark, Robert E.; Johnson, Lin; and Sloat, Allyn K.: *Christian Education: Foundations for the Future*. Chicago: Moody Press, 1991.

Clarke, Judy, et al. *Together We Learn*. Scarborough, Ontario: Prentice Hall, 1990.

deBenedittis, Suzanne M. *Teaching Faith and Morals—Toward Personal and Parish Renewal*. Minneapolis, Minn.: Winston, 1981.

Dunn, Rita and Dunn, Kenneth. *Teaching Elementary Students through Their Individual*

Learning Styles. Boston: Allyn & Bacon, 1992.

———. *Teaching Secondary Students through Their Individual Learning Styles*. Boston: Allyn & Bacon, 1993.

Guild, Pat Burke, and Garger, Stephen. *Marching to Different Drummers*. Alexandria, Vir.: ASCD, 1985.

Hale-Benson, Janice. *Black Children: Their Roots, Culture, and Learning Styles*. Baltimore: The Johns Hopkins University Press, 1988.

Harmin, Merrill. *Inspiring Active Learning: A Handbook for Teachers*. Alexandria, Vir.: ASCD, 1994.

John, David W.; Johnson, Robert T.; Holubeck, Edythe Johnson; and Roy, Patricia. *Circles of Learning*. Alexandria, Vir.: ASCD, 1984.

Kagan, Spencer. *Cooperative Learning Resources for Teachers*. Riverside, Calif.: University of California, 1988.

Kolb, David. *Experiential Learning: Experience As the Source of Learning and Development*. Englewood Cliffs, N.J.: Prentice-Hall, 1984.

Lawrence, Gordon. *People Types & Tiger Stripes: A Practical Guide to Learning Styles*. Gainsville, Fla.: Center for Applications of Psychological Type, Inc., 1982.

LeFever, Marlene. *Creative Teaching Methods*. Elgin, Ill.: David C. Cook Publishing Co., 1985.

———. *God's Special Creation—Me! Camp Curriculum*. Wheaton, Ill.: Harold Shaw, 1988.

———. *Survival Kit for Growing Christians: Camp Curriculum*. Wheaton, Ill.: Harold Shaw, 1988.

McCarthy, Bernice. *The 4MAT System: Teaching to Learning Styles with Right/Left Mode Techniques*. Barrington, Ill.: Excel, Inc., 1987.

Pazmino, Robert W. *By What Authority Do We Teach? Sources for Empowering Christian Educators*. Grand Rapids, Mich.: Baker, 1994.

Perrin, J. and Santora, S. *Elephant Style*. Jamaica, N.Y.: St. John's University.

Polette, Nancy. *Picture Books for Gifted Programs*. Metuchen, N.J.: Scarecrow, 1981.

Slavin, Robert. *Using Student Team Teaching: An Overview and Practical Guide*. Baltimore: The Johns Hopkins University, 1986.

Snyder, Chuck and Snyder, Barb. *Incompatibility: Grounds for a Great Marriage*. Phoenix, Ariz.: Questar Publishers, Inc., 1988.

Learning Style Inventory (TSI). McBer & Company, Training Resources Group, 137 Newbury Street, Boston, MA 02116.

Learning Style Inventory (LSI). Available through St. Johns University School of Education and Human Services, Grand Central & Utopia Parkways, Jamaica, NY 11439.

Learning Type Measure (LTM) and Teaching Style Inventory (TSI). Excel, Inc., 23385 Old Barrington Road, Barrington, IL 60010.

Productivity Environment Preference Survey, St. Johns University, Grand Central & Utopia Parkways, Jamaica, NY 11439.

Media

4MATION—Lesson Plan Software (Macintosh and Windows). Barrington, Ill.: Excel, Inc.

Learning Differences: Designing Instruction with the 4MAT System. Video. Barrington, Ill.: Excel, Inc.

A Morning with Bernice McCarthy. Audiocassette. Barrington, Ill.: Excel, Inc.

Teaching to Learning Styles. Video. Alexandria, Vir.: ASCD.

Newsletters

Learning Styles Network Newsletter. St. John's University, Grand Central & Utopia Parkways, Jamaica, NY 11439.

Teacher Touch. Marlene LeFever, ed. Elgin, Ill.: David C. Cook Church Ministries.